THE
HOUNDSDITCH
MURDERS

and the Siege of Sidney Street

THE
HOUNDSDITCH
MURDERS

and the Siege of Sidney Street

DONALD RUMBELOW

To the memory of my Mother and Father

First published 1973
This edition published 2009

The History Press
The Mill, Brimscombe Port
Stroud, Gloucestershire, GL5 2QG
www.thehistorypress.co.uk

© Donald Rumbelow, 1973, 2009

The right of Donald Rumbelow to be identified as the Author
of this work has been asserted in accordance with the
Copyrights, Designs and Patents Act 1988.

British Library Cataloguing in Publication Data.
A catalogue record for this book is available from the British Library.

ISBN 978 0 7509 5072 5

Typesetting and origination by The History Press
Printed in Great Britain

Contents

Preface

Some years ago, chance put in my way the police documents on which this book is substantially based. Most of them have now been deposited in the Records Office of the Corporation of the City of London, Guildhall. Some of the more general photographs, such as those of the policemen's funeral, needing more sensitive storage, have been deposited with the Guildhall's prints and pictures collection. The original documents were scattered about in old cardboard boxes, thickly coated with dust, but had managed to survive not only the Blitz and the wartime paper salvage collections, but also years of neglect; they were earmarked for destruction.

These papers are the investigative records of the Houndsditch murders, and several months of spare time were spent in trying to put them into some sort of order. They consist of original statements, typewritten copies and handwritten notes, some from the prisoners in Brixton, and one roughly-scrawled note which helped to identify the Sidney Street informant. There are notebooks containing shorthand translations and normal handwritten translations of letters and papers which were seized by police; the originals are missing. Possibly they were returned or have been destroyed. Though these have only been partly translated, the references make it clear that they were to and about fellow revolutionaries in Latvia. The backs had broken on these notebooks and the pages had become scattered, but the pages were numbered and arranged as near to the original order as possible. The documents included photographs that were seized from the conspirators, chiefly from Grove Street, the lodgings of Fritz Svaars, and which Sara Trassjonsky was trying to burn. Some of the photographs have now been successfully used to identify international revolutionary groups of the time. The maps that were with these papers were extremely brittle – the binder thought that they had been baked!

Later I thought I would write a short account of the Siege from these documents. I didn't expect to find anything new as the story was so well known. However, once I had started to work on the papers, the errors and omissions in former versions of the story became only too apparent; it is for this reason that I have kept almost exclusively to the original documents and quoted, with few exceptions, only from incidents in which the writers were personally involved and when they were not speaking from hearsay.

Some of the more personal documents have survived only in the very stilted translations which were made at the time. I have preferred to paraphrase these letters, which have been used very sparingly and which do not affect the main line of the story, rather than quote from them directly.

Much new information has come to light about the early background of some of the revolutionaries and here I must express my total indebtedness to Andris Mellakauls and Philip Ruff who have generously shared their researches into the Latvian and Russian sources. Andris additionally made a fresh translation of Svaars' last letter from Sidney Street.

I should like to thank the following: Charles Perel, a sprightly 76-year-old when I met him, for his remembrances of his father and of the young revolutionaries who lodged with them. I still recall the shock, because I thought he knew already, of explaining to him the precise part his father had played in the Siege. Also Catherine Golden for filling in an important part of the story with her memories and photographs of her parents, Karl Hoffman and Luba Milstein. Frank Clarke for tying up the Australian end of the story in his book *Will-O'-the-Wisp*. Professor William J. Fishman for help and encouragement as always. And special thanks, for more reasons than one, to Menna Wilders, for her recollections of her visits to May and Igor Peters in Moscow.

My former thanks go to the following: L. C. Dixon, W. J. and L. J. Piper, G. A. Freeman, Mrs Leader, Sam Hart, Keith Andreang, Donald McCormick, Dale Wilkinson, Peter Simmonds, Betty Masters, the Commissioner of the City of London Police, the Commissioner of the Metropolitan Police, Polly Rumbelow and James Wright.

I should also like to thank the following for the use of photo-graphs: the Commissioner of the City of London Police; Radio Times Hulton Picture Library; Press Association; United Press International; Mrs M. Wilders; Mrs Catherine Golden.

My final thanks go to my editors Mike Bailey and Bill Massey and my literary agent, Michael Shaw, as always.

List of Characters

I have noted the main characters in the story in the hope that this will be helpful to the reader. Many of the individuals operated under various aliases. I have, for interest, given them in parenthesis.

Wanted Men, Relations and Friends

Tottenham Outrage
Hefeld, Paul (nickname 'Elephant')
Jacob (surname Lepidus or Lapidus?)
Salnish, Christian (also Jacob Fogel or Vogel, Jan Sprohe, Grishka Sander)
Vanoveitch, Evan (?Jan Janoff Palameiko, nickname 'Bifsteks'. Also Janis Zakie)

Houndsditch Murders
Dubof, Yourka (real name Yourka Laiwin)
Federoff, Osip
Gardstein, George (also P. Morin, Poolka Mourrewitz or Mourremitz, or Mouremtzoff, George Garstin; carried passports in names of Schafshi Khan and Yanis Karlowitch Stentzel)
Gershon, Betsy (lodger, 100 Sidney Street, where Svaars and Joseph hid; she was Joseph's mistress)
Hoffman, Karl (also Janis Trautman, Chochol and Masais; carried passport in name of Peter Trohimtchick, which was an alias used by Fritz Svaars; real name Alfred Dzircol, later anglicised to Driscoll)

'Joseph', *see* Sokoloff, William

Levi, Joe, *see* Smoller, Max

Milstein, Luba (Svaars' mistress)

Molchanoff (or Molacoff), Pavell (friend of Peter Piatkow)

Peters, Jacob (cousin of Fritz Svaars; in England, as secretary of the Lettish Social Democratic Federation, used the workname Jacob Colven or Kolnin. In Russia his party name was Svornoff)

Piatkow, Peter (alias Peter Schtern; 'Peter the Painter')

Rosen, John (also John Zelin or Tzelin, nickname 'the Barber')

Smoller, Max (also Marx or Marks Smellor; rented 11 Exchange Buildings as Joe Levi)

Sokoloff, William (surname also spelt Sokaloff, Sokolow, Sokolov and Solokoff, commonly known as 'Joseph' or 'Yoska')

Svaars, Fritz (cousin to Jacob Peters; also known as Karl Davidoff Dumnieks, Louis Lambert and Peter Trohimtchick, which was an alias also used by Hoffman)

Trassjonsky, Sara ('Rosa'; carried passport in name of Sara Davidowna [Tuwiena], daughter of David Tuwic Treschau)

Vassilleva, Nina (also Lena Vasilev; carried passport in name of Minna, daughter of Indrik Gristis)

Police and Witnesses

Abrahams, Mr and Mrs (tenants of 12 Exchange Buildings)
–, Solomon (their son)
Bentley, Police Sergeant Robert (murdered at Houndsditch)
Bluestein, Mrs (landlady, 102 Sidney Street)
Brown, Wolf and Fanny (36 Lindley Street, where Hoffman lived)
Bryant, Police Sergeant (wounded at Houndsditch)
Choate, Police Constable Walter (murdered at Houndsditch)
Clemens (or Clements), Mr and Mrs (lodgers of Fleishmann's)
Dixon, Detective Constable (involved at Tottenham)
Eagles, Police Constable (involved at Tottenham)
Fleishmann (or Flieschmann), Rebecca (landlady, 100 Sidney Street)
–, Samuel (her husband)
Freedman, Dr Mengle (acquaintance of Nina Vassilleva)
Gordon, Isaac (Nina Vassilleva's landlord)
–, Fanny (his wife)

–, Polly (their daughter)

Harris, H. S. (jeweller)

–, Harry (his son)

Hart, Sam (witness at Houndsditch)

Hayes, Chief Inspector (stationed at Bishopsgate on the night of the Houndsditch murders)

Jacobs, Harry (tenant, Exchange Buildings)

–, Bessie (his sister)

Johnstone, Dr Nelson (Sidney Street)

Joscelyne, Ralph (boy murdered at Tottenham)

Katz, Max (landlord, 59 Grove Street)

–, Mrs (his wife)

Kempler, Jacob (44 Gold Street, where Gardstein lodged as P. Morin)

Keyworth, Albert (Schnurmann's factory wages-clerk)

Leeson, Detective Sergeant Benjamin (wounded at Sidney Street)

Levy, Isaac (witness at Houndsditch)

Martin, Detective Constable James (Houndsditch)

Mulvaney, Divisional Superintendent (Metropolitan Police)

Newman, Police Constable (Tottenham)

Ottaway, Detective Superintendent John (City)

Parker, Ada (tenant, Exchange Buildings)

Perelman, Charles (Carlusha)

Petter, Elsa (Dubof's landlady)

Pilenas, Casimir (interpreter from Thames Police Court)

–, Peter (his brother)

Piper, Police Constable Walter (Houndsditch)

Reitman, Morris (lodger, 36 Lindley Street)

–, Mrs 'Grobber'

Scanlon, Dr John (attended Gardstein)

Schiemann (also Sheinmann, Shiesmann, Schiesbann), David and Mrs (lodgers of Fleishmann's)

Silisteanu, Michail (rented 10 Exchange Buildings)

Smolensky, Abraham (Svaars' landlord at Newcastle Place)

Stark, Superintendent John (City)

Strongman, Detective Constable Arthur (identified Peters at Houndsditch)

Thompson, Detective Inspector

Tucker, Police Sergeant Charles (murdered at Houndsditch)

Tyler, Police Constable (murdered at Tottenham)

Weil, Max (trader in Houndsditch)
Wensley, Detective Inspector Frederick Porter ('Weasel')
Wilson, Joseph (chauffeur, Schnurmann's rubber factory)
Woodhams, Police Constable Ernest (wounded at Houndsditch)

Informers

Perelman, Charles (also spelt Pearlman; landlord at Great Garden Street
  and Wellesley Street)
Tomacoff, Nicholas (also spelt Tomazeff; balalaika-player)

1

The Tottenham Outrage

In 1909 nearly two million Londoners were officially classed as poor or very poor. Most of them lived in the East End. For centuries the City of London's stringent corporate and guild restrictions had forced new labour to live and work on the open marshland outside the City wall. Immigrants fleeing continental persecutions, notably the seventeenth century Huguenots, settled in East London. Steadily the number of immigrants increased. By the end of the nineteenth century the brickfields and the pleasant weavers' houses had become rack-rented ghettos. Nearly fifty per cent of the workers paid from a quarter to half of their wages for poky little one-room hovels for themselves and their families.

From the 1870s the East End began to expand to the east and to the north. The railways brought growth to the villages on the periphery of London. The old village main streets with their half-timbered cottages and bow-fronted homes on either side were rapidly expanded from behind with two-storeyed houses, mostly jerry-built. Soon these became microcosms of the East End. Walthamstow was called Little Bethnal Green. The familiar pattern of brawling, street markets with naphtha flares, nightly drunkenness was once more repeated. Rapidly these new areas degenerated into slums. Fresh waves of immigrants from Central and Eastern Europe, from Poland and Tsarist Russia, moved into these areas in the 1890s and the first decade of the twentieth century. Wages, which were already low, were depressed still more. Unable to compete at these low rates, the workers in some areas rioted. In Tottenham, in 1902, they smashed factory windows with stones. They achieved nothing by their action. Seven years later large numbers of immigrants were still being employed by the rubber factory, Schnurmann's, in Chestnut Road at the corner of Tottenham High Road. The factory façade of bleak quarried stone, now painted grey was more suited to a prison than to a factory, despite the ornamental pineapples on the roof. The only openings in the street wall were some small mitre-windows. Between the side walls of the gate was stretched a thick cable and from it was suspended, like a pendant, a monster gas-lamp faceted with panes of glass like a diamond. The gates beneath it had a forbidding fringe of metal spikes.

On Saturday, 23 January 1909 these gates were open. Two young political refugees from the Baltic state of Latvia, Paul Hefeld and Jacob, both in their twenties, one dark and the other fair, were lounging on the pavement outside, one on either side of the entrance, insolently eyeing the police station opposite as they waited, with guns in their pockets, for the factory car to return from the London & South Western Bank in Hackney with the week's wages, about £80, as it did every Saturday morning at 10.30.

The car was a few minutes late. As it turned the corner they noted the gleaming brasswork, the monster headlamps and the carriage lamps on the hood supports. The rear of the car was boxed in with leather like a hansom cab, which it closely resembled, and the only protection the driver had from the weather was from the roof and the full-length glass panel in front. In wet weather he had to look through an oval incision in the glass. Huddled behind the glass (the front half of the car had no doors) were the driver, Joseph Wilson, in his heavy motor-coat and gauntlets, and the seventeen-year-old wages-clerk Albert Keyworth.

Keyworth paused as he stepped onto the pavement with the wages bag in his hand. Seeing the two men on either side of the entrance made him suspicious. Hefeld saw him hesitate and nodded his head in greeting. Keyworth nodded back as he recognised Hefeld as somebody who had recently worked at the factory. He knew him by sight but did not know his name. Nobody did. Hefeld had contemptuously refused to give it. The management had been indifferent as to what he was called so long as he did the work. All immigrants lied anyway. In the blank name-space on his time-sheets they put down, in allusion to his great bulk, his nickname of 'Elephant'.

As the car pulled away Keyworth walked across the pavement to the factory yard. Before he could reach the entrance Jacob's arm locked around his throat from behind. Keyworth shouted and plunged forward with Jacob clinging to his back. Frantically he tried to throw him off but Jacob hung on and with his free hand tore at Keyworth's arm and at the canvas bag he held just out of reach. Wilson heard the shout, and as the two men staggered backwards into the roadway he leaped out of the car and ran towards them. He threw his arms round Jacob's head and pulled him off the boy. Then, throwing all his weight forward, he tried to force the man's head down between his knees. In so doing, he himself was completely off balance and a sudden sideways movement rolled him over Jacob's head and shoulders onto his back. As he sprawled, momentarily winded, in the roadway he looked up and saw Hefeld, who until then had taken no part in the fighting, moving towards him with a gun in his hand. Jacob, meanwhile, had managed to wrench away the wages bag from the boy and was also pulling out a gun.

Hefeld fired at the chauffeur several times in rapid succession. Wilson rolled desperately over and over shouting for help. Miraculously he was not hit. His ankle-length motor-coat was riddled with holes, and a slanting shot across his stomach cut through everything he was wearing including his vest.

The police station is on the corner of Tottenham High Road and Chesnut Road. From the office window there is a clear view across the road to Schnurmann's. The shots were heard inside the station and two policemen on Reserve, 403 'N' Tyler and 510 'N' Newman, ran into the High Road. 'Guv'nor, you're wanted,' shouted a passer-by and pointed down Chesnut Road. They ran round the corner just in time to see a passer-by, a burly stoker called George Smith, bring Jacob crashing to the ground with a flying tackle. Smith had run down the street using the car as a cover and had taken the two gunmen completely by surprise. As Hefeld spun round to face this new threat the driver seized his opportunity, staggered to his feet, and ran towards the policemen less than forty yards away.

Smith and Jacob were still wrestling on the ground, with Smith on top, and there was not even time for Hefeld to take aim. He straddled the two men and fired four times at Smith's head. Two shots went through his cap tearing his scalp, one completely missed and the other shot wounded him in the fleshy part of the collar bone. Incredibly Jacob was not hit. Catching hold of the startled Smith by the throat he rolled him over and grabbed the wages bag. Hefeld fired once more and then the two of them began running down Chesnut Road with the two policemen close on their heels.

X Some passers-by joined in the chase. One woman further down the road, buying greengroceries at her gate, flung a potato at them as they ran past. More help came from the police station, which was also a section house. Some of the night-duty men were woken by the shots. Others heard Police Constable Bond, who had been shaving and seen the robbery from an upstairs window, shouting the alarm as he ran downstairs. He grabbed a truncheon, leaped through a window into the yard below, and over a wall into the street. The others quickly followed. Most of them were on foot, but some of them commandeered bicycles and pedalled furiously down the road. Most of them had not understood what had happened.

Hefeld and Jacob took the first turning to the left and ran through the small streets of terraced houses towards the marshes by the River Lea. All the time they kept firing back at the policemen on their heels. In Scales Road Tyler and Newman recklessly closed to within nine yards but were again beaten off by the gunmen's fire and forced to shelter behind a stationary dust-cart. Moments later, the factory car turned the corner with Wilson at the wheel. Newman climbed in while the manager and Tyler ran alongside, holding on to the car as it slowed down to a walking pace. They followed the gunmen into Mitchley Road. As one of them stopped by the Mission Hall to reload Wilson shouted that the gun was empty. Newman excitedly told him to run the gunman down if he could.

Jacob and Hefeld crouched down as the car accelerated towards them. They took careful aim and fired simultaneously. A leather-cutter's wife, who had heard the police whistles and the shots, was standing by her gate with her baby in her arms when the gunmen opened fire. She saw a small boy run to the car for cover as everyone ducked.

One shot tore through Newman's cheek and the lobe of his ear as the bullets smashed the windscreen. Another cut across Wilson's neck and collar and a third burst the car's water-pipe. The small boy had almost reached the car when he lifted his hand to his mouth and fell heavily onto the edge of the pavement. Jacob and Hefeld took to their heels once more. Thrusting her baby into someone's arms, the leather-cutter's wife ran into the roadway and took the child from a passer-by who had picked him up. Blood was trickling from his mouth. Cradling him in her arms she ran to the car, but because of the burst water-pipe it was impossible to drive on. Newman looked bleakly at the child as he dabbed the blood on his cheek and then ran on after Tyler and Bond, who were still dogging Jacob and Hefeld as they headed for the marshes. Somebody with a bicycle took the child to hospital, but it was too late. He was already dead from a slanting shot through the body.

Somebody else was sent back to the police station for firearms. These were locked in a cupboard, but as they had never been wanted nobody knew where the key was kept and the lock had to be smashed to get at them. Thrusting the guns into their pockets, more policemen headed for the marshes on bicycles.

The two gunmen were now in Down Road heading towards the marshes. This meant that they had to cross over the railway footbridge by the Council Depot and Refuse Destructor at the end of Down Road; it was surrounded by a wall about five feet high. Concealed by this wall Tyler, Bond and Newman tried to head off their quarry by cutting across some waste ground behind the houses. Tyler, the most athletic of the three, was in the lead when the gunmen ran out from behind the wall. As they converged on the footbridge there was only twenty yards between them.

'Come on; give in, the game's up,' shouted Tyler.

Hefeld turned, lifted his Bergmann automatic and pulled the trigger. Tyler's head snapped back and he fell forward onto his face. Newman shouted for a gun as the rest of the pursuers ran up. Snatching one, he ran forward and fired three shots at Jacob and Hefeld as they scrambled over the footbridge.

Tyler was picked up and carried to a nearby cottage. The owner's daughter had been kneeling at the back window as the gunmen raced by. 'Look, mama, there's some men racing!' she called. She saw some 'sparks' and the policeman fall to the ground. He was carried into the scullery a few minutes later. Tyler opened his eyes and groaned but he could not speak. He rapidly lost consciousness. Nothing could be done for him. The bullet had gone through the right side of his neck and he was bleeding to death.

The Divisional Inspector asked the Superintendent of the Refuse Depot to telephone police headquarters at Stoke Newington for reinforcements while he returned to the station for his horse. Policemen from the surrounding stations were told to converge on Tottenham marshes. Some of them were armed by their station and a few of them borrowed firearms. Most of them were armed only with truncheons.

Jacob and Hefeld continued firing as they crossed the bridge and gained the marshes on the other side. The footpath weaved away in front of them to Stonebridge Lock. The stubby grass underfoot was green in contrast with the bleached acres of wind-beaten rye-grass and couch-grass about them. Scraggy green nettles and brown shafts of sorrel were not so yielding and stood in clumps waist-high, against the wind. As they bobbed along the footpath they could see the black rooftops of the barges moored on the canal. Coming steadily nearer, they gained some height and began to see the brightly painted panels and the brittle walls of the canal. Behind the canal was the long, even slope of Lockwood Reservoir.

They crossed over Stonebridge Lock. For a few minutes they rested on the gates and fired from the rails at their pursuers. Some footballers on the marsh had now joined in the chase. Crossing over they continued along the footpath on the east side of the canal. The ground sloped down to their right to Tottenham mill-stream about twenty feet below them. Before they could get to the open space around Banbury Reservoir they had to cross yet another bridge and this was now threatened by some labourers on the other side of the canal who were demolishing some rifle-butts. Flinging down their picks and shovels they started running along the opposite bank to head them off. Jacob and Hefeld ran parallel with them and, firing continuously across the canal, succeeded in wounding several of them. Once on the bridge they rested and again kept the crowd at bay by firing from the parapet. A policeman crept through the scrub on the mill-stream bank and got within firing range, but his gun was faulty. Before he could get back he was spotted from the bridge and shot in the calf and thigh.

From the bridge, the footpath swept round the south side of Banbury Reservoir. On either side of the footpath was a high fence, and the risk for the pursuers was greatly increased, as once they got between the palings there was no room for them to spread out. Instead they had to keep well back against the fence, especially on the bends, and they could hear shots repeatedly hitting the palings. One man got too close and was shot in the thigh. Through the hedges on the slope of Banbury Reservoir above them, one of the policemen saw a party of sportsmen out duck shooting. He called to them to shoot the man with the green

The Tottenham Outrage: the route taken by Hefeld and Jacob as they tried to escape.

cap (this was Hefeld, who was doing most of the firing) but at first they failed to take in the situation. Some of them then hurried to the top of the reservoir for a better view. Looking down they could see six police-men in front; every time the gunmen fired they took cover. The duck shooters fired through the hedges at Jacob and Hefeld; one of them was seen to put his hand to his face as though hit and his cap was later found to have been riddled with shot.

Jacob and Hefeld hurried on until they saw the open ground around the base of Higham Hill in front of them. Reaching some cottages they rested once more and then ran across some fields in the direc-tion of Folly Lane. As they cut through the fields and the adjoining allotments they ran into a small gypsy-encampment with two round-top caravans. 'You have some too,' shouted Hefeld and fired at one of the gypsies who ran out. They had now almost reached Billet Road, but as they ran towards it they suddenly saw more of their pursuers appearing in front of them over the hedgerow on bicycles, horses, in motor-cars and on foot.

Forced to retreat once more, the two men hurried on as fast as they could across the fields to Salisbury Hall Farm. They were too exhausted to run. Hefeld was still doing most of the firing. He would halt every so often and use his left arm as a rest for his automatic while Jacob reloaded the other gun. Then they would walk a little way and jog-trot a similar distance. In the farmyard they took temporary shelter behind a haystack. From either side of it they kept firing at their pursuers, who at this point had dropped down to about twenty and who were forced to throw themselves into the furrows as the bullets swept across the field at waist-high level.

Behind the gunmen was the Chingford Road. Running down it for some two or three miles was a single-track tramline. At vari-ous stages there were loops for trams to pass each other. The trams passed Salisbury Hall Farm which was about a mile from Chingford, and on Saturday mornings they were little used. Jacob and Hefeld saw a tram approaching. Suddenly they broke cover and dashed for the road.

As he passed Salisbury Hall Farm the driver of tramcar number 9 saw a crowd of excited people running across the farm in his direc-tion. He could hear cries of 'Murder' and somebody shouting to him to stop. As he slowed down a man (from his story it is not clear who, but the indications are that it was Jacob) jumped over a hedge or ditch and rushed onto the platform. In his hand he held a revolver and he was calling to a man who was running along the road about fifty yards behind the tram. 'Stop,' shouted Jacob, pointing his gun at the driver and conductor. The driver braked and, as Hefeld ran nearer, some of the crowd, which now included the duck shooters, opened fire on the stationary tram with shotguns as well as revolvers. The tram's three passengers – an elderly man, a woman and a child – flung themselves face downwards in the aisle as the windows were shattered and flying glass littered the interior. The driver, too, was caught in the cross-fire. Convinced that death was inevitable if he stayed where he was, he managed to scramble up some steps at the front of the tram without being seen by Jacob and hide behind the seats on the top deck. The conductor had to stay where he was on the platform with Jacob until Hefeld scrambled on board. Only then did Jacob realise that the tram had no driver. Thrusting his pistol into the conductor's face he told him to drive the tram. The conductor, unhappily, and quite truthfully, told him that he had never driven anything in his life. Jacob placed the pistol against the conductor's head and as Hefeld opened fire on the men behind the hedges, he told him once more to drive the tram. Knowing that he would almost certainly be shot if he refused again, the conductor walked to the front of the tram and fumbled at the controls as bullets flew about them. As the tram pulled slowly away Jacob held his gun-barrel against the conductor's cheek and Hefeld kept up a steady fire from the platform at the back. Most of their pursuers were now being left behind but some of them were already looking for ways of continuing the chase.

The conductor's main worry was whether the driver upstairs would do anything silly to jeopardise his life. He could, if he wanted to, stop the tram by pressing down the trolly bar and cutting the circuit. Meanwhile, the conductor racked his brains to think of some way of bringing the nightmare journey to an end. Jacob stood by his side the whole time, occasionally turning and firing at some imaginary pursuer. His ammunition seemed inexhaustible. No sooner was his magazine empty than he dipped his hand into his pocket and pulled out a fresh supply. Hefeld came up to the front to join them for a few minutes just as the tram reached a loop and was forced to slow down to let another tram pass in the opposite direction. The woman passenger and the child were able to scramble off unseen, but the elderly man had to stay on. He was becoming increasingly agitated.

The other tram had not gone very far when it was stopped by some of the pursuers running towards it who immediately put it into reverse to come after them. Meanwhile, the captured tram was fast being caught up by a horse-drawn advertising-cart which had been commandeered by an armed policeman. It came up behind the tram at a sharp trot, but before it could get near enough for the policeman to open fire Hefeld killed the pony with one carefully aimed shot, spilling the occupants into the road and throwing the can of paste which was in the cart on top of them.

As the tram approached a bend in the road the conductor suddenly had an idea. 'You'd better get off here,' he said, 'as there is a police station just round the bend.' Jacob did not know whether to believe him or not and his uncertainty was increased still more by the conductor's apparent indifference. The situation was unexpectedly resolved by the elderly passenger. As the tram came to the bend, Kite's Corner, the strain proved too much for him and he stumbled forward as if he meant to snatch the gun. Jacob was too quick for him. He turned and shot the old man in the throat. As he collapsed in the aisle Jacob and Hefeld leaped off the tram and ran for a milk cart standing by the kerb. The milkman came running towards them and was instantly shot in the chest. They jumped on the milk cart and, lashing the horse with a whip, drove off down Kenilworth Avenue in the direction of Forest Road and Epping Forest.

Somehow they managed to wreck the milk cart. It was said that they overturned it by taking a corner too fast. Abandoning it they stopped a greengrocer's van and ordered the teenage driver out at gun-point. Jacob grabbed the reins and Hefeld climbed onto the tailboard with both pistols. Hefeld sat with his wrists on his drawn-up knees and the guns hanging limply down. Almost immediately they were chased by some policemen on bicycles, one of them carrying a cutlass, who were part of the larger force steadily closing in on them. Whenever they came too near Hefeld opened fire. In Forest Road he shot at a policeman on foot. The policeman immediately chased after them blowing his whistle and within minutes had commandeered a chauffeur-driven car. Two more policemen and two passers-by jumped in from behind. (Later the police had to pay a bill for bending both wings.) The car kept steadily behind the cart. It was never more than a hundred yards away and sometimes crept up to thirty yards whenever one of the passengers wanted to fire the shotgun.

In spite of the savage lashing he was giving the horse – the owner later complained that the pony was so overstrained that he could not work it for four days – Jacob could not work up any more speed. He had not realised that the chain-brake was on and that one of the wheels was running dead. The horse was soon spent, and as the steepness of the road increased it rapidly became clear that they would have to abandon it. They did so in Winchester Road and once more retreated on foot with their pursuers close behind.

A narrow, shallow stream known as the Ching Brook ran under a very tall railway-arch. One bank, on the Winchester Road side of the arch, was open but on the other side were six-foot palings forming part of the boundary of the yard of some newly erected houses. The two men ran along the fence not realising that the footpath converged on the fence and got steadily narrower until it disappeared altogether. When they realised their mistake it was too late to turn back and they tried instead to climb over the fence. They were both exhausted by the long chase. Jacob managed to scramble over but Hefeld stumbled and fell back just as the first of the pursuers ran up. Seeing that he was about to be captured Hefeld shouted to Jacob to save himself and then fired his gun into his brain. The bullet went in half an inch above the right eye and exploded out through the forehead on the other side. He was badly wounded but still alive. Before he could fire again the gun was wrenched from his fingers. Struggling violently he was overpowered and taken to the Prince of Wales Hospital covered in blood. His shirt was ripped up to bandage his wound. On the way he would not speak beyond remarking that he felt cold.

Jacob, meanwhile, had managed to scramble up the steep incline and cross over the railway line. He cut through Beech Hall Estate, where some houses were being built, ran across Oak Hill, through the hedge, and headed across some fields towards Oak Cottage where he was temporarily lost sight of.

Oak Cottage was a small, old-fashioned house belonging to a coal porter, Charles Rolstone, and consisted of four rooms and a lean-to. Mrs Rolstone was home with the children. Shortly after noon, she heard police whistles and went to her front gate and stood there with her little boy. A policeman hurried by looking for Jacob and curtly told her, 'Woman, go in and shut your door; there is a murderer about.' She went back to the cottage and pushed the door of the lean-to which was to the left of the cottage and formed a sort of scullery. To her astonishment she found it locked. She pushed it again and then to her horror saw a blood-stained face and 'wild staring eyes' staring back at her through a hole six inches square at the side of the door. She began to scream. Her two other children, aged 2½ and 6, were locked inside with this monster.

After Jacob had cut across the field he had scrambled over the back fence into Oak Cottage garden and run into the kitchen. He immediately bolted the front door and locked the door of the lean-to. The children were terrified by his blood-stained appearance as he stood in the kitchen drinking from the mug that had been put on the table for them. He savagely told them to be quiet and then went into the sitting-room.

The cottage was hurriedly surrounded. Police Constable Eagles, when he reached Oak Cottage, heard a crowd of people shouting out, 'He has gone into that house.' He borrowed a double-barrelled breech-loading gun from a bystander and went into the scullery. Moments before another policeman had smashed the glass with a brick and gone in and brought out the children. Hearing a noise upstairs, Eagles went into the yard and got a ladder from the garden of the next house. Meanwhile, two detectives, Dixon and Cater, had crept through a ground-floor window into the cottage. One of the first things they noticed was the number of sooty handprints on the walls and furniture. As the chimney was one of the large old-fashioned type they thought it might be Jacob's hiding-place and fired a shot up the chimney to flush him out. All they did was to dislodge more soot. Then they moved over to the staircase door and Dixon slowly crept upstairs to the landing. Cautiously he opened the front-bedroom door and then sprang back, slamming the door behind him, as he saw Jacob open fire. Dixon shouted to him to surrender and throw out his gun, but Jacob mumbled that he would do no such thing.

Outside the cottage, Eagles dragged the ladder into the yard and put it up against the back wall. He climbed up to the bedroom window and opened it. At the suggestion of an onlooker, a collie dog that was tied up in the yard was passed in to Dixon and sent up the stairs in the hope that it might flush Jacob out or at least divert his attention. Eagles, looking in through the window, saw the dog come out onto the landing and then beyond him Jacob appear in the bedroom doorway pointing a gun at him. Eagles pulled the trigger of his double-barrelled gun but nothing happened. He quickly slid down the ladder before Jacob could fire and tumbled into the house. Jacob had not fired because he had only two bullets left.

Dixon crept up to the landing again with a double-barrelled shotgun which someone had passed in through the window. One of the barrels did not fire, but with the other he peppered the front-bedroom door with shot. He and Cater then began firing through the thin door with their revolvers. Creeping nearer they looked through the bullet holes they had made and saw Jacob hysterically flinging himself about the room. Eagles joined them on the landing. According to Dixon, Eagles did not value his own life as much as he, Dixon, did his, and was anxious to have a shot. 'Let me have a pop at him,' he begged.

At first Dixon would not hand over his revolver as he wanted to defend himself. But Eagles begged again and after some persuasion Dixon allowed him to take it. Eagles, without hesitation, flung his whole weight against the door and burst it partially open. Thrusting his arm around the door until it was well inside the room, he fired two shots. Jacob was leaping about wildly shouting 'Come on now.' His face was spattered with blood and his head and shoulders black with soot; he looked like a blood-stained crow. He peered out of the window and instantly every pane of glass was shattered with shot. He flung himself back on the bed and tried to pull a sheet over his head. 'Come on now,' he screamed as Eagles shouldered the door open and charged into the room. The two men fired simultaneously. Jacob fell back shot in the head.

The child's bedroom was spattered with blood. The ceiling by the window was ploughed up with shot. The pictures on the opposite wall had been smashed and the floor was littered with fragments of smashed ornaments. Eagles snatched Jacob's pistol out of his hand and Dixon grabbed him by the throat. They dragged him backwards along the floor and downstairs into the yard. The crowd gathered round him as he lay there on his back. Some flicker of life still existed, but for a few minutes only. As he hovered between life and death everyone who saw it remembered the horrible grin on his face. He never stopped grinning. That awful look, with the staring eyes, was still on his face when he died a few minutes later. So intense was the feeling against him that had it not been for the police, the crowd, so Dixon believed, would have poured paraffin on him and burned him where he lay.

The chase had lasted more than two hours, and had covered a distance of six miles. Hefeld and Jacob had fired over 400 rounds of ammunition. Two people had been killed and twenty-one others, seven of them policemen, had been wounded or injured in some way. Several of them were in a critical condition.

Up until 4 p.m. Mrs Tyler still expected her husband home to dinner. A friend who had heard that her husband had been shot hurried round to console her, and was startled to find that nobody so far had told her what had happened. He told her that he had heard that there had been a bit of bother and that her husband had been shot in the leg. He had seen a constable being taken to hospital. Mrs Tyler hurriedly put on her coat and set off for the hospital. Before she got there the friend took her into his own home and broke the news that her husband was dead. He was thirty-one. They had been married twelve months.

For some hours nobody knew who the boy was. In the evening somebody heard that a boy named Ralph Joscelyne was missing. A policeman went to the boy's home, taking with him a piece of clothing from the body, and asked the parents if they recognised it. Husband and wife rushed to the hospital. A photograph of the father was taken as he stood outside the coroner's court a few days later. He is standing on the edge of the pavement, rigid with grief. His wife never got over the shock. She kept the shoes that her boy was wearing on the day he died. When she herself died, nearly fifty years later, they were buried with her.

On 26 January the inquest opened on Tyler, Ralph Joscelyne and Jacob. Throughout the proceedings the latter was referred to simply by this name. *The Times* reported that Special Branch officers present believed that his surname, Lepidus, was false. The post mortem on Jacob showed a bullet wound on the right temple, about an inch in front of the right ear, on a level with the upper part measuring one inch by about half an inch. There was no sign of singeing or powder-burns. Some bruises on the face had been caused by gunshot, but only one piece of shot had penetrated the skin and that was above the left eye. There was a wound on the right knee, which had not penetrated the joint. Both hands were covered with black powder, particularly the right.

The principal witness was Eagles who, until the inquest, mistakenly believed that he had killed Jacob. But the jury were handed three bullets to inspect – one from Jacob's automatic, one from Eagles' service-revolver, and the bullet which had been extracted from Jacob's head by the doctor. The difference in bullet size made it perfectly clear that Eagles had missed and that Jacob had fired his own gun into his head. The jury's verdict was *felo de se*.

The shootings intensified local feelings against immigrants, particularly Russians. An English shopkeeper in a mainly immigrant area told one newspaper reporter that the foreigners living around his shop were no use to anybody. His complaint has a familiar ring. 'They change their homes every two months. If the guardians relaxed their vigilance for a single week they would go back to their old trick of sleeping twenty-five in a room. Here and there you find a decent, clean man or woman, but nearly all of them are downright riffraff. I have been here a good many years and I have watched this and other roads go down since they infested them.'

Meanwhile, an armed guard was being kept inside and outside the hospital in case Hefeld tried to escape. He was guarded on either side of his bed by an armed policeman. He frequently tried to get up. According to the hospital governor, he would glare around the ward with an expression of terrible ferocity as if maddened by his impotence.

The bullet had entered his head just above the right eye, and for half an inch around the skin was charred. The bullet had passed out of the other side of the forehead lacerating the exit-wound. Although it had passed over the roof of the eye and had caused a fracture, the eye itself had not been injured. There were also some smallshot in the front of the right leg and two pieces of shot in the forehead under the skin.

His wounds closed up and for nearly two weeks he made excellent recovery. But on 9 February it became necessary to operate to remove some pieces of bone at the entrance to the wound which were causing compression of the brain and which had set up meningitis. He died three days later at 9.15 in the evening. Death was due to meningitis caused by laceration and shock. The coroner's jury brought in a verdict of *felo de se*.

While in hospital he had maintained a stubborn silence as to his own identity and history. The only words he is known to have spoken were those at his capture and those he uttered in hospital just before he died.

'My mother is in Riga,' he whispered.

2

Heirs of the Revolution

From Tottenham Station, which is where Tyler's funeral procession entered the High Road, it is approximately two and a half miles to the cemetery gates. Stretching from end to end, on both sides of the road, stood an unbroken crowd of silent men and women. Hundreds more watched from windows, balconies and rooftops as the procession, taking twenty-five minutes, passed by. A column of three thousand policemen paced slowly behind the black-plumed hearse which had postilions in black velvet riding on the backs of the leading horses. Leading the procession were high-ranking police and government representatives, and behind them the funeral carriages conveying the family and friends. So many wreaths had been sent that extra carriages had had to be hired. Tyler's coffin itself was covered with the Union flag. Close by was a wreath of white flowers from his wife, which the florist had shaped into a lyre with one string broken to symbolise her husband's death. Behind all this pomp Mrs Tyler was already having to face up to the harsh economic reality of her situation: as a policeman's widow the most that she would get would be a meagre pension of £15 a year. Once this was realised a public appeal was made on her behalf which raised the sum of 1,055, but only the interest was paid to her. On her death the capital sum was paid into the Metropolitan and City of London police orphanage fund.

Later that same day, after the crowds had dispersed, the gates were locked at Walthamstow cemetery and in the presence of just the under-taker's men, the cemetery superintendent, two policemen and a Baptist minister, who said a few words, a plain elm coffin was lowered into the ground. The silver coffin-plate was inscribed 'Jacob, died January

23rd, age about 30'. Three weeks later Paul Hefeld's coffin was lowered into the same unmarked grave. As far as the newspapers were concerned, the interment was worth only a cursory paragraph or two, even though there was intense speculation as to their true identities and backgrounds.

'Who are these fiends in human shape, who do not hesitate to turn their weapons on innocent little boys and harmless women?' the *Daily Mirror* cried, and then answered its own question. 'The answer is: they are foreign Anarchists, men who have been expelled from Russia for their crimes, whose political creed and religion is that human life is of no value at all.' Such a response was not unexpected but was about as useful as coding the political parties and groups according to colour, i.e. red for socialists, black for anarchists and white for Tsarist supporters. Anarchism seems to have been a blanket expression used by the press to label any underground resistance to the Tsar, particularly if violence was used. Whether or not this resistance was justified was a question that was frequently ignored and public feeling was greatly influenced by the widespread prejudice against aliens, especially Jews, and the willingness of the revolutionaries to use their bombs and guns on other people's doorsteps.

Part of the problem was that the anarchists' successes in their heyday of the 1890s had created the image of some great international terror network, whereas in reality such acts tended to be carried out by individuals without any coordination from a central organisation. The idea behind such bombings and assassinations – propaganda by the deed – was that they were economical (they did not need mass support) and that by putting the lives of the policy-makers at risk the anarchists could not only shake the existing regime but bring it down and usher in a new society where there would be 'no persecution, no hunger, only warmth and generosity'. This violence, although designed to show the masses the way to revolution, never won mass support and the effect has been described by one of those involved as like a storm taking place in a confined space: the waves got higher and higher but did not break.

As other groups began to use similar methods, anarchism, because of its early successes, still tended to be blamed for the violence. But this popular image of the bomb-throwing anarchist revolutionary was rather unfair, as much of the violence was actually due to one or both of the other two major revolutionary organisations – the Social Revolutionaries (non-Marxist) and the Social Democrats (Marxist).

All three parties believed in 'individual terrorism' – the seizing and retaining of power by striking at government officials, ministers, the Tsar and his family, the aristocracy, the military, and anyone who might be considered as part of the official establishment. Where the Social Revolutionaries and the Social Democrats differed from the anarchists was in their support for 'mass terror' where not just individuals but classes or groups of people were considered as legitimate targets solely on the grounds of property or wealth.

This upsurge in terrorism had its origins in the rising tide of nationalism and democracy not only within Russia itself but inside its satellite countries such as Latvia and Poland. Everywhere there was growing unrest, with recurring demonstrations which could only be controlled by frequent use of an armed police force and the army. The first distinct period of terror initiated by the Russian revolutionaries was from 1878 to 1881 and culminated in the assassination by a bomb of Tsar Alexander II. One immediate consequence of this was the beginning of the pogroms which sent hundreds of thousands of Jews into exile. This foretaste of the Holocaust was a natural extension of the anti-Semitic edicts of successive Tsars, some of them stretching back to the eighteenth century. Jews had ultimately been restricted to what was known as 'The Pale of Settlement' on the Polish–Russian border, to stop them moving any further eastwards. As William J. Fishman wrote in *East End Jewish Radicals,*

> Jews were debarred from employment on government projects such as roads, railways, state manufactories, that is any project related to modernising industrial growth. By the 1870s the Jews were a dispossessed class – mainly artisans, tailors, bootmakers, cigarette hands, in cut-throat competition with each other … Other insecure occupations were forced on them – carriers, cart-drawers, and a growing army of 'peddlers and fiddlers', middlemen with no economic base with the vast majority living on the margin of subsistence.

Jewish boys and young men could be conscripted into the army at any age between twelve and twenty-five and compelled to serve the colours for a term of thirty-one years before release. So many died through cold or hunger or the brutal attempts at 'de-Jewification' that on leaving home the prayer for the dead was often intoned over these unwilling cantonists.

The pogroms began in earnest after the assassination of the Tsar in 1881. Between April 1881 and June 1882 225,000 Jewish families fled abroad. The new Tsar proposed killing a third, converting a third and expelling a third, and fifty villages were burned to the ground in one province alone. Violent resistance resulted in token sentences for the attackers and heavy sentences for Jews attempting to defend themselves. It was said that some of the revolutionaries tried to exploit the situation by forcing the army into a situation where it would have to defend the Jews against the Christians. It was hoped that either the soldiers would refuse to do this, or that the people would be so outraged that a general uprising might occur.

Terror was not intended to replace the long-expected revolution but to maintain the discontent that would one day lead to it.

The Social Revolutionaries were behind the second wave of terror that took place between 1902 and 1911, and in the peak years from 1905 to 1907 the SRs were responsible for the murder of more than two hundred people. However, these were also the years of the abortive 1905 uprising and its bloody repression when, so it has been calculated, some four thousand people were murdered. The right-wing counter movement to the revolutionaries was the forming of the Black Hundreds, supporters of the Tsar who saw it as their duty to use every means, including murder, to suppress the opposition. With the active help and encouragement of the police they initiated and carried out pogroms against the Jews, and after the 1903 Kishinev pogrom and the 1905 uprising the number of Jews escaping the country rose to over two hundred thousand each year.

Russia's humiliating defeat by the Japanese added to the general discontent that led to the abortive uprising of 1905. Strikes and protests spread throughout the empire to the Baltic, Poland, the Ukraine and the Caucasus resulting in whole areas having to be placed under martial law. In the Baltic States such as Latvia revolution and nationalism were virtually synonymous. Latvia was a country that had been fought over and dismembered in turn by Poland, Sweden and Russia and was now divided into three – Livonia in the north, Courland in the south, and Latgale by the Russian border. It had remained under Russian domination ever since Peter the Great had driven out the Swedes and managed to 'break the window' to the Baltic. Despite the policy of Russification – the deliberate suppression of the Lettish language and culture and its attempted replacement with its Russian counterpart – there had been a slow but growing revival of Lettish nationalism.

With the outbreak of revolution in 1905 the Letts saw their chance of freedom at last and demanded an independent Latvian state, with the result that the country was put under martial law. Suspected revolutionaries were shot or hanged within twenty-four hours of trial; whole villages were sacked as if by an invading army, while police and troops, using the Jews yet again as scapegoats for the failure of Tsarist autocracy, carried out hundreds of pogroms against enemies of the regime, whether Jews or non-Jews, forcing many of them to escape to safety abroad. In Riga, the Latvian capital, fifteen thousand demonstrators provoked a clash by marching through the streets in defiance of a military ban. Some of the demonstrators were armed and when police and troops fired on them to disperse them they fired back. The demonstration was quickly suppressed. Some of the demonstrators died in the streets; others, in their panic, tried to escape across the river but the ice was too thin and many drowned in the attempt. Other outbreaks were just as brutally punished. Within the next twelve months an estimated fourteen thousand people were killed, another thousand were hanged and a further seven thousand imprisoned or exiled. Among those arrested was Jacob Peters, who had been an agitator in both the army and the dockyards. He spent eighteen months in prison awaiting trial and while he was there he had had his fingernails torn out under interrogation. He later told of another prisoner, imprisoned and tortured with him, who had his fingernails pulled out, his eardrums punctured and his genitals torn off. In such circumstances it was courageous, as well as a sign of his desperation, that Peters led a prisoners protest demanding that when prisoners were transferred outside the prison they should be more heavily handcuffed and chained. What lay behind this extraordinary demand was the knowledge that the Ochrana (the Tsarist secret police) were using these transfers to shoot prisoners, later explaining these deaths by saying that the prisoners had tried to escape. Peters' demand was made in order to deny them this excuse and to guarantee the safety of prisoners. Altogether he spent eighteen months in prison before being tried and released, but on hearing that he was to be rearrested on account of articles that he had written he escaped to England, arriving in London in 1909. Another escapee was Yourka Dubof who, like Peters, had also been an agitator but when caught had been flogged by the Cossacks and released.

The favourite escape route was through Libau, as this avoided a long railway journey and a border crossing where, if stopped, they were likely to be stripped of anything of value before being allowed to continue. The route was used mostly by the Jewish emigrés, and the Russian government turned a blind eye to many of the port's irregularities. This made it easier for the revolutionaries to slip in and out of the country as seamen. Conditions were much the same at Riga where, the English consul explained, each ship had its recognised quota of stowaways: ships sailed with '160 passengers who were provided with passports ... more likely about 200 will land in London. The emigrants are supposed to be bound for either the United States of America, or South Africa, and might produce vouchers to this effect, but for a great part these vouchers are blinds and are given gratis by the emigration agents here.'

Escaping abroad, for Jew and non-Jew alike, was simply exchanging one prison for another. Certainly the laws were less harsh and there were fewer restrictions, but this time they were imprisoned by their language and culture. Inevitably they only tended to mix with others from the same background and the sense of danger that many of them got from knowing that they were being watched by agents of the Ochrana only tended to make them even more suspicious of strangers. Nor, for the Jew, did the fear of pogroms recede. At the time of the Jack the Ripper murders in 1888 there had been the serious risk of riots in London's East End as it was popularly believed that only a Jew could have committed such murders. Anti-Jewish feeling became anti-alienism and vice-versa. A foreign news editor said of the East End at the time that just by watching the eyes of passing Englishmen as they saw the Jewish girls in their Sunday finery, with golden rings on their fingers, sitting outside in the street, already you could 'discern the look – which is already half indicative of the pogrom'. He went on, 'A pogrom in Brick Lane, in the crossroads of Commercial Road can be a more bloody and terrible affair than one in the Baltic.'

For many of the escapees London was simply a staging post to somewhere else. For others Britain's toleration of political exiles together with its proximity to Europe and the sea routes to the Baltic ports made it a convenient place from which to continue the struggle for revolution. The Russian authorities could have applied for their extradition, but any attempt to do so would have led to international protests. Russian pogroms and barbaric treatment of political prisoners were a world scandal and one of the reasons why Great Britain had such lenient alien laws. For a long time it was policy not to interfere with foreign political groups as long as they did not use Britain as a centre for open propaganda. It was only occasionally that the police came down heavily on the political refugees.

In the three decades up to 1914 about three million Jews passed through Britain with about 120,000 of them finally deciding to settle, the biggest settlement being in London's East End. Few of them moved nearer to the docks than Cable Street or north beyond the track and goods yard of the Great Eastern railway. The boundaries to the east and west were Jubilee Street and Aldgate pump. Since the 1880s many of the old slums, the old rookeries of crime, had been demolished, as big business realised the economic advantages of being so near to the capital's centre. Although more factories and warehouses were built, this commercial redevelopment meant that there were fewer houses to be had, resulting in greater overcrowding. In Whitechapel the maximum limit of 204 people to an acre had risen by the turn of the century to more than 6,000. There was a tremendous displace-ment of population with more and more people crowding into smaller amounts of accommodation.

Inevitably the Jews became the scapegoats for some of the worst excesses. There was a saying that give a Jew an inch and he put a bed in it; give him two and he took in lodgers. Where there should have been back gardens there were, so Jack London wrote in *The People of the Abyss* in 1903,

> one-storey hovels, cowsheds, in which people lived. The roofs of these hovels were covered with deposits of filth, in some places a couple of feet deep – the contributions from the back windows of the second and third storeys. I could make out fish and meat bones, garbage, pestilential rags, old boots, broken earthenware, and all the general refuse of the human sty.

Beds were let on the three-relay system – three tenants to a bed, one every eight hours, so that it never went cold. The space under the bed was let on the same system. Such ghetto overcrowding was common-place. Six, seven, eight and nine people could share one room. London quotes a notice saying, 'A part of a room to let'. Not only were rooms overcrowded with individuals, but frequently they also shared them with their goods because they had nowhere to leave them overnight. Mouldering fruit and veg were a minor hazard; the rag pickers brought their scraps home with them, herrings and gherkins were processed by the pickle men. One of the worse cases quoted by a Whitechapel Sanitary inspector was of a family of four sharing their living room with twelve fowls roosting under the bed and a further 127 in the adjoining room; the previous week there had been 212!

Jewish immigrants quickly adjusted to the new way of life as they had the advantage of the common language of the ghetto; they had their own synagogues, their own school, their own newspapers, and boards of guardians, headed by the great banking families, to help and to advise them. Their presence ultimately imposed a certain respectability in some quarters. In Hanbury Street, where one of Jack the Ripper's victims had been murdered, the prostitutes were forced to quit their rooms because of the higher rents paid by the sweatshop traders. Some could be found in nearby Christchurch Gardens, Spitalfields, where they were willing to sell themselves, as London put it, 'for thru'pence, or tu'pence, or a loaf of stale bread'. Others used St Botolph's, Aldgate, at the bottom end of Houndsditch as a pick-up point for the passing east–west trade, but they had to keep circling the church to avoid the charge of soliciting.

The better life that many of the immigrants had hoped for soon proved to be illusory. They were sorely exploited, the language barrier disqualifying them from any but the most menial jobs. Even then they had to put up with the native hostility where it was felt that to give a job to a foreigner was a betrayal of the English working man. They had to work twelve to fourteen hours a day for a starvation wage, primarily in the 'needle trades'. They became tailors, hat makers, cobblers and watchmakers. Some trades were almost exclusively Russian such as the bamboo workers and slipper makers. The women found work as seamstresses, tailoresses, bow makers and milliners. The clothing trade predominated simply because the trade was so heavily sub-divided; there were twenty-five different processes involved in making a suit and each of these could be quickly and easily learned by the unskilled. (Peters, for instance, became a tailor's presser.) Because the competition was so fierce the labour was sweated. George Sims explained what this meant in 1901 in his book *Living London*:

> There are more than two thousand sweaters in the East End of London. Some have workshops, others use their own dwelling room. Let us enter a 'dwelling' workshop. It is a room nine feet square. In it fourteen people are at work. There is a coke fire, and seven or eight gas jets are burning.

Ventilation there is none. The sweater is at work himself. Hollow-eyed, gaunt-visaged men and women are toiling in various ways. Some have a sewing machine, others are doing handwork. It is evening when we enter. The poor wretches have been at work since six o'clock in the morning. They will go on probably till midnight, for it is the season, and the sweater has his hands full. The wages these poor foreigners can earn by their ceaseless toil will perhaps be eighteen shillings at the week's end. For that they will work on Sunday also.

Sims also made the point that despite these hard conditions their thrift was phenomenal. He calculated that from just one bank (he calls it the Ghetto Bank of Whitechapel) nearly a million roubles was sent each year to family and friends in Russia and Poland. The bank had agents in every town of importance in Russia and dealt with queries in Russian, Polish, German and Dutch. The immigrants, Sims added, had the satisfaction of knowing that, 'If they live on a piece of black rye bread and an onion, or a piece of fish fried in olive oil by way of luxury, they at least know that their frugality and economy will, bye-and-bye, enable them to alleviate the wants of their old people at home or bring some young and cherished relative out of the "land of bondage".'

An additional hardship imposed on the non-Jewish immigrant was the fundamental clash between his beliefs and those of his Jewish neighbours which could and sometimes did lead to the odd pitched battle in the streets. Socialist beliefs, particularly those on free love, were widely viewed as a threat to traditional teachings and were actively condemned from the pulpit by the rabbinical priesthood. In addition the priesthood was seen as putting a brake on anti-Tsarist activity. Some confrontations were deliberately provoked. The East End anarchists in particular would hold their dances on Yom Kippur and provoke their elders to howls of rage and fistfights by standing outside the synagogues eating pork and ham sandwiches. Equally offensive was the anarchist view of free love which not only attacked the whole idea of the family but ran counter to the widely held belief that the girl who lost her virginity was fit for nothing else but prostitution. Jewish hostility was further aroused by dances that went on until 3 a.m. Eventually the Jews were provoked enough to hire their own gangs of thugs to break up anarchist and Social Democrat meetings.

The main hostility was focused on the Anarchist Club which was opened in 1906 by the doyen of anarchist leaders Prince Kropotkin.

Although it was called the Anarchist Club, not all of its members were anarchists. The building had originally been the Jubilee Street Methodist Free Church and subsequently a Salvation Army depot. It was a large building with two halls. In the great hall there was a stage and refreshment counter. The lower hall, which had a gallery and adjoining classrooms, was capable of taking more than eight hundred people. The second floor had a library and reading room. The finance to make it possible had come from dances, subsidies and the pennies donated by 'slaves of the sweatshop'. The overall organisation was the responsibility of the contradictory-sounding Federation of Yiddish Speaking Anarchists. The club provided lectures, recitals, plays, chess competitions and wide ranging debates, and was hardly ever empty. Over countless glasses of tea, as William J. Fishman quoted, 'discussion would go on far into the night between Buddhists, Zionists, Anarchists and Social Democrats who argued excitedly together.' Another meeting place was the Communist Club in Charlotte Street, off Tottenham Court Road. There were other smaller organisations in and around London of which those at Tottenham and Edmonton were the strongest. Outside London the most active centre was probably that at Liverpool.

One of the early problems the Jubilee Street club had to face, as possibly did the others, was that of the foreign revolutionaries who joined. According to Fishman,

> Young expatriates, from the Russian underground, were the most attractive and the most dangerous. They could not adjust to a freer life in London. Convinced that they were the vanguard in the battle against established society, they could see no difference between governments, Russian or British, since all bourgeois authority was the implacable enemy. They also provided an entrée into the revolutionary movement for Ochrana agents, double agents, spies and agents provocateurs.

An early warning of the risks involved centre on a comrade called Tschiskcoff who had allegedly been carrying out expropriations inside Russia itself but had escaped to London where he persuaded other young Russians to join him in underground missions to Russia. While he was in London he had an affair with a young worker and then threw her out of his rooms when his wife joined him a couple of months later. Such behaviour was tolerated so long as his private life did not interfere with his underground activities. Funds were provided for Tschiskcoff to return to Russia to organise an underground conference which he then betrayed to the Ochrana whose agent he had been all the time. The Ochrana had even organised his original escape from Russia. Eventually the underground caught up with him and he was shot for his treachery.

Another Ochrana attempt to smear the revolutionary movement was discovered when agents persuaded four youths and a girl to throw a bomb at the Lord Mayor's Show in November 1909, some months after the Tottenham Outrage. Fortunately the plot was discovered in time and they were persuaded to call it off.

Some of the revolutionaries, Jews and non-Jews alike, drifted into what has been termed 'illegalism' as a way of getting money to continue the fight. Reminders of the struggle were constantly about them in the East End. Russian revolutionary postcards were openly for sale; one might be of the Tsar trembling in front of the headless corpse of Louis XIV. Another might depict him as the instigator of the flogging of women, the shooting of old men and the crushing of liberty. Money could be obtained by the carrying out of 'expropriations' of State and private funds for party purposes. In Russia, as a result of these activities, banks and bureaux de change had to be protected day and night by armed guards. It seemed only logical that these 'exes' should come from the better off. The maxim was to let the Tsar pay for the revolution.

Firearms were subject to very few restrictions in Britain and surprisingly easy to come by. One newspaper told how in December 1905 a Russian bound for London had been stopped by customs at Dover because he had in his luggage forty-seven automatic pistols and nearly 5,000 rounds of ammunition. Astonishingly, none of this arms cache was confiscated and he was allowed to bring it all into the country. A more simple way of obtaining a firearm was to buy the gun – they could cost as little as sixteen shillings – over the counter and conceal the fact by having the sale put down to 'Repairs' on the invoice. If the buyer was caught the maximum penalty was a fine of £5.

One of the strongest condemnations of 'expropriations' had actually come from the anarchist leader Prince Kropotkin who had pleaded in 1904, 'Bourgeois money is not necessary for us, either as donations or as thefts.' But these words had largely been ignored. Both wings of the Social Democratic Party had benefited from 'exes', although they did not usually carry them out themselves, leaving them to specialist groups within the underground movement. However, at a Congress in 1906 the Mensheviks had argued against the Bolsheviks that expropriations should not be used, winning the vote by a large majority. To subvert the ruling Lenin persuaded the conference to set up a small group to be known as the Military Technical Bureau whose business it would be to fight back against the Tsarist Black Hundreds. Lenin took control of the Bureau, ignored the ban on expropriations and channelled the money that was raised from 'exes' directly to his own party. Some of it went to finance his own supporters' attendance at the next Congress which was held in London in 1907. The meeting place was the Brotherhood Church in Whitechapel, which belonged to a religious group known as the Christian Socialists. Originally planned for three days, the delegates stayed there for nearly three weeks. Among the three hundred or so delegates were Trotsky, Voroshilov (a future Soviet field marshal), Maxim Litvinov (future ambassador), Maxim Gorky and a minor delegate from Georgia called Joseph Vissarionovich Dzhugashvili who was to use the pseudonym of Stalin. Within weeks of the Congress breaking up he was to organise the biggest of the Bolshevik expropriations in the Caucasus.

Such a gathering attracted the attention of both police and press, including photographers. Among the unofficial observers were twelve detectives from the Tsarist Embassy in London in addition to the large numbers of Tsarist policemen, so it was reported in the press, who had been sent over to watch the delegates. Additional British detectives were watching not only the delegates but the Tsarist detectives too. So openly was this being done that on one occasion a group of delegates sat down with their British detectives in a pub, struck up a conversation, bought them beers and questioned them as to whether they were working for the British or the Russians. The detectives swore that they were watching both the delegates and the Russian detectives. Other detectives would have had much deeper cover.

Alan Moorehead has said of the 1907 conference that although its arguments were wrung out to their last drop of meaning, it was argument without power or responsibility behind it. The revolutionary movement was running down. He went on:

One has a queer picture of the exiles over the next few years. They hunt in packs. They coalesce only to split up again and form new patterns in another way. The best of friends turn into the bitterest of enemies. They drift from conference to conference throughout Europe, and when they are not together they wrangle at a distance in their newspapers. And all of them from time to time suffer from the chronic melancholy of the exile: the ennui and frustration of never being on their native soil, of watching the years go by and nothing apparently accomplished. The need for money presses upon them continually, and every city where they pause briefly on their wanderings is like any other: the same back room in the same boarding house in the same back street. They live life at second hand, constantly talking about the Russia they cannot see and the revolution that has not happened, endlessly reading newspapers and awaiting news from Russia. But Russia keeps receding.

As far as the British press was concerned anarchism was still a convenient brand label for the different groupings of revolutionary activity. They still tried to invest the movement with its old anarchist bomb-throwing image. The heights of absurdity had been reached during the 1907 Congress when a photograph was published of a cotton weaver, one of the delegates, with the caption 'Princess so-and-so, daughter of a Governor-General' who always carried bombs in her muff when in Russia, and had personally done away with several governors and other high officials'!

Much the same confusion still prevailed after the Tottenham Outrage. For the press, anarchists, Social Revolutionaries and Social Democrats were simply labels meaning much the same thing and therefore interchangeable.

According to *The Graphic*, a local band of anarchists had been in existence in Tottenham for the past two or three years. The membership consisted almost entirely of Letts and was part of the Lettish Socialistic Revolutionary Party. In an interview a well-known but unidentified member of the Russian revolutionary movement said that he had no doubt that the two men responsible for the Outrage were members of the Lettish League which corresponded in Russia to the Social Democratic Party. This League, however, went much further than its English counterpart inasmuch as its members advocated political terrorism. He argued that the two men did not hold anarchist views but were in favour of expropriation. He went further and said that they probably belonged to a Russian society known as Bolsheviky which was the most extreme section of the Democratic Party. (If ever there was an interview that could be said to have blurred the trail, then it was this one. They had been labelled in turn as anarchists, Social Revolutionaries, Social Democrats and finally Bolsheviks.) *The Star* reported that after the shootings the local anarchists had held a meeting in their club room near Ferry Lane; half of those present had repudiated the two men while the other half had praised them to the skies. *The Times* confirmed that the membership of this particular club was entirely made up of Letts who worked at two unnamed establishments (Schnurmann's was possibly one) where, so it was said, foreigners were employed in preference to Englishmen. The group, however, denied *The Star*'s report that it consisted of anarchists and stated that it was part of the Lettish Social Revolutionary Party. They repudiated the shootings and claimed that both Jacob and Hefeld, despite having links with the local branch, had only been connected to it through the central finance organisation which could be traced to an unnamed Communist club in the West End. In another interview, a member of the Social Revolutionary Party said that the two men were members of the Lettish League. He did not think that they were anarchists. Probably they were Bolsheviks. There was no doubt, however, that they were criminals before they joined. He added that he had seen Jacob Lepidus at meetings at a Communist club and believed that he was a Russian outlaw.

There was further confirmation from someone who had known both men and had been taken to the mortuary to make the formal identifications. Subsequently he told a reporter that the police would never find out Jacob's true name, even though he had been closely linked with the revolutionary movement in England for about four years. Members, he said, never knew each other's true names. Jacob was a member of the Bolshevik section of the Lettish revolutionaries but he was not a member of whom they were very proud. He had been a criminal in Russia and merely joined the party to provide cover for his acts of robbery. His family was thought to live near Riga and he was believed to be the younger brother of the anarchist Leiser Lepidus, who had been killed two years before in a bomb explosion in Paris on 1 May 1907. Apparently he had been on his way to plant the bomb that killed him when it exploded in his pocket, blowing him to pieces and badly injuring his companion. Special Branch officers who went to the inquest on Jacob were not convinced by the story and thought that his name was a false one; when pressed for reasons, they would not say why. The few details that did emerge were not particularly helpful.

His lodgings, in the three months before Christmas, had been at a house in Ashby Road, Tottenham. His landlord was Stanislaus Golenski who said that Jacob was a Russian who came from Riga and that he had worked in a timber yard. He had been sacked from his job and shortly afterwards Golenski had evicted him as he did not have any money.

Hefeld's identity was almost as elusive. Schnurmann's had taken him on as an unskilled labourer; his job had been to clean up old rubber for reprocessing. He had lived in lodgings for the two weeks prior to the robbery. He told his landlord that he had started work when he was fourteen (he was now twenty-one) and had been an apprentice of some kind until the age of sixteen. He was equally vague about his movements. He had spent four years in a certain country (Russia?) and one year in Britain. He had travelled widely in Britain, including Scotland, where he had been just prior to the robbery. He had come south with an unidentified man who was a cabinet-maker. His story was partly confirmed by one newspaper which said that both Hefeld and Jacob had travelled south from Manchester or Scotland and that they had left Russia about eighteen months to two years before.

What did emerge was that both men were believed to have been couriers for smuggling propaganda into Russia. So much of this material was found in Hefeld's room that a special car had to be hired to take it away. It was known that Hefeld had been a ship's fireman and that from April to 30 November he had been on board a ship which he left at Christiania. He was also said to have been a block-maker, which would have explained this dual background of printing and sailing. It was thought that both men sailed to Riga and the other Baltic ports and then smuggled the propaganda ashore in their seabags. The press said that it was well known that anarchist literature was produced in large quantities in private houses in Hackney, Hammersmith and certain places in Whitechapel. The *Daily Mirror* dubbed Hefeld somewhat grandiloquently 'the emissary of the Anarchist Secret Service Corps'! Despite the press's use of the catch-all term anarchist, it is doubtful given the known backgrounds of the two men, that it was actually anarchist propaganda that they were carrying. It is far more likely that both men were Lettish Social Democrats, which is largely confirmed by the anonymous press interviews, and that they belonged to the Bolshevik section of the party. Possibly, at a certain level, they could have had dealings with other groups out of mutual self-interest and might even have mounted a joint operation to carry out this particular expropriation.

What is puzzling is that the robbery was so badly bungled. Hefeld made no attempt at concealment, and since he knew that identification was certain if he left anyone alive, this suggests that murder as well as robbery had been the intention of both men from the beginning. Had they been better marksmen murder certainly would have been the result. Possibly the raid had been precipitated by Jacob's obvious cash crisis. He had no job, no money and no lodgings. Although only a small amount of money was involved, it would undoubtedly have tided them over for living expenses and helped to fund another expropriation. The problem they faced, and the desperate means they used to try and solve them, were well illustrated by one of their contemporaries, Victor Serge, who described in *Memoirs of a Revolutionary* how he had found himself in the same situation:

> We had to win our food, lodging and clothing by main force; and after that, to find time to read and think. The problem of the penniless youngster, uprooted or (as we used to say) 'foaming at the bit' through irresistible idealism, confronted us in a form that was practically insoluble. Many comrades were soon to slide into what was called 'illegalism', a way of life not so much on the fringe of society as on the fringe of morality. 'We refuse to be either exploiters or exploited,' they declared, without perceiving that they were continuing to be both these and, what is more, becoming hunted men. When they knew that the game was up they chose to kill themselves rather than go to jail.
>
> One of them, who never went without his Browning revolver, told me, 'Prison isn't worth living for! Six bullets for the sleuth-hounds and the seventh for me!'

The Expropriators

Special branch investigators suspected that a young Lett named Jacob Fogel had been the organiser of the Tottenham Outrage. According to their information he had been a militant anarchist and an active 'expropriator' since his early teens. He had taken part in several bank raids and was wanted for five murders. On one occasion he had been captured by government forces but had managed to escape. This information was only partly true. Fogel's real name was Christian Salnish. He was not an anarchist but a Social Democrat and had been active in the revolutionary movement since the age of thirteen. He had been a party member since 1902 and at the time of the 1905 uprising was only twenty years old. He was a professional revolutionary from 1905 onwards. In the two years following the Baltic state's revolt he organised the resistance fighters in Riga, Libau, Terbata (in Estonia) and in St Petersburg itself. Initially the role of the fighting groups was to protect the strike movement in Riga and then the revolution itself. Punitive government expeditions roamed through Latvia from December 1905 carrying out field courts martial and executions to crush the dissent. This became a guerilla war of such savagery that Jacob Peters, who took part, recalled it as being worse than the Red Terror unleashed nearly two decades later. Prisoners were not brought to trial until over a year had passed, in 1907. Burnings, firing squads and torture were commonplace. Salnish was a vain man but also one of great daring. In September 1905, to release two party members, he led a group of fifty-two armed fighters of the Latvian Social Democratic Workers Party, including Russian members, in an attack on Riga Central Prison. They scaled the prison walls and, after an armed fight with the guards, got them out. Among the attackers, who may have included Peter Piatkow (Peter the Painter), were four or five men who normally worked with Fritz Svaars, suggesting that Svaars himself may have been present.

Svaars was a legendary expropriator. In appearance he was broad-shouldered with grey eyes and light-brown hair and moustache. He tended to hunch his shoulders as he walked. In October 1905 he was arrested with four or five others on suspicion of sabotage (pulling down telephone wires), robbery and two murders, one victim being a shopkeeper and the other a policeman. A couple of days later there was a mass round-up of suspects, with eighteen to twenty in a cell. In the confusion Svaars broke out or bribed his way past guards. More serious was his arrest in January 1906. Because there had been so many mass arrests that week he was taken to the Directorate of the Secret Police offices at Riga police station where, because of the overcrowding, he and some prisoners were kept under armed guard in the corridor of the detective department. He was interrogated and tortured. Somehow Salnish was informed and plans were made to rescue Svaars. The risks were appalling. Not only were there armed guards throughout the building but also troops; in fact there were 160 in the canteen directly over the corridor where Svaars was held! Salnish turned up with only eleven men to get Svaars out. All of them were armed with Mausers. Eight were posted in the street to guard their retreat, two more held up a policeman and a soldier in the waiting room at the entrance, while Salnish and one other bluffed their way up to the detective department as if they were there on official business. They knew precisely where Svaars was. As they entered the corridor Salnish shot the soldier guarding him and then, arming Svaars and some of the other prisoners, they shot their way out of the building. In his haste to escape Svaars left his cap behind, and once they were out in the street this made him a conspicuous target. With great presence of mind one of his rescuers snatched a bowler hat off a passer-by and pressed it on Svaars' head! Altogether five people were rescued, but reprisals were quickly inflicted on those who had been left behind. Two days later four of them were put against the wall of Riga Central Prison and shot.

On party instructions (i.e. under the command of the 'Battle's technical office') Salnish travelled abroad and organised the transportation of weapons and literature from England. In the search for funds to finance these operations he continued to be involved in expropriations and after these had been condemned by the party he came directly under the control of Lenin, who for part of the time was based in Paris. In 1906–7 an unidentified Lett was involved in the attempted purchase of 150,000 rounds of ammunition for Mausers and rifles. Four people were arrested at addresses in Newcastle and Sunderland. Three were convicted of the illegal storage of explosives and given derisory fines ranging from £2.1 7s 6d to £20. The Russian Consul in Newcastle was involved in the investigation which would also have involved by association the Ochrana. The unidentified Lett, who had posed as a German, was never found.

The men engaged in these underground activities travelled backwards and forwards between Europe and America (particularly Boston which was the main American centre for Latvian organisations) and as seamen it was easy for them to smuggle through their guns and propaganda. One of them, Karl Hoffman, was a gun-runner who worked as second mate on board the SS *Veliki Kniaz Alexander Michaelovitch*. Another was Bifsteks whose real name may have been Janis Zakle (pronounced Shakle). Another alternative was Evan Vanoveitch but if his name was Zakle, as seems likely, then he too had been part of the resistance in Riga. He had been the commander of militia of the Riga Federative Committee which had taken over the city for two months in the late autumn of 1905. As with some of the others involved, the 1905 revolution had profoundly influenced his political thinking. He had become more radical and moved away from the centralisation policies of social democracy towards anarchism. Svaars too was turning to anarchism.

At some unknown date Bifsteks escaped abroad, and when he surfaced again it was in London, where he was living in a sailors' hostel in High Street, Poplar. The landlord was an anarchist like himself. Bifsteks was regularly away at sea, usually for a month at a time on a cargo ship to America, but when on leave he would go to the Anarchist Club in Jubilee Street. It was there in the summer of 1908 that he met a young teenager named Fanny Perelman and started an affair with her. (Possibly this was a piece of deliberate manipulation, however, as there may have been links with her father going back to the uprising.) According to Charles Perelman's subsequent statement to the police, he brought his wife, three sons and three daughters, from Srfrtov, Volga, in Russia to London in July 1906. He moved house four times before moving to 29 Great Garden Street, which was a bigger house than his previous one, as he intended to take in lodgers. This was about six months after Fanny had introduced him to Bifsteks. The latter moved in with them as a lodger and occupied the front room on the ground floor. He said that he had got a holiday from his ship. About two weeks later he introduced Perelman to a friend of his, Greasha, who needed lodgings. Perelman took him in and he shared the same room on the ground floor with Bifsteks. This would be about ten days to a fortnight before the Tottenham Outrage. Greasha or Grishka Sander was another of Christian Salnish's aliases.

In view of the subsequent comings and goings, it is unlikely that Perelman was the innocent bystander he pretended to be. It is extremely likely that he shared the same background as the others and there is indeed some evidence for this. In December 1905 there had been an armed uprising in Tukums with a fiercely fought battle between the local population and 2,000 troops. In order to capture the town the troops knew they would have to raze it to the ground, but after three days' fighting they were running short of ammunition. Calling a temporary ceasefire the attacking commander General Huronshenkov promised the insurgents that if they evacuated the town they could keep their arms and there would be no reprisals. After the insurgents had marched out, however, the general's commander, Baron von Reke, reneged on the agreement and executed sixty townspeople including several women and children. At the same time General Huronshenkov pillaged and bombarded the nearby town of Telsin, which is where Peter the Painter is supposed to have come from. Among the sixty named as being executed was one Karlis Perlmanis or Charles Perelman. Possibly this is a mistake as the same source also wrongly lists Hoffman as being killed. Some of Svaars' friends were active in Tukums as was Rudolph Lemkins who was a friend both of Salnish and of Svaars' cousin Jacob Peters.

According to Perelman's son Carlusha (Charles) the family had been brought over through the good offices of the Rothschild family and Rufus Isaacs. It was unlikely to have been through their personal sponsorship and more probably through some relief agency to which they lent their names. Perelman, now nearly seventy, tried to look the rebel that he always claimed to be, affecting a black sombrero and cloak as part of this image. He was still a good looking man with dark grey hair, a neatly trimmed 'artist's' beard, black eyes ('big like a deer's') with the beautiful speaking voice so necessary to being a good confidence-trickster, which is how his son remembered him. Carlusha, when small, would sit on his father's knees just to listen to this voice which was so beautiful that he never heard its like until the occasion, some years later, when he met a Russian officer.

Perelman obviously had considerable charm which is what had possibly attracted his wife in the first place. Deborah Maichihoff was the daughter of a poor man's lawyer (because of the Tsarist edicts Jews were not allowed to enter into the professions). She was thirty years his junior and had been only sixteen years old when he met her for the first time. She was a very pretty teenager with blonde hair and blue eyes. Perelman was then forty years old. He had been a student at Warsaw University and claimed to be a Doctor of Philosophy. He also claimed to speak seven languages. Clearly there were strong family objections to any marriage between them, his age being the obvious barrier. Eventually the couple were forced to elope, but the children's ages suggest that they waited for six years, until she was twenty-two, before doing so; after that there is almost one birth every year for the next six years, three boys and three girls, from 1894 onwards.

Whether Perelman was the rebel he pretended to be, or whether it was part of an act to get money, is not clear. Certainly his behaviour suggests that the latter was nearer the truth. He had a limited talent for painting. Even his son, who was then an admiring but streetwise nine-year-old, remembers the paintings as amateurish. The only one that Carlusha could remember later in life was a painting three feet by two called 'Pogrom in Minsk'; hardly a painting for hanging at home. It was a street scene depicting forty to fifty terrified people at the mercy of Cossacks. Furniture was being thrown into the street (Carlusha remembered a broken piano) while the Cossacks rode up and down whipping some of the people and hanging others from lamp posts. Perelman apparently charged £50 a time for such paintings, but the wealthy Jews to whom he sold them got fed up with seeing him and the money given to him seems to have been out of charity or embarrassment rather than as any reflection of the paintings' true worth. When the money from this source dried up Perelman tried for other work but his attempts never lasted very long, either because of laziness or rheumatism, and eventually, in 1910, he acquired a place in Montague Street where he found an outlet for his artistic talents by enlarging photographs and touching them up.

Another of Perelman's lodgers was a man called William Sokolow or Sokoloff but who was better known as Joseph. He was a tall, dark-skinned man with a long thin nose and face, and he walked with a limp. His body twisted with each step he took so that his right foot always seemed to be dragging along behind his left. Possibly there was some shortening of the leg from a fracture in the right thigh bone. By profession he was a watchmaker, but since coming from Russia eleven years before, he had worked for twelve different jewellers up and down the country. Apart from two long periods of employment, his average length of time with each varied from three to six months. In October 1908 he was employed as the manager of a jeweller's shop in Old Street. Within the month the shop was burgled, the safe broken open and jewellery and watches worth about £150 stolen. The police suspected that the burglary had been faked but it was much later before they guessed that Joseph had probably organised it together with Bifsteks and Salnish.

The Tottenham robbery followed three months after this burglary, and Salnish, who seems to have already been under some kind of observation from the Special Branch, was immediately suspected of being implicated in the Outrage. None of the money had ever been recovered and it was widely believed that it had been passed to a third accomplice in the early stages of the chase when this would have been possible. The police were apparently convinced that Salnish was the third man, but they did not have any evidence on which to arrest him. Presumably the fact that his lodger was under suspicion was communicated to Perelman, and to protect himself he ordered both Bifsteks and Salnish to leave. Significantly, however, he didn't deliberately distance himself from them, as might have been expected, but instead took in one of their friends as lodger in their place, suggesting again that he was far more involved with them than he would have admitted publicly. Before Salnish and Bifsteks left, this friend stayed the night with them. He was Fritz Svaars. After they had gone he took the upstairs room facing the street. (Where we have the information, it is a common feature of all their lodgings that they take front rooms with easy access to the street to avoid being trapped in an emergency.)

Apart from his cousin's statement that at some time in 1906 he was a sailor, not much is known about Svaars' life during the intervening years. Between his two escapes in October 1905 and January 1906 he was one of twenty-five guerillas who attacked a detachment of dragoons outside a factory in Riga. In February 1906 six of the people Svaars normally worked with carried out an expropriation in Helsinki. Whether he was involved is not known. However, he was certainly continuing to carry out expropriations, because by the time he resurfaced in 1909 he was wanted for a bank raid in Pennsylvania where a reward of $20,000 was being offered for his capture. Within two weeks of moving into Great Garden Street he was joined by George Gardstein (this was one of several aliases), who was to effectively replace Salnish as the organiser of future expropriations in London.

Gardstein was subsequently found in possession of a membership card for the 'Leesma' or 'Flame' group of Lettish anarchists. A Special Branch report estimated that there were only eight or nine members altogether, but another source puts the number at fifteen. They had no known meeting place and none of them were known to any of the recognised groups. The card was in the name of Grunberg, who had been an organiser of the fighting groups in Latvia. He had been one of the five rescued with Svaars from the secret police headquarters and had subsequently taken part in the Helsinki expropriation. Gardstein was certainly an anarchist but it is unlikely that he was actually Grunberg, as he was reported to have gone to Warsaw at the end of 1905 and organised several acts of terrorism there. He was then using another of his aliases, Morountzeff or Murontzeff. According to the *Daily Telegraph*'s Warsaw correspondent, 'It was further discovered that Murontzeff had offered himself to all the advanced parties, including the "Black Flag" group of Anarchists, as instructor for their "fighting organisations". His offers, however, were declined. Thereupon he collected together a number of hooligans and thieves and organised a special party known as the *Zmowa Robotnicza* (Workers' Conspiracy), which devoted its baleful energies to robberies with violence and attacks upon banks and commercial houses. In these outrages seven persons were killed.' The police successfully broke up his gang and as his behaviour compromised the revolutionaries abroad, efforts were made to 'remove' him. These failed, and in one attempt Gardstein killed the two Social Democrats who had been sent to murder him. Ultimately, in 1907, he was forced to escape from Poland. Subsequently he was wanted for robberies in Germany.

Gardstein seems to have been a freelance 'Mr Fixit' who, while working for himself, could pull together people of different political persuasions and beliefs, and get them to work together in a common enterprise. It was as such an organiser that he had offered his services to the anarchists, and that was how he had worked in Warsaw. He was now to do the same in London.

Gardstein and Svaars stayed with the Perelmans for three months. Among the visitors was John Rosen (real surname Tzelin) who had been born in Riga but came to London in January 1909. He claimed that it was while staying at the sailors' lodging house in Poplar that he first met Bifsteks, and then Fanny Perelman and subsequently Svaars, Hoffman and Peters. He earned his living as a hairdresser which is why his nickname was the 'Barber'. He lived in a small back room behind the barber's shop at 112 Well Street, Hackney, which his employer wanted him to work up into a profitable business. Many people thought that he and Svaars, because they looked so alike, particularly in profile, were brothers.

Fritz's only relation known to be in London was his cousin Jacob Peters who had arrived in October 1909. He was then twenty-three years old. Up to 1905 he had been employed as a grocer's assistant in Libau; he then worked as a dock labourer and in a butter factory. As an active member of the Lettish Social Democratic Party he had carried out propaganda work in the army and among the workers. According to an article he wrote about his experiences, events in Courland moved very fast from the spring of 1905 onwards. The city workers suddenly became conscious of their own industrial strength and increasingly used the weapon of the strike. At this time Peters was working in Libau. He and his fellow party members were widely known to the workers and they agitated among them quite openly, with virtually no opposition from the workers themselves, though Libau was one of only three towns where the military still had control; elsewhere there were peasants' risings and workers' strikes. The plight of people like Peter's own father, who was a hired farm labourer, was wretched under the oppressive rule of the landowners, particularly the German Baltic barons. But the successes of the 1905 revolution were swiftly followed by reaction and retribution, and a terror worse than the Bolshevik Red Terror which followed the 1917 revolution and in which Peters himself played a leading part. Punitive expeditions made up of mounted Cossacks were led by the Baltic barons. Many young revolutionaries took to the forest and became known as the 'woodland brethren'; they formed units and carried out raids to execute provocateurs or to rob post offices. Although hunted by the barons they were helped to safety by the peasants, and in the cities the party helped them to emigrate or to live under false identities. Peters was arrested, held in Libau prison and tortured by having his fingernails pulled out.

He was held for eighteen months before being brought before a court martial and acquitted.

He was released on 1 September 1908, but on hearing that he was to be rearrested on account of some subversive articles he had written he fled to Germany, intending to go on to the United States. But he did not have sufficient money to make the onward journey so instead he went to Denmark and, not able to get any work, finally to London. The cousins soon quarrelled – to Peters his cousin's conversion to anarchism must have been anathema – and Peters moved to other lodgings, although the two men did continue to meet in other people's rooms.

Other visitors were Yourka Dubof and Karl Hoffman. Dubof (real name Yurka Laiwin) had known Svaars for about two years. He was the son of a small farmer and in 1905 when he was eighteen he had gone to Riga to become an art student. Like Peters he was a member of the Lettish Social Democratic Party and must therefore have been caught up in the revolt. In the autumn he went back to the farm, but he was arrested and flogged with *nagiakas* or Cossack whips which left him permanently scarred. He escaped first to London in June 1907 and then to America, to New Jersey, before returning to Riga in June 1909. He came to London again in January 1910, and then made a journey to Switzerland before returning on 20 September to find lodgings in Shepherd's Bush.

Hoffman, however, was actively engaged in gun-running. He had run away to sea when he was twelve. His real name was Alfred Dzircol, which he subsequently anglicised to Driscoll. Although he was not an intellectual, he had a lot of common sense and a highly developed instinct for sensing danger. Sometimes, even in a safe house, he might wake up, and if this instinct told him to get up and go he would do precisely that without trying to analyse the reasons.

The back room of 29 Great Garden Street was rented to another underground revolutionary named Nina Vassilleva. Her father had been a chef in one of the Tsar's palaces. She was then or would soon become Gardstein's mistress. Meeting her in later life young Charles Perelman (Carlusha) said that he found nothing glamorous about her but what he did sense in her, even when he was a boy, was 'a rare, rare dedication'. She too was wanted in Russia. What for, we don't know and neither apparently did the British police, which suggests that the name she used was false. She would only go so far as to say that if sent back to Russia she would be hanged. She was great friends with the Perelman family, particularly with Fanny, who one day gave her a photograph of herself taken with her father and Gardstein, dedicated 'To dear Nina from the "wicked" Fenia'.

The Perelmans' youngest son, nine-year-old Carlusha Gregoria Barlosav Carloivish Perelman, knew instinctively that his father was a fraud and, worse, there was the dark side to him which he detested. Perelman was frequently brutal to his wife, and he could be equally brutal to his children. Once he pinned one of his teenage daughters to the floor with his foot on her throat, after which Carlusha wanted to kill him. In revenge he stole his father's tobacco tin, hid it in his pillow and slept on it every night for the next two weeks.

The boy's strongest relationship was with his mother. His father was a womaniser even in his old age and this, together with his brutality, explains the apparent disintegration of his marriage. An equally important factor was probably the thirty-year gulf between husband and wife, and Carlusha soon became aware of his mother's fondness for other men. When they had first arrived in England, soon after the move to Plumbers Row, his mother had started doing sewing work for Solomons, who had a factory in Great Garden Street. Her wages at that time were seventeen shillings a week, and that is what they lived on. As Carlusha got older his mother would take him to the factory 'bastings' to help out; he would use a little stick to pull out the 'bastings', or cotton threads, that were used to tack the cloth together before sewing. He quickly became aware of his mother's relationships with various men, particularly with Mr Solomons, into whose office she would often disappear, with her work in her hand, while the other women would sit sewing and muttering about the length of time she had been gone. Their suspicions were not misplaced and on several occasions Carlusha caught his mother with her skirts up around her waist with different men. Instead of recoiling with shame or embarrassment, the boy would stand his ground and refuse to go away; it was the men who had to leave and not him. Nor, surprisingly, did his mother seem to mind when they went.

Although they were Jewish, the Perelmans were not part of the surrounding community. According to Carlusha, he was fourteen or fifteen years old before he even knew that he had met another Jew. Such a remark is open to various interpretations. As a boy who was street-wise he could not have avoided seeing them and recognising them. Meeting them in the sense of knowing them to speak to is clearly what was meant, and this is confirmed by the fact that he would not mix with or associate with neighbouring children. He was a little snob, he said in later life, although he was not aware of it at the time. His unorthodox upbringing was partly to blame. Educationally and culturally the family were well above their neighbours. The family, so he said, were 'classical' in their outlook. Politics was another reason for their isolation. Perelman was part of the generation that had rejected Judaism as conflicting with their socialist beliefs. 'The progressive intelligentsia eschewed religion as obscurantist and reactionary, bound by the rigidity of ritual and orthodoxy and a priesthood who acted as a brake on anti-Tsarist activity. (The rabbis persisted in fulminating against the Socialists from the pulpit!) For them the Jewish tradition was associated with the unedifying physical and mental stagnation of the Ghetto.'

Carlusha was fascinated by the family's lodgers and could not stay away from them. He knew that the men were adventurers who carried revolvers, and though his father warned him not to, he was always listening at keyholes and peering under doors. They had a closeness which he had never seen before and he instinctively knew that if necessary they would have given their lives for each other. Gardstein was his particular hero. Not only was he the cleverest but he was tremendously strong and on occasion he would show off by lifting three people – Perelman, Fanny and Carlusha – at one time in a straight armlift off the ground and holding them there for five seconds.

To his delight Carlusha became useful to his father's lodgers because he had a smattering of English and could translate for them when they wanted to go out. Possibly they exaggerated his importance to them, but the boy was pleased and he would walk happily behind them when they went to a pub in the afternoon. What was seems odd was that thirty yards back there would be one or more policemen shooing them along the pavement. Such conspicuousness seems odd, but is confirmed by Arthur Harding, a local villain, living in the same area at the time. According to him the group – he calls them Gardstein's mob – were part of the landscape in Brick Lane. Gardstein used the Warsaw restaurant in Osborne Street, but collectively the group would go to the restaurant in Sclater Street next to the King's Arms near Clark's coffee shop, which is where Harding and his friends used to meet. Harding was attracted to the 'two or three lovely girls with them, all good lookers, nice, shapely girls, all blonde'. Conversation between the two groups was difficult, because neither side could understand the other much;

in an apparent row over one of the girls, Harding was pulled away by one of the Gardstein men and in retaliation Harding gave him a right-hander and knocked him down. In retrospect, Harding said somewhat dramatically that he never knew how close he was to getting a bullet in him, though at the time he did not know that they were armed. One thing struck Harding about the group:

> The most peculiar thing about them was that they always walked in the road, never on the pavement. I can see the idea, if anyone's waiting for you to arrest you, they wouldn't wait out in the road, they'd wait in a doorway which they could see in the road. They always marched along in the roadway with their womenfolk in the middle of them; they numbered sometimes as many as twelve or fifteen people, men and girls – the girls were good-lookers, gypsy-style. We would have liked to be friendly with them. We knew they were crooked, but we were told they were on the run from the Russian secret police; that fact alone gained them our sympathy. They had to live, they had to pay their lodgings, and they needed the money for their politics when all's said and done. That's why they did these robberies.

Nina, certainly, and Fanny Perelman, were probably two of the blondes that Harding saw. The friendship between the two was one of the reasons for Nina moving into the back room of the house. Before that she would stay the occasional night and, despite his father's warnings, the continually curious Carlusha would watch her. The boy was not deterred from his spyings even when he was caught by Fritz who came up the stairs and saw him peering under a door. 'You little bastard' he shouted in his gruff voice and caught hold of him. Fortunately Gardstein was coming up the stairs behind Fritz and had to tell him several times to leave him alone. The boy knew, although he could not have put it into words, that Nina's overnight stays had some sort of sexual connotation for the group. What the boy saw when he peeped under the door were 'shadows making images'. In the centre of the room was a basin and around it he could see four pairs of legs, one of them Nina's. The room would suddenly acquire a stillness and although he never saw what happened, as an adult he surmised that Nina had been masturbating each of the men in turn.

Such behaviour seems less surprising if one recalls some of the details of the Patty Hearst kidnapping by the Symbionese Liberation Army in

1974. She explained in her book, *Every Secret Thing*, 'Free sex was one of the principles of the cell. It was obvious … that revolutionaries operating underground could not go out in the street and find sex in the usual way. Therefore everyone in the cell had to take care of the needs of the others. No one was forced to have sex in the cell. But if one comrade asked another, it was "comradely" to say yes.' She added, 'It was ironic that all of the SLA sisters believed in the liberation of women, and yet the men in this cell acted as though the women were there to serve them sexually. It was even more peculiar that none of the other women appeared able to see what I could see.' Possibly because Nina was his mistress, Gardstein was never one of those that took part in this ritual.

Perelman moved his lodgings yet again, this time to 74 Wellesley Street. Prior to the move he gave Gardstein and Svaars notice to quit and used the move itself as an excuse for getting rid of Joseph also, though they kept in contact. Yourka Dubof was one of the lodgers who replaced them. Nina's friendship with Fanny survived only a little longer, until February/March 1910, and with the change of relationship Perelman ordered her to leave.

Gardstein found lodgings at 44 Gold Street where he rented a back room in the name of P. Morin. In March 1910 the tenancy changed hands. The new landlord was an Austrian Jew, by profession a 'boot-clicker', named Jacob Kempler. Kempler agreed to keep him on as a lodger at a rent of four shillings a week but understandably he was puzzled by Gardstein's long, unexplained absences. From the quantity of laboratory equipment and chemicals in his room he thought that he might be a chemist. Gardstein encouraged him in this belief and, as if to stress the dangerousness of his materials, always asked that the room of his door should stay locked whenever he was away. In fact the only key that Gardstein possessed was the key to the street door.

There were two unexplained absences during Gardstein's stay. The first was from May to July 1910 and the second from September to the middle of October of the same year. On both occasions Gardstein only took away with him a small portmanteau. Significantly he promised to pay the rent on his return. Inevitably this only fuels speculations that he was carrying out an 'expropriation'. The first time that he went away Joseph turned up at his lodgings with a letter from Gardstein saying that he could sleep in his room in his absence. Joseph stayed for five weeks until the landlord became so exasperated by the amount of rent owing that he ordered him out.

Meanwhile, Fritz Svaars dropped out of sight for almost a year. During this period he returned to Riga and in January 1910 was captured by the Russian secret police. He had various aliases and so was able to keep his true identity hidden. He was only in police hands for eleven days but in that time he got so many beatings that his head, so he later wrote to his sister Lisa, felt quite soft. He was released on bail and followed everywhere until he managed to give his trackers the slip and escape abroad once more. But the damage had been done. The beatings had apparently broken his spirit and from then on the spectre of betrayal began to haunt him as he knew that if captured again he would break under interrogation and tell everything he knew. By the time he returned to England in June 1910 he had made up his mind to send for his wife, who was still living somewhere in the Baltic, and emigrate to Australia.

For the rest of the year much of his limited social life was centred on the Anarchist Club. It was in the club, through a personal introduction by Gardstein, that Fritz met Luba Milstein, and they soon became lovers. Theirs was a stormy relationship. They quarrelled so fiercely in the first month that Fritz walked out on her without saying where he was going and disappeared for two weeks. When he returned he was in possession of several watches that were apparently part of the proceeds of an expropriation. He gave one of the watches to Luba and kept the rest for pawning. While she may have suspected what he was up to, that was not the cause of their quarrelling which continued for the whole of the relationship. The root problem was his admission that he was a married man and that he was planning to emigrate to Australia with his wife. Fritz had never attempted to conceal these facts which were known to even casual acquaintances.

However, Luba, who was only 19, was so besotted with Fritz that, as she later wrote, if he had told her at midday that it was midnight she would have believed him. Ultimately she moved in with him, though knowing that this could only be on a temporary basis. Possibly she was hoping that such a move would make him give up his wife. Fritz found lodgings for them at 35 Newcastle Place and rented a single room on the first floor; the landlord, Abraham Smolensky, a Hebrew teacher, lived in the two rooms below them. Gardstein painted, papered and whitewashed the room for them.

Luba's family were Russian Jews. She herself had been born at Leipowitz near Kiev. Her father, who was a commission agent, had

died in Russia in 1906. His widow and family were living at 2 Cecil
Court off the Mile End Road. Luba's brother Jack had a tailor's shop
in Branch Yard, Whitechapel, where she worked for him twelve
hours a day with an hour's break for lunch. She would normally
finish about 8 p.m., but sometimes sooner if the work was slack.
She would then hurry away to meet Fritz. It was not long before her
brothers Jack and Nathan learned that she was living with a married
man but they could not find out from her where or with whom
she was living, and she refused to break off the relationship. Despite
the family pressure she carried on working for her brother finish-
ing skirts. One of the persons she worked with, and who seems to
have had a stabilising influence on her life, was a small hunchbacked
Polish Jew, who had left Russia about three years before, named Sara
Rosa Trassjonsky. She herself was highly-strung but what was to
follow would drive her insane.

Although Luba was passionately in love with Fritz, it is doubtful
whether he returned her affection. When they were together in their
room his friends constantly intruded, her presence being no deterrent.
Gardstein, Karl Hoffman and John Rosen were regular visitors; and in
the autumn, for five weeks, until their final move, their room was used
on a daily basis by Peter Piatkow (alias Peter Schtern, alias Peter the
Painter) who had recently arrived from Paris. It is extremely doubtful if either Piatkow or Schtern was his real name, but it was known
that he came from Pskow in the province of Courland. Like others
in the group he had been imprisoned for his part in the 1905 uprising but had escaped and gone into hiding in his hometown where he
knew he would be safe. He could not stay hidden for long and when
he surfaced he earned a living by painting street doors and numbers,
hence his nickname Peter the Painter. (As someone later caustically
remarked, if he had been called Albert the Greengrocer nobody would
have remembered him.) Peter's father died in 1908 while he was still on
the run but his mother and sisters were still living at the family farm
somewhere near Talsen.

Peter made use of his exile and travelled widely. While he was living
in Marseilles, an uncle, who was also an army colonel, told him that if
he would go to Paris and study – anything but politics – he would send
him a regular sum of money each month. This offer was apparently
rejected (because the uncle was a Tsarist officer?) and Peter continued
to earn his living as a painter. He was apparently a hard worker and

in Marseilles he earned a fair living at his trade. His personal habits were fairly modest. He was a vegetarian but enjoyed smoking and playing cards. There was a girlfriend, Anna Schwarz, but she was living out of reach in Russia. Such an innocuous-sounding individual seems to acquire a greater depth of personality with the official report that was subsequently forwarded by the French Chief of Police. According to this report, while searching the residence of one of an international group of anarchists who had been captured at the railway station at Maisons Alfort where they had gone to obtain dynamite, the French police came across Peter Piatkow. His real name, they said, was Peter Piatkoff, though he was then using the name of Paul Pavloff. He had been born on 20 June 1884 at Povsk in the Grand Duchy of Courland. He was fluent in French, German, English, Russian and Yiddish and when resident in Jewish houses he used a Jewish name. Despite expulsion from France he had reappeared in 1909 and was known to have been living in a house in the 14th Arrondissement but shortly afterwards he disappeared again.

Why he suddenly turned up in London in the autumn of 1910 has never been satisfactorily explained. Was he one of the group's leaders? Certainly he seemed to have been given the status of leader from the way that he took over Fritz's lodgings for five weeks, almost as if he were holding meetings and conferences on a daily basis. (At night he slept in Karl Hoffman's lodgings at 36 Lindley Street.) Others believed he was an agent provocateur acting under instructions from Russia to incite expatriates to some outrage which would create sympathy for the Russian government's anti-revolutionary measures and at the same time smear the revolutionary cause.

On 4 November Fritz, Luba and Peter moved to new lodgings at 59 Grove Street; to two first floor rooms which had been found for them by old Mr Reuben, the grocer. Smolensky later said that he gave them notice to quit because of the number of visitors (ten to twelve at a time), as well as the mandoline playing and the late hours that they kept, though according to Luba they moved because Fritz and Peter did not want to be separated. Either explanation could be true. Gardstein helped them to move their possessions, which they trundled through the streets on a costermonger's barrow. Possibly it was during this move that Fritz went round the room tearing the wallpaper off the walls in strips. He said the room was not fit for pigs to live in. 'We'll show the bastards,' he said.

Svaars' lodgings at 59 Grove Street.

At the new lodgings Peter took possession of the front room, which was the biggest, for himself; Fritz and Luba had the smaller back room despite the fact that they were paying the rent.

Soon there was the usual run of visitors; Gardstein, Joseph, Hoffman, Rosen and a newcomer, Max Smoller, whom Luba had seen loitering about Reuben's grocery. Luba knew Fritz was a locksmith, but living with him – and as work slackened off at the tailor's shop she spent more and more time at home – she began to realise that Fritz had little, if any, regular employment. The same was true of Peter the Painter, although Fritz told her that he was studying art and that his parents were sending him money. (His poverty and total dependence on Fritz indicate that his uncle was not.) She asked Fritz how he earned his money but he told her curtly to mind her own business. She must have guessed. She knew that Fritz occasionally carried a Browning, and Gardstein the less compact but more deadly Mauser which he concealed in a specially constructed trouser pocket. She knew nothing of the group and began to resent their presence. She had no keys, not even to the street door, and often she was excluded from the meetings in the front room, which were never explained to her; conversations were whispered or switched into another language, which she did not understand, if she came near. Occasionally she was allowed into the front room but at other times, coming home weary from work and worried by the persistent nagging of her brothers, she would scream at the constant noise and muddle, and humiliate Fritz in front of the others. Worse still was the knowledge that Fritz had sent money to his wife, who would be joining him in January 1911.

Her behaviour was an added reason why Nina Vassilleva and Jacob Peters stayed away. Fritz did not particularly like Gardstein's mistress, and she never visited his new lodgings, although Gardstein was a daily visitor. Peters only came a few times, but it was their political differences basically that kept the cousins apart. Only Gardstein held the group together and, in Salnish's absence, he assumed the leadership. Salnish, if he were needed, could still be contacted through Bifsteks' fiancée, Fanny Perelman, or through Karl Hoffman whom he apparently saw on rare occasions. Gardstein was the obvious choice as leader, particularly as Fritz was still suffering from broken nerves and planned to emigrate. He was the group's Mr Fixit.

The information for the next expropriation came from Joseph. He had once worked for a jeweller in Houndsditch in the City of London and he now heard that since May a new jeweller's, 'H. S. Harris', had opened which was reputed to be the wealthiest in the street. Access would have to be from one of the empty houses in Exchange Buildings, behind the shop, which would have to be rented. Cutting equipment would also have to be bought to open the large iron safe that was visible from the street. But the group's finances were parlously low. It was possibly on the understanding that he would provide extra finance that Joseph introduced Max Smoller to the group.

Smoller lived with his wife and two children in Wellesley Street, not far from Perelman's lodging house. According to Nina Vassilleva, he and Joseph had once been caught and tried for a fur robbery in which they were both implicated. They were great friends still – in fact, Joseph had such great admiration for Max that he boasted that he was his pupil. Both men were said to be wanted in the Crimea for a number of jewel robberies similar to the one they were now planning.

The houses in Exchange Buildings, a cul-de-sac at the back of Houndsditch, were owned by Millard Brothers in Houndsditch.

On 21 November a pimply-faced man with thick lips and the appearance of an East European Jew called at the office to ask whether they had any houses to let, as he was in business in the West End and he wanted somewhere handy for himself and his wife. He spoke fairly good English and said that his name was Joe Levi; in reality it was Max Smoller. He said that he was anxious to move in quickly; but two or three days later, when he called back to ask if the house was ready, he was told that a better one, No. 11, would be vacant by the end of the week. Having looked over it he said that he would take it as it did not need so much doing-up. His rent was ten shillings a week, and he took possession on 2 December.

The hesitation over the choice of house is understandable as No. 10, which backed on to the jeweller's, had already been let. The exact position of the shop was uncertain. The back yards were only three feet wide and the view was obscured by a wall which was higher than the houses. No. 9 was still empty but to rent that too was beyond the gang's means at that time.

Gardstein's plans had not included Fritz, but now he had to be involved. Money was also needed for extra equipment. He asked Fritz to lend him 100 roubles (£10) for two weeks. Fritz had already spent 160 roubles on his boat tickets to Australia and sent 100 roubles to his wife to join him; he could only manage 60 roubles, which left him a meagre 20 roubles (£2) in cash. He gave Gardstein the last watches he had kept for pawning from the last expropriation, and even took back from Luba the watch he had given her to raise the extra money. After several months of boring inactivity and domestic squabbles it was not too difficult for Gardstein to persuade him to take part in the expropriation, although Fritz's experiences earlier in the year had made him terrified of being caught. On 6 December, Fritz, using the name Goldstein, speaking broken English and carrying an umbrella, rented No. 9 Exchange Buildings. He explained that he only wanted it for two or three weeks to store Christmas goods and paid five shillings deposit. He took possession on 12 December. Gardstein, meanwhile, used some of the money borrowed to buy a large quantity of chemicals, a book on brazing metals and cutting metals with acid.

Most of the inhabitants of the other houses in Exchange Buildings assumed that the new tenants were a newly married couple and wished to be left alone. Occasionally they saw Nina Vassilleva in a white blouse and blue skirt taking down the shutters or walking out of No. 11 with a shawl pulled over her face. Max and Joseph, who stayed with her, were rarely seen; they slept in the first-floor bedroom and Nina on the sofa downstairs. Their furniture was borrowed from Fritz and Gardstein. Luba's reaction – she still did not know what was happening – can easily be guessed.

Now they had the two houses the only obstacle in their way was the occupied house in between directly backing onto the shop. It had been rented by a Romanian, Michail Silisteanu. He was an ex-journalist who for the past three years had been trying to interest the British public in a game he had patented called 'Flyscout'. He occupied only the top room of the house which contained a bed, table and chairs and a large quantity of cardboard boxes. Fortunately for the group's plans the police intervened and brought an unexpected solution to their problem. Silisteanu's office was in 73 St Mary Axe near by, and he hired girls to demonstrate his game in the window. When crowds started to block the pavement there was the inevitable brush with the law. The police told him that the City's bye-laws empowered them to stop the demonstration. Nor would they allow him to give out handbills. Silisteanu left for Paris in disgust on 12 December. The owners, Millard Brothers, used No. 10 temporarily for storing goods but planned to take the last of them out by Friday, 16 December.

Gardstein organised the final details of the robbery, including the purchase of a cylinder of oxygen, and a final briefing was held in Fritz's lodgings on the afternoon of 16 December. The only people absent were Nina Vassilleva, who was already at Exchange Buildings, and Jacob Peters, who didn't finish work until after 8 p.m.

Gardstein counted on thirty-six hours at the most in which to break into the shop and rob the safe. Apart from the rear wall adjoining No. 10, a second wall had to be broken behind the safe, which then had to be cut open from behind; it was in full view of anyone who happened to look through the shop window, including the policeman on his beat. Obviously it was likely to be a lengthy business and they might have to work through two nights and a day. Those taking part were split into two groups. In the first was Gardstein himself, Max Smoller, Jacob Peters and Yourka Dubof. The last named was one of the gang's three locksmiths and was a logical inclusion in case they broke through sooner than expected. The other two locksmiths were Fritz and Osip Federoff.

Fritz and Joseph were in the second group. They were both bad risks to take on the initial breakthrough. Fritz's fear of being caught made

View across the roofs from the break-in point in Exchange Buildings to the jeweller's shop (marked H) in Houndsditch.

him a bad risk at any time, and Joseph's lame leg was likely to stop him escaping if anything went wrong. The others on standby were Karl Hoffman in 36 Lindley Street, Osip Federoff (it is not known where he was) and John Rosen, who later told his fiancée that if anyone had gone sick he was the next to be called.

Clearly there had to be a prearranged meeting-place in case anything did go wrong, and Fritz's lodgings were a natural choice. The others either lived in rooms which they shared with strangers, or in rooms which were too far away or totally unsuitable for their purpose. Besides, Fritz's landlord was accustomed to his late hours and the comings and goings of his friends. The only problem was Luba. Fortunately she would never go into the front room if she knew that anyone was there, and it was a simple matter to arrange for Peter the Painter, who was only a bystander to the robbery, to be there and keep her out. Both doors opened onto the landing and unlit staircase, and there was no connecting door between the rooms. Because Peter would be covering for them, Fritz could hide there unknown to Luba and Joseph wait with him.

The initial breakthrough did not begin until after 7 p.m. which was the time Millard Brothers took the last of their Christmas stock out of No. 10 and locked the door. In the darkness the men scrambled over the lavatory roof from the yard of No. 11 and soon began to hammer away at the lavatory wall, which was also the back wall of Harris's shop. The noise, since it could be heard in the shops in Houndsditch, must have sounded even more exaggerated to the men making it. Dubof, whose sensitive fingers might be needed for the safe, went outside and wandered about the adjoining streets, in Cutler Street and Houndsditch, to see if there was any reaction to the noise and, if the police were called, to give the others warning to get out. But it was the eve of the Jewish Sabbath and the streets were almost deserted.

4

The House with Green Shutters

Late Friday evening, 16 December 1910. There was a high wind blowing through Houndsditch. Gas lamps flickered, and the streets were deserted. The street was all that was left of the protective moat or ditch that used to run outside the City wall from the Tower of London, in the east, to Blackfriars in the west, and which at one time stretched as far north as Moorgate and Cripplegate. It was called Houndsditch, or Dogditch, because the Common Hunt used to fling into it the carcases of the dogs he slaughtered and which were believed in the sixteenth and seventeenth centuries to carry the plague. Gradually the ditch had been built over until all that was left was a strip running north and south from Bishopsgate to Aldgate. At the northern tip was the church of St Botolph-without-Bishopsgate and at the southern end the church of St Botolph, Aldgate. Outside the church prostitutes solicited for customers – they kept within the law by never stopping but walking all the time around the surrounding piece of burial ground; inside the church, in a glass case, was the mummified head of the Tudor Duke of Suffolk, severed on Tower Hill. In Mitre Square near by the locals would point to Ripper's Corner where in the autumn of 1888 Jack the Ripper disembowelled one of his victims.

Max Weil closed his shop door and, stepping out into the street, peered through the window of the shop next door. The centre of the window was empty except for the velvet-covered shelves displaying on either side ornaments and scattered bric-à-brac. High up, in the centre of the window, was a large ornate clock, with a case shaped like the Eiffel Tower partly masked by the words 'ESTD 1865' on the window.

The overhead sign creaking in the wind and projecting from the first floor window read 'No. 119 H. S. Harris. Jewellers from 1865'. This particular shop had only been open since May and old man Harris had left the management of it to his son Harry. The bostwick gate was locked and there was an observation light burning in the inner office. Peering through the window, Weil could see the office door open flat against the wall, and in the corner, under the light, a jeweller's heavy iron safe. Everything appeared to be in order and yet Weil felt uneasy. He lived next door in a flat over his fancy-goods business with his sister and their maidservant, Edith Chard. He had been out until about 10 p.m., and when he returned home had found the two women agitated by unusual noises coming from downstairs at the back of the shop. Weil had immediately gone down to his counting-house, where the noises seemed to be coming from, but finding nothing wrong had gone into the street to see if anyone was still working in the jeweller's. Finding nobody, he thought he had better report the matter to the police. If people were trying to break in they would have nearly thirty-six hours in which to do so; next day was Saturday, the Jewish Sabbath, and the shop would stay closed. Besides, he too had heard the rumours about the Tsarist crown-jewels.

In Bishopsgate he found a young City constable, Walter Piper, who followed him back. Together they listened to the noises for a while and both agreed that they sounded like the 'drilling, sawing and breaking away of brickwork'. Piper thought there was probably some innocent explanation but went to the rear – to the small cul-de-sac, Exchange Buildings – to investigate. The lights were on in the Cutlers' Arms on the north-east corner and he knocked on the door immediately opposite, which was No. 12. He asked if anyone was working in the yard at the back and, drawing a blank, he moved on to the next house and knocked again.

The ground floor of No. 11 Exchange Buildings had an old-fashioned folding shop-front and each of its three windows was covered by a green shutter except for a gap of about six inches at the top through which the gaslight was gleaming. The door was opened so quickly, and the manner of the man who opened it was so furtive, that Piper's suspicions were immediately aroused. Instead of repeating his question and arousing the man's suspicions, he said the first thing that came into his head: 'Is the missus in?'

Gardstein shook his head. 'She has gone out.'

Piper shrugged indifferently. 'Right, I will call back,' he said and walked away.

When he heard the door close behind him he tapped lightly once more on the door of No. 12. 'How far is Harris's from here?' he asked. He went through into the narrow yard at the back and tried to judge for himself; then he left. As he walked towards Cutler Street he could see a man lurking in the shadows at the entrance of the cul-de-sac watching him. He approached the man, who walked away; there was something about the way he walked that made Piper feel he could identify him if he saw him again.

In Houndsditch Piper saw two constables from adjoining beats, Walter Choate and Ernest Woodhams. He told them of Weil's suspicions but not that he had been to Exchange Buildings or that he had spoken to Gardstein and so put the gang on their guard. Choate stopped in Houndsditch to watch the front of the jeweller's shop and Woodhams placed himself at the entrance to the cul-de-sac, while Piper went back to Bishopsgate Police Station for help. Nobody could get in or out of the buildings without being seen by either of the two policemen. On his way into the station, which was only a few minutes' walk, Piper met one of the duty sergeants, Robert Bentley, and two plain-clothes constables, James Martin and Arthur Strongman. Strongman was sent back to the station with a message for the Night Duty Inspector to telephone Harris and ask him to come and open his shop.

Weil took Bentley through to his counting-house to listen. As they were talking the hammering stopped and there was some conjecture later as to whether their voices had been heard through the none-too-thick wall. By now, other people had also heard the hammering and had become alarmed. Mrs Jones and her daughter, at the dairy shop on the other side of Harris's, saw the policemen waiting outside the shop and told them what they had heard. Strongman was waiting outside with two sergeants, Bryant and Tucker (affectionately known as 'Daddy'), and Constable Smoothey, and had a message for Bentley from Chief Inspector Hayes. Hayes was suspicious of some foreigners living on the right-hand side of the Exchange Buildings where the noises were coming from; Bentley was to find out if they were making the noise.

Piper was only a probationer constable and he was ordered to take Choate's place in front of Harris's shop out of harm's way. Constable Smoothey was positioned at the corner of Houndsditch and Cutler

Street, and Woodhams was left where he was, at the entrance to the cul-de-sac. In this way there was a connecting chain between the two points and instant communication. Bentley went with the others to No. 11 Exchange Buildings. None of them knew that Piper had been to the house fifteen minutes previously. The time was now about 11.30 p.m.

Bentley knocked on the door of No. 11 and slowly the bar of light on the pavement outside widened as the door was pulled back. 'Have you been working or knocking about inside?' he asked. Gardstein peered at the policeman suspiciously and ignored the question. 'Don't you understand English?' Still there was no answer. 'Have you got anybody in the house that can?' persisted the sergeant. 'Fetch them down.' Gardstein pushed the door partly to. Constable Martin who was standing outside guessed that he had gone upstairs, as he could see into the room and Gardstein did not cross his line of vision.

Almost directly opposite, at No. 5, sixteen-year-old Bessie Jacobs peeped through the door to see what was happening. In spite of the heavy winter greatcoats and the combed helmets she instantly recognised the burly figure of Constable Choate. 'Hello missie,' he said. Bessie opened the door a little wider.

'Nice to see you after all this time,' she called out.

Choate ignored her. His mother had just died and he had been to her former home in the country, settling her affairs. He nodded towards the partly open door. 'We've got a little something we have to do.' Bessie's mother called downstairs and asked what was happening. She was ill in bed with pneumonia and her daughter was supposed to be making coffee and fetching coal for the bedroom fire. Bessie left the door partly ajar. As she went inside she heard one of the policemen further down the cul-de-sac, who could not see what was happening, growl, 'Open the door or we're going to smash it in.' His words must have carried. At the same time the lights in the Cutlers' Arms were turned off.

Bentley pushed open the door of No. 11. There was no connecting door between the small lobby at the foot of the stairs and the room on his right. There was a large fire burning in the grate and on the table there was a cup of fresh tea, some bread and some paste. There was also a pressure gauge, rubber tubing and blowpipe. Otherwise the room was empty. Sergeant Bryant stepped into the doorway behind him for a closer look. Suddenly both men realised that they were being watched from the stairs. They could not see the man's face because the stairs were very dark, only the bottom of his trouser legs.

'Is anybody working here?' Bentley asked.

'No.'

'Anyone in the back?'

'No.

'Can I have a look in the back?'

'Yes.'

'Show us the way.'

The man on the stairs pointed to the room and spoke for the last time.

'In there,' he said.

Bentley stepped further into the room. As he did so the back door was flung open and a man, mistakenly identified as Gardstein, walked rapidly into the room. He was holding a pistol which he fired as he advanced with the barrel pointing towards the unarmed Bentley. As he opened fire so did the man on the stairs. The shot fired from the stairs went through the rim of Bentley's helmet, across his face and out through the shutter behind him. 'Gardstein' by now had closed to within three or four feet and was firing just across the table. At point-blank range he could not miss. His first shot hit Bentley in the shoulder and the second went through his neck almost severing his spinal cord. Bentley staggered back against the half-open door and collapsed backwards over the doorstep so that he was lying half in and half out of the house. Bryant, who had been standing partly behind him, glimpsed the pistol turning towards him and put out his hands instinctively, as he said later, 'to ward off the flashes'. He felt his left hand fall to his side and then, stumbling over the dying Bentley, he fell into the street. He had only a hazy recollection of what followed but he remembered getting up and staggering along the pavement. Fortunately he walked away from the entrance of the cul-de-sac, which probably saved his life. He was very dazed and fell down again. He regained consciousness some minutes later and found himself propped up against the wall of one of the houses. He had been shot in the arm and slightly wounded in the chest.

Constable Woodhams saw Bentley fall backwards over the doorstep and ran to help him. He could not see who was doing the shooting. Suddenly his leg buckled beneath him as a Mauser bullet shattered his thigh bone and he fell unconscious to the ground. Constable Strongman and Sergeant Tucker saw him fall but neither could see who was doing the shooting. Only a hand clutching a pistol protruded from the doorway. 'The hand was followed by a man aged about 30, height 5 ft 6 or 7, pale thin face, dark curly hair and dark moustache, dress dark jacket suit, no hat, who pointed the revolver in the direction of Sergeant Tucker and myself, firing rapidly. P.S. Tucker and I stepped back a few yards, when the sergeant staggered and turned round.' Strongman caught him by the arm and Tucker staggered the length of the cul-de-sac before collapsing in the roadway. He had been shot twice, once in the hip and once in the heart. He died almost instantly.

Martin, who like Strongman was in plain clothes, had been standing by the open door when the shooting started. As Bentley then Bryant staggered back bleeding from gun wounds, he turned and ran for the partly open door behind him. Bessie Jacobs' first thought when she heard the opening shots was that the high wind had blown the chimney pot off. But then she saw the gun flashes through the tops of the shutters. She pulled her nightclothes tighter round her and as she reached the door it burst open and Martin leaped inside. He slammed the door behind him and she began to scream. He covered her mouth with his hand. 'Don't scream, I'm a detective,' he pleaded. 'I'll protect your mother and I'll protect you.'

In the darkness, some of the targets were little more than shadows, and bullets splintered and gouged the wooden fronts of the houses as the gang raced for the entrance. Twenty-two shots were fired. Gardstein had almost reached the entrance when Constable Choate caught hold of him by the wrist and fought him for possession of his gun. As Gardstein pulled the trigger repeatedly Choate desperately pushed the pistol away from the centre of his body and the shots were fired into his left leg. Others of the gang rushed to Gardstein's assistance and turned their guns on Choate. He was a big, muscular man, 6 feet 4 inches tall, and in spite of the darkness, a target impossible to miss. He was shot five more times. The last two bullets were fired into his back. As he fell backwards he dragged Gardstein with him and a shot, fired at Choate, hit Gardstein in the back. Choate was kicked or punched in the face to make him release his grip on Gardstein, who was seized by two of the group and dragged away. But already he was a dying man.

When the shooting stopped, the dazed inhabitants came out of their houses. In No. 12 Mr Abrahams muttered that he knew that there was something up and blew a whistle as his fourteen-year-old son ran outside in time to see Sergeant Tucker die in the arms of Harry Jacobs, the second-hand-clothes dealer. His mother had hysterics, ran screaming out of the house and fell over one of the bodies. The door of No. 5

opened cautiously and Constable Martin slipped outside after begging Bessie Jacobs to promise not to say anything. Almost the first thing they saw was the shattered figure of Constable Choate struggling up on his hands and knees for just a few seconds before collapsing; in spite of his terrible wounds he was still alive. Martin went over to the dying Bentley still sprawled in the doorway and when he saw the wound in his neck unbuttoned his tunic. He was helped by a young tailor's-presser, Sam Hart, who lived in Artizan Street. Like most people who heard them, he had thought at first that the shots were chimney pots blowing down in the wind. As he ran through Harrow Alley he had seen two men coming towards him, dragging what he thought was a drunk between them. There was a woman walking, behind them and when she saw him running she had screamed, 'Go back, go back.' Hart had only run faster and it was not until later that he realised that the 'drunk' was Gardstein and the escaping gang. In Exchange Buildings he saw Bentley sprawled in the gaslight, lying with his head and shoulders on the pavement. Hart helped Martin do what he could for Bentley and then turned his attention to Bryant, who was walking about in a state of shock. He sat him down, propped him up against a wall and undid his tunic. For some unexplained reason, Hart thought that the police had been shot while raiding a gambling den.

Constable Piper, who had been in Houndsditch when the shooting started, ran to Cutler Street and saw Sergeant Tucker fall to the ground – a minute or two at the most after he had been shot, according to the doctor. He ran back to Houndsditch, stopped a motor-car, bundled the passengers out and sent Constable Smoothey with Sergeant Tucker to the London Hospital. Tucker was already dead when he was examined by Dr Rainey in the Receiving room at about 11.50 p.m. His tunic was open and the third button from the top had had a piece taken out of its edge. There was a small puncture wound two inches from the centre of his body, right over the position of the heart. This was the bullet that had killed him. There was a second bullet wound in the left lateral line of the body, four inches above the hip bone.

Dr Rainey had just finished his examination when Constable Choate was brought in on a stretcher. He was obviously suffering from shock and loss of blood and was immediately taken to the wards. He was conscious but had no memory of what had happened. His mouth, nose and eyes were bruised, which could have been caused by a fall or a blow. There were eight bullet wounds. The first was just above the spine of the right scapula; the second an inch to the right of the tenth dorsal spine; the third in the left loin an inch below the tip of the tenth rib, which was larger and more lacerated than the other wounds; the fourth and fifth were in the left thigh, one on the outside and one on the inside; the sixth, seventh and eighth were in the right calf, the outer side of the right foot by the toe and on the inner side about centre. He did not feel any pain. He was not losing blood externally but he was obviously suffering from haemorrhage and the rupture of some hollow organ. Some fluid was injected in the veins of his arms. He was operated on immediately. An incision was made in the right side of his abdomen and a ragged fragment of bullet was found just beneath the skin. Three feet of the upper part of the small intestine was found to be lacerated in five places; that piece was removed. He was too ill to withstand further surgery. He was taken back to the ward where he died two hours later, at 5.20 a.m., Saturday, 17 December 1910.

Bentley was carried to St Bartholomew's Hospital where he arrived just before midnight. He was suffering from cerebral irritation and was struggling and calling out. He was only semi-conscious when he was examined. There were two bullet wounds, one in front of the right shoulder-joint and one in the neck. The spinal cord had been partly severed and by morning his lower limbs were paralysed. He regained consciousness at some time during the day and was able to answer quite rationally the questions put to him, and he probably spoke to his wife, who was expecting a baby. At 6.45 p.m. his breathing became more difficult and his condition worsened rapidly. He died forty-five minutes later.

Within minutes of the shooting policemen were rushed from Bishopsgate Police Station to Exchange Buildings. Among the first on the scene was Sergeant Bayley, who should have been out with Bentley and Bryant that night. They were known as the three Bs. By a twist of fate he had been required inside to do the divisional pay sheet and Sergeant Tucker had taken his duty. In the early hours they were hampered by the lack of information. Bryant had wandered away, still in a daze and clutching his arm, to find a doctor, and the only other witnesses to the shootings were Woodhams, who was still unconscious from the crippling shot to his leg, Strongman, who had caught the dying Tucker and helped him away, and Martin, who lied that he had not seen anything because he had stumbled and fallen. Piper had come into Cutler Street from the Houndsditch end and must have realised that the wanted men could only have gone out through Harrow Alley, but was too busy sending the dead and wounded men away to hospital and raising the alarm. There was no way of passing this information on. The only police-box system in use at the time was an ambulance call-box. Anyone could communicate with the headquarters telephone-room simply by lifting the receiver, but there was no flashing light or other signal by which the telephone room could get in touch with them. Messages had to be passed on by foot or by pedal-cycle. The only mechanised transport the police possessed was an electric ambulance.

Shortly before midnight Detective Superintendent John Ottaway took charge. Like the detectives with him he was armed. Possible witnesses were taken into the Cutlers' Arms – where the fact that the police never paid for the brandy that was consumed that night was remembered for years afterwards – and the cul-de-sac was sealed off. At the blind end a large quantity of timber planking was stacked against the warehouse wall, and this was thoroughly searched in case any member of the gang has been unable to get away and had hidden there. After Bentley had been carried out of the doorway, the door of No. 11 had been left open and watery gaslight was still flickering over the pavement when the first detectives entered the house. The fire was banked up. On the table was a cup of freshly made tea, some bread, paste, jam and sardines, together with a pressure gauge, a double blowpipe fitted with seven feet of flexible metallic tubing, a similar length of rubber tubing and two stop-cocks. There was a clutter of chairs in the room and a gas stove; on the floor were pieces of oil cloth. The most distinctive piece of furniture was a chest of drawers belonging to Fritz.

Two panes of glass had been broken in the window by the door, one apparently from a bullet fired from the stairs. There were also two bullet holes in the ceiling, so that it looked as if one of the men had paused by the door and fired two warning shots into the air. One of the bullets had gone through the ceiling and lodged in the ceiling of the first floor bedroom, which was the only one of the two upstairs rooms, one above the other, which had been used. White lace and green-cloth curtains covered the windows, and on the black and brass bedstead were two red feather pillows and a plaid quilt.

The back door led into a small yard about fourteen feet long by three feet wide with a sink at one end and a lavatory at the other.

There were marks on the wall and pipe near the sink where somebody had scrambled over into No. 10, which was empty. Again there were signs that somebody had climbed from there into the next-door house, over the wall into No. 9. In the yard was a cylinder containing forty feet of oxygen-compressed gas; broken bricks littered the ground and blocked the lavatory pan. The seat was covered with brown paper on which were diamond-pointed drills, a carpenter's brace, chisel, crow-bars and a special wrench with jagged jaws, similar to a tin opener, for ripping metal. In the wall, reaching through to the matchwood at the back of Harris's shop, a gaping hole had been torn in the brickwork, twenty-four inches high by twenty inches across and nine inches deep. In the house was sixty feet of rubber tubing, fixed to the gas pipe, some mortar, wax candles, sand and asbestos boards. The bolt working the street-door handle had been fastened back with a screw so that the door could only be opened with a key.

The robbery would have been possible, but only just. The distance to the safe was sixty feet and the tubing was sixty-three, which would have only given them a clearance of three feet to the back of the safe. The night's most important witness was fourteen-year-old Solomon Abrahams, who lived next door at No. 12, and who claimed to have seen the killings. He stated he was standing by the door when he

> heard a smash of glass at No. 11. A man then opened the door, I did not see his face, I only saw his arm and heard a report of a firearm and immediately saw the policeman fall into the doorway. A man then ran out of the door with a revolver in his hand and fired about eight shots at the officers and four of them fell. Sergeant Bentley ran towards the man and caught hold of him by the shoulders and threw him to the ground. The man caught hold of the Sergeant's legs and pulled him down. They struggled and the man got on top of P.S. Bentley. Another man, whom I cannot describe, ran out of No. 11 and fired at Bentley, the bullet struck the man in the back and he fell backwards with his arms up in the air. I then went inside my house where I remained until the firing ceased. I heard about 15 shots fired in quick succession.

His story was plausible enough but hard to reconcile with the facts. It could not have been Bentley who caught hold of the man since he was found lying in the doorway. Possibly the boy meant Choate, but if so why did he not see Tucker and Strongman who were standing

Map of the break-in from Exchange Buildings to the back of Harris's safe. Nos 9 and 11 had been rented. No 10 was empty.

between him and the gunman? Nevertheless, the newspapers publicised him as the boy who had raised the alarm, and photographed him in youthful bowler, Eton collar, knee breeches and boots. The other inhabitants had equally sensational stories to tell. Ada Parker, at No. 2, said she was sweeping the floor when she noticed in the wooden front of the ground-floor room a small hole, about fifteen inches from the floor. Later she found a bullet at the back of the room and declared that it had passed through the bottom of her mother's long skirt and the leg of the chair she was sitting on at the time. However, Bessie Jacobs always swore that it was common knowledge the hole had been made in the chair with a red-hot poker to get money out of the reporters.

Throughout the night the police took statements and collected what evidence they could. They searched the cul-de-sac with lanterns and picked up spent ammunition-cases. Five were believed to be Mauser bullets and five Browning, and two more were unidentified. With daylight, newspaper reporters came flooding to the scene and by late morning Houndsditch was choked with sightseers.

Two more witnesses were soon found. A workman flushing gullies in Cobb Street had seen four men hurry by soon after the killings. He had heard the shots but the sound had been partly muffled by the wind and he had mistaken them for the sound of hoardings blowing down in the wind. One of the men was being supported by his friends and from his dazed expression the workman had assumed him to be drunk. Another workman made a similar statement that he had seen the same four men in Wentworth Street a little later.

The most important witness was not found until late the next afternoon. He was Isaac Levy, the manager of a tobacconist shop in Walthamstow. Immediately after the shootings he had run into Exchange Buildings and seen the policemen taken away. In the Cutlers' Arms he listened afterwards to the excited babble. 'Look what a bit of luck I have had,' said Mrs Abrahams breathlessly. She had almost recovered from tripping over one of the bodies and was rapidly becoming aware of her son's importance as the only eyewitness to the killings. 'My people could have been shot down.'

Levy could no longer control himself and burst out, 'Look at mine. The men pointed revolvers at me and told me not to follow them.' Suddenly fearing that he had said too much, he hurried away and next morning caught his usual train to work. He was badly shaken by what he had read. Choate and Tucker were dead, Bentley was dying, and the condition of Bryant and Woodhams was critical. His nervousness increased. He was too afraid to go to the police but he had to tell somebody what he had seen. His later explanation for not going to the police was that he was not sure what view his firm would take of one of their managers being implicated in such an affair. He told his story again and again to his customers; one more enterprising than the rest telephoned the *Star* newspaper, and they published a story in the afternoon edition that the hue and cry was for three men and a woman. By the time a *Daily Mail* reporter reached the shop, Levy had locked up, but not before telling his employers his story and asking for the rest of the afternoon off to recover his shattered nerves. His original intention had been to go home, but he steeled himself to go to Exchange Buildings, where he spoke to Chief Inspector Hayes. He was escorted by two detectives to Bishopsgate police station and after making his statement was allowed to go home, where he was run to earth by the *Daily Mail* reporter.

Levy told him that he had worked late the previous evening and his train home had pulled into Liverpool Street station at about 11.28. He followed his normal route home through Devonshire Square, Borers Passage, alongside the Port of London warehouses, and then into Cutler Street; it took him only a few minutes. As he was walking through Borers Passage he heard a single shot followed immediately by a succession of shots – fifteen or twenty he guessed – 'there was a slight interval between the first and second shots, but the others were very rapid, without any stoppage'. He ran down the passage, not very fast as he was tired, and into Cutler Street. As he turned the corner he almost bumped into the three men coming towards him. Behind them was a woman wearing a fur toque on her head and carrying a large muff. The men were in the middle of the road, only about four steps away, and he saw their faces quite clearly as there was a light burning over the carpet-maker's on the corner of the passage. The man in the centre was being supported by the other two; he seemed dazed, or exhausted, and was holding his head down. The two men on the outside both pointed revolvers into Levy's face. 'Don't follow us,' they said in broken English. 'Don't follow.' For a moment or two Levy went physically blind with fear and could see nothing. He then stood and watched them walk away down Harrow Alley, dragging the man between them, with the woman hurrying after.

In the few minutes Constable Piper was away looking for assistance, Dubof, who had been watching him from the shadows, slipped into Exchange Buildings to tell the others that the policeman had also been to No. 12. Possibly he had made a genuine mistake and called at the wrong house, but they could not be sure. Suddenly it became impossible for them to leave. Constable Woodhams strolled into Exchange Buildings and stood in the entrance to the cul-de-sac. Now they could not get out without being stopped or seen. Still uncertain as to just how much, if anything, the police suspected, they decided to brazen it out. Max climbed back into No. 10 and resumed hammering, pausing every now and then for breath and to listen for the warning shout that would send him scrambling back over the lavatory wall. The others got ready to leave. Nina Vassilleva put on her coat and the fur toque and muff she had been given by a sick friend. The men took out their guns.

None of them had any scruples about shooting policemen. Peters had had his fingernails torn out by Tsarist police and Dubof his back torn by Cossack whips. In their own country policemen had killed, tortured and condoned the most outrageous brutalities, and there was no reason to assume that the English police were any different. Why assume they were unarmed? Fritz and Gardstein both had special pockets for concealing their guns so why shouldn't the police? Any chance of allaying their fears, which were common, not only to them but to most of the East End's immigrant population at this time, was completely destroyed by their ignorance of the language.

When Bentley knocked at the door the second time Gardstein delayed opening it long enough for Nina Vassilleva, who was in the upstairs bedroom, to lean out of the back window and signal to Max to get clear. Gardstein opened the door and then went back upstairs and waited at the top of the stairs in the darkness, with only his trouser bottoms showing, as Max scrambled over the lavatory wall into the yard. Gardstein had already taken out his Mauser and was standing with it partly concealed by the folds of his overcoat when the unsuspecting Sergeant Bentley pushed open the door and stepped into the house. Less than two minutes had passed since Bentley knocked at the door. As Max scrambled clear Peters, for reasons which will be explained later, flung open the back door and walked rapidly into the room firing his Dreyse pistol. In the same instant Gardstein lifted his long-barrelled Mauser and fired at Bentley's face. His shot went through the rim of his helmet and through the shutter behind him. He saw Bentley stagger backwards, shot in the shoulder and throat by Peters. He swung his Mauser to the right and fired into Sergeant Bryant's chest as he put out his hands in front of him to ward off 'the flashes'.

Stepping over the dying Bentley sprawled in the doorway, Peters went into the street and, walking towards Sergeant Tucker, wounded him with a bullet in the hip and then shot him through the heart. As Constable Strongman dragged him away Peters followed them along the street, still firing, into the light of the street lamp where Strongman had a good look at him before Peters turned back to help Gardstein.

Gardstein had been firing from the doorway as Peters cleared the street for their escape. He shot Constable Woodhams in the leg, and he was now lying unconscious in the roadway. As Nina Vassilleva scrambled downstairs and into the street Gardstein fired two more shots into the ceiling as a warning and then followed her out. Suddenly the burly figure of Constable Choate loomed out of the darkness in front of him and gripped him by the wrist. Possibly he shouted or Nina screamed for help. He pulled his Mauser trigger four times as the policeman towering over him pushed his hand down and the pistol away from his body deflecting the shots into his thigh, calf and foot. At that moment Max and Dubof ran out of the house into the street firing their guns. Peters ran behind Constable Choate and fired two closely spaced shots into his spine in the same instant that Max loosed off a shot with his Browning and hit Gardstein in the back as Constable Choate dragged him down. Max was appalled as he realised what he had done. Peters and Dubof grabbed Gardstein by the arms and, yanking him to his feet, half dragged, half carried him into Cutler Street as Constables Piper and Smoothey pounded towards them from Houndsditch. The only way they could get out now was through Borers Passage or Harrow Alley. They had almost reached Borers Passage when the tobacconist, Isaac Levy, ran out in front of them and almost collided with them head on. He had a clear view of the three men and Nina Vassilleva, but did not see Max who was out of the light, somewhere in the darkness behind them, covering their retreat. Peters and Dubof lifted their pistols and pointed them at Levy's face.

Incredibly, for the next half-hour they were able to drag the badly wounded man through the East End backstreets to Grove Street. Shortly after the last sighting in Harrow Alley, Nina and Max slipped away to see if they could get help from Dr Mengle Freedman, whom Nina had known for about three years and who lived on Whitechapel Road. It is not clear how much she told him, but the doctor flatly refused to help and threatened to call the police if she didn't go away. Now they had the added burden of not knowing if he would betray them. At some point (again the details are not clear) Fritz and possibly Joseph met Peters and Dubof, who were still carrying the dying Gardstein. One can only guess that as part of the plan they had slipped out to join the others in Exchange Buildings around midnight, by which time the first phase of the breakthrough would have been completed. Dubof and Peters were seen dragging Gardstein out of Exchange Buildings. Later, there was an argument about dumping Gardstein in the street. Fritz subsequently told Luba that he had carried Gardstein like a baby; he had wanted to leave him near Commercial Road but he had started screaming. A glance at the map shows that the Commercial Road was as far as they could take him without a decision being made as to their final destination. They must have been carrying or dragging him for about half an hour, and by then the others must have made it clear to Fritz that the logical place to dump Gardstein was Grove Street. Except for Max, who was already making his own plans to get away and would be gone within a matter of hours, the others were single people living in lodgings with little or no privacy, where it would be clearly impossible to hide the wounded man.

The East End. Principal locations from Houndsditch to Sidney Street.

Somehow Fritz was made to accept the situation and they made their way to Grove Street. They dragged Gardstein up the dark, unlit staircase, stumbling as they did so, because there was no hand-rail to grip. Peters and Dubof must have still been carrying Gardstein as Fritz went ahead of them and held the back bedroom door shut in case Luba or Sara, who were listening, decided to come out onto the landing. Once they were in the front bedroom Luba, who had been terrified, came out and tried the front bedroom door. 'Don't come in,' said Fritz. She was surprised to hear his voice as she thought that he was out. She retreated to the rear bedroom and closed the door.

Meanwhile, Peters and Dubof had gently eased Gardstein onto the bed. Without the others noticing Peters slipped his Dreyse between the mattress and the palliasse. They pulled off Gardstein's boots but left him in his overcoat as he was pale, shivering, weak from shock and loss of blood, and clearly too ill to move. Minutes later they were joined by Max. Either he had borrowed a spare key or the street door had been left ajar. As the two women heard him come upstairs Luba opened the back bedroom door to see who it was, her curiosity overcoming her fear. She noticed that Max's hands were black with brickdust where he had been breaking through the wall. Fritz opened the front bedroom door and let him in. She shut her door again and minutes later the women heard two people – Peters and Dubof – go downstairs and hurry away into the night.

5

The Way to Dusty Death

On the day before the murders, Thursday, 15 December, Fritz Svaars had woken at nine o'clock and crept out of the house at 59 Grove Street leaving his mistress still in bed. There was little point in waking her.

Work had been slack and she had not gone to her brother's shop for nearly a week. She was still asleep when he returned nearly two hours later and only woke when he touched her with his cold hands. She heard him chuckling and opened her eyes to see him standing by the bed, his cheeks red from the raw wind that was blowing outside. 'Where were you?' she said, huddling deeper into the bedclothes.

Fritz laughed. 'You'd better not ask me where I've been,' he said, and bending over her whispered, 'Get up. It's two o'clock.'

She was so much in love with him that she believed him implicitly. She got up and began to dress, but Fritz was in a playful mood and threw her clothes about the room. Luba scrambled after them and eventually lost her temper, but not for long. Fritz's good humour was infectious and they both ended up laughing. Only when she had finished dressing did Fritz show her the correct time. Luba was annoyed again, remembering how deeply asleep she had been, and when Peter the Painter came into the room she complained to him about how Fritz had fooled her, and then pushed them both out of the bedroom while she tidied it up. Afterwards she joined them in the front room. She had not heard Gardstein come in, but when she went into the room she found him playing chess with Peter, and Fritz was in the background practising the mandoline for his part in a Christmas play at the Anarchist Club. She took some money to buy food, and Gardstein asked her to buy him some cigarettes. She jokingly replied that she would not, and when she returned and found them all drinking tea she hid the cigarettes until Gardstein laughingly pushed her onto the landing and told her that she should stay there until she gave them to him. She gave the cigarettes to Fritz instead but, before he and Gardstein went out, he told her to stay at home as someone was supposed to come and see him and he was to be asked to wait. After they had gone Luba made dinner and finished making a black velvet blouse for herself.

When Fritz returned at 5 p.m., Luba could see that he was not as happy as he had been in the morning. She started questioning him, but he told her curtly that he was hungry and the best thing that she could do was to give him something to eat. Then, seeing that he had hurt her, he immediately put his arms around her and took her over to the food cupboard. 'Don't be angry but give me something to eat,' he said.

Fritz had spent the afternoon at 15 Duncan Terrace, Islington, in the workshop of one of the leading militant anarchists of the day, the Italian Errico Malatesta. For the past fifty years Malatesta had conspired and agitated not only in his native Italy but in England, Spain, the Levant, the United States and Argentina. On two occasions he had escaped from prison by boat – nailed up in a packing-case, if the legend is to be believed – and for the past twelve years he had lived quietly in London, running his small electrician's business, after a comrade in America had tried to shoot him. His workshop had been used for the past twelve months by a man he knew as 'the Russian'. Sometimes this unknown man used his workshop two or three times a week to finish off some little job. When he was questioned later, Malatesta always denied that he knew the man's name, or that the names he was known by – George Gardstein, Poolka Mourremitz and P. Morin – meant anything to him. He had met him at the Anarchist Club and understood that he was a Russian political refugee and engineer.

Malatesta had been under the same close supervision as Carlusha alleged that Gardstein and the others had been. When he escaped from Italy to London he was under close surveillance by two plain-clothes detectives.

Fritz had gone down the back staircase into the workshop and introduced himself as Louis Lambert. In very bad French he had asked Malatesta to sell him a cylinder of oxygen for a lantern show he was giving. Only three days before, according to Gardstein, Malatesta had exchanged a six-foot cylinder of oxygen gas for a forty-foot cylinder. When they came to cut through the safe the extra footage would give them a burning-time of about forty-five minutes. Malatesta arranged to sell him the cylinder as well as a pressure gauge, a valve and about fifteen or twenty yards of rubber tubing for which he was to pay £5. Fritz paid him £1 on account and asked for them to be ready by the following afternoon when he would send a man to collect them and pay the balance. Next day he sent a young boy, who fetched the things away on a coster's barrow. Malatesta's unknown friend, 'the Russian', was busy at the work-bench when the boy came. Possibly Gardstein was making sure that nothing had been missed.

Fritz's nervousness had shown itself in a more marked form the previous Saturday when he had gone to the British Asbestos Company, Commercial Road, to buy the asbestos boards they needed to guard against the heat when they were cutting open the back of the safe. His English was even more limited than his French. When he could not make himself understood he began to shout at the woman who was trying to serve him. He made so much noise that the Company Secretary came out of his office and personally intervened. He called the warehouseman to assist and told him to show Fritz some asbestos boards but none of them, it seemed, were thick enough, and Fritz had only the vaguest notion of what he wanted. Eventually he chose four boards but refused to pay the price (17s 3d), saying it was too much. The Company Secretary again had to intervene; he told Fritz that he had better make up his mind as they were closing in a few minutes and, more bluntly, that he was going to a football match and would not serve him. In the end, Fritz picked two cheaper boards, paid 8s 6d and left.

He was obviously in the same tense mood when he came back from Malatesta's. Luba ignored him but after they had eaten he and Peter, who ate with them, started talking in Lettish. She railed at them for talking in a language which they knew she did not understand. Peter went back to his own room and left her with Fritz, who quietly washed up, put the things away and then sat down on the bed beside her, talking about the concert he had arranged for the Russian emigrants. She heard him rehearse his lines for the Russian socialist play he was appearing in on Boxing Night. He had reluctantly agreed to take the part of a policeman hunting down socialist revolutionaries, a part which nobody else would play. He translated his lines from the Lettish into Russian for her so that she could follow the story. The original play, *Matteo Falcone*, was the story of a Corsican brigand whose son betrayed one of his comrades to the soldiers. To wipe out the dishon-our Matteo Falcone must kill his son Fortunato, and makes him stand on a small mount while he prepares to shoot him. From the mount Fortunato sees the captured Brigand escape from the soldiers and run back towards him. Fortunato wipes out his dishonour by fighting the soldiers and defending the brigand he has so recently betrayed. In the version in which Fritz was playing, the soldiers became policemen and Fritz was the inspector leading them. There was one important change in the text. The boy who betrayed the brigand/social revolutionary could not wipe out the dishonour. He was shot.

They sat on the bed until it grew dark. Luba listened to him as he softly repeated his lines in Russian; she might not have been so happy had she known that the boy's part was being played by a Russian girl and that Fritz had told her that he was unattached. She nestled closer. Suddenly somebody outside the room shouted, 'What are you doing in there?' and broke the mood. The door was pushed open and Joseph and Gardstein came into the room. One of them struck a match and said, 'We shall not disturb them.' As Luba swung her legs off the bed to light the gas her face filled with disgust as she saw Joseph bend over Fritz and whisper in his ear. Fritz spoke low and then, seeing the look on Luba's face, told her to go into the other room as Joseph had something to show him which it would not be nice for her to see. He followed her to the door and told her that he would explain later. She went sul-lenly into the other room where Peter sat reading. She stayed with him for a bit and then went out. She returned just before midnight. Fritz looked at her coldly and asked where she'd been. Luba smiled wanly. 'Fat lot you care about me,' she said. She waited for him to say some-thing else but he ignored her and continued to leaf through the papers he had taken from the drawer he normally kept locked. He put some on the fire and watched them burn. 'Papers lie about here for a hun-dred years,' he said. And then with a change of emphasis. 'They ought to be burned.'

'Whose fault is it?' Luba snapped, and walked out onto the landing and into Peter's room. Her head drooped, she subsequently wrote, as if the whole world had come to an end. Peter looked at her thoughtfully for several minutes and then went into the other room to speak to Fritz.

She stayed in bed the next morning, the day of the murders, until 12.30 p.m., and then went to her brother's shop to ask him to cut out a dress for her. In the street she passed Gardstein and Hoffman.

She deliberately ignored them but guessed that they were on their way to see Fritz. Possessiveness, as much as curiosity, made her hurry back to find out what they were doing. From the murmur in the front bedroom it was obvious that there were a number of visitors. She went in and asked Fritz for some money to buy food; she then complained that she was not feeling well and asked her friend, Sara Trassjonsky, who was in the back room waiting for her, if she would go to the shop instead. Sara had been working for Luba's brother since her arrival from Paris a few months before, but she was showing increasing signs of mental instability. Part of her condition was certainly physical. Her right shoulder blade was deformed, as was her left hip. She was a willing little creature and went to the shop readily enough. She had only been gone a few minutes when Luba, on the pretext that she wanted some rubber heels, went once more into the room to call to her from the window; but Sara was too far down the street to hear. Maddeningly she next insisted on taking down the curtains as she wanted to send them to the laundry. The men had ignored her previous remarks that she was not feeling well, but now one or two faces were tinged with amusement and several pitying glances were thrown at Fritz, who went on talking animatedly to Gardstein.

The talk became even more restrained when an unexpected visitor dropped in, a young balalaika-player who had been teaching Fritz for the past three weeks to play the mandoline for his part in the Boxing Night play. He was a thin-faced twenty-one-year-old named Nicholas Tomacoff, with dark hair and a small moustache, who had arrived in England in June from St Petersburg where he had been living with three maiden aunts who owned a tailor's business. Tomacoff played regularly with a local group of Russian balalaika-players and singers, the Slavonics, who were well known in the area. In November Fritz had called at his lodgings and asked if he would play the mandoline one evening at the club in Jubilee Street. Tomacoff had agreed, although his only payment would be lemonade, and on the night of the performance Fritz had worked the stage curtains. They had spent the rest of the evening talking, and a casual friendship had sprung up between them. Sometimes they used to meet four and five times a week. It was several weeks before Fritz trusted him enough to give him his address, but after that they visited each other's lodgings very frequently. Tomacoff learned that Fritz carried a Browning revolver, that he also possessed a Mauser which he had bought in Antwerp (there was a broken one lying openly on a shelf) and that there were several hundred rounds of ammunition in the room.

Tomacoff knew some of the other men slightly; he had met Gardstein, Dubof and Hoffman several times. John Rosen was pointed out to him as 'the Barber'; he had stripped off his coat and waistcoat and was playing chess with 'the Painter'. Joseph was sitting on the bed and Osip Federoff lying down. He stayed till about 2 p.m., walking about the room, strumming his mandoline and listening to the conversation.

The others stayed talking till about five, finalising the arrangements for the robbery; they drifted off in ones and twos, and when most of them had gone Fritz told Luba that he was going to the West End to collect some money that was owing to him. She pleaded with him not to go, but he told her that he could only get the money by going there personally. He said that he might stop the night but that he would be back by eleven the next morning. Seeing that he was determined to go, Luba pretended a sudden indifference and asked for some money to go to the pictures. She watched him leave the house with Joseph, and only Peter Piatkow was left behind when she went out at 5.30 p.m.

Sara joined her and they returned at about 9.30 p.m. In their absence Fritz and Joseph came back and waited in the front bedroom with Peter. When the women came in Peter played his violin. As expected, Luba stayed away; the relationship between the two could not have been worse. Luba's dislike of him stemmed from the fact that Fritz gave preferential treatment to Peter instead of to her. After the quarrel between Luba and Fritz the previous evening, Peter had simply got up and walked out. And when she and Sara had returned home from the pictures there was no friendly greeting, no suggestion that he should join them for a bedtime drink, no friendly word shouted through the closed door as might happen in a normal relationship. From the gang's point of view it was an ideal situation.

Sara left the house for a brief time but soon returned; she was staying the night with Luba. After supper she and Luba sat in bed reading. At about 12.30 a.m. they heard two or three people struggling up the stairs in the dark. There was no hand-rail and one false move could easily tip them into the staircase well. The women were terrified and listened as the footsteps reached the front bedroom where Peter was. Luba slipped out onto the landing and nervously tried to open the front bedroom door. Someone was leaning against it and to her astonishment she heard Fritz's voice. 'Don't come in,' he called out. She went back to her room and closed the door but opened it again a moment later when she heard someone else on the stairs. It was Max Smoller. His hands, she noticed, were black and he was in a highly excitable state. He too went into the front bedroom. Soon afterwards – it was only minutes at the most – she and Sara heard two people going downstairs. Then silence.

Suddenly Fritz opened the door. Ignoring Luba he said to Sara: 'Mourremitz is shot; make him a cold compress.' Only then did Fritz turn to Luba and ask her for one of the two sovereigns he had given her to buy a dress with earlier in the week. She begged him to tell her what had happened, but he ignored her questions and told her that she had better get out of the house. He stayed only five minutes and then left with Max, Peter and Joseph, who had been watching silently from the background.

Gardstein was fully conscious and lying on the bed. His overcoat had been flung to one side, and Sara pulled off his boots. She lifted his shirt and gently placed a wet towel in position on his back. Luba shuddered when she saw him and said that she could do nothing for him as she was feeling too ill. The gang meant nothing to her and not even out of pity would she stay with him. It was obviously best to get her out of the way altogether. Sara told her to go away and gave her the key to her own rooms in 10 Settle Street.

Instead Luba went to 36 Lindley Street where Karl Hoffman lived; she and Fritz had frequently fed him when he had no money. Hoffman was also in love with her and probably she knew this. He rented one room on the first floor; he was so poor that the rent had been reduced from 3s 6d to 3s a week. On the ground floor was Morris Reitman, his wife and three children. Mrs Reitman, or Mrs Morris as she was generally known, was so fat that she was known as 'Grobber' Morris. Her size had become even more startling in the last nine months and when Luba knocked at the door she was just starting a difficult labour. The midwife was with her in the back room, and Morris Reitman was sitting in darkness in the front room with his three children when he heard Luba knock at the door. He listened for the number of knocks. Twice was always for Hoffman upstairs, although he did not know his name. Curious to see who was knocking at this hour, he peeped into the badly lit passage. He saw that the woman was not wearing a hat and that her coat and hair were dark.

On the way upstairs Luba could hear 'Grobber' Morris groaning in labour and the midwife fussing about her. Stepping into Hoffman's room she was staggered to see Fritz, Peter and Joseph. She had not expected them to be there and had only come to ask Hoffman for advice. Fritz caught hold of her by the arms. 'What are you doing here? Get out of it at once,' he shouted. Luba became hysterical. 'What have you brought a wounded man to our rooms for?' she sobbed. Fritz quietened her down. He told her to go to her brothers', but first she was to go back to Grove Street and bring away her collection of family photographs. Peter Piatkow, he said, would fetch a doctor. Luba was not to stay with Gardstein. He gave her his door key.

Fritz took out the Browning that Max had given him and said that he must see if it was fully loaded. This was an extra gun. He already had a Mauser, as did Joseph. For them the situation was and always had been

59 GROVE STREET

0   5   10 feet   15   20

GROUND FLOOR   **1ST FLOOR**

akin to that in Russia 'where every policeman and every public dignitary was an instrument of despotism and oppression'.

Fritz had been appalled when Smoller told him that Nina's doctor had not only refused to help them but that he was going to the police. Fritz could not prove that he was innocent of the murders. Luba did not know that he had been in the house all the time. There was nothing he could say without implicating himself, or the others, still more. If he was caught, even supposing he escaped hanging in England, he could still be deported to Russia where he would have to face a capital charge. Besides, he was afraid of being made to talk. He had confessed to something when he was beaten up by the Russian police earlier that year – this was common knowledge in the group – and he firmly believed that the British police would further beat him up if he fell into their hands. He was ready to kill himself rather than let that happen. In view of what Max had said, neither he nor the others dared to go back to Grove Street, if, as they believed, the doctor was arriving with the police, even though they had left behind them letters and photographs which could incriminate them all. It was safer to use Sara and Luba who were not involved, as very little would happen to them even if they were caught.

Luba hurried back to Grove Street and snatched up some photographs. She was too agitated to make a thorough search and told Sara to leave at once. Gardstein was writhing on the bed in terrible pain and begged Sara not to leave him. He was so ill that Sara felt that she could not abandon him and told him that she would stay with him. But Luba scuttled away to Sara's lodgings. At 3 a.m. Gardstein's condition worsened still more, but the pain was more manageable and he told Sara to leave him as he knew that he was dying. Instead she went to her lodgings and insisted that Luba help her to find a doctor. Luba thought that she knew where there was one in Whitechapel Road. She did not know the number, but there was a brass plate outside which was in both Yiddish and English.

They pulled their shawls over their heads and hurried through the dark, deserted streets until they found the doctor's house just before 3.30 a.m. There was a speaking tube from the street to the upstairs bedroom where the duty doctor, John Scanlon, was sleeping. Although the brass plate was inscribed in both Yiddish and English, Dr Scanlon could only speak English, which neither woman knew. Fortunately he could speak French and Sara, who had lived in France for some time, told

him, 'A man is very bad at 59 Grove Street.' She gave no further explanation. As Scanlon came out Luba pulled her shawl further over her
face so that she would not be recognised. After she had walked along
with them for just a few minutes, she felt that she had done enough and
slipped quietly away and went back to Sara's lodgings.

It was not until they got to 59 Grove Street that Sara realised that Luba
had taken the door key with her. Reluctantly she knocked on the door
to wake up the landlord. She tried several times to attract his attention.
Dr Scanlon became tired of waiting and rapped imperiously on the
wooden shutters with his stick. At last the door opened. As Dr Scanlon
climbed the stairs, keeping well over to one side away from the missing
hand-rail, he heard the door slam behind them in protest.

He noticed that the front bedroom door was slightly ajar. The gas
light was faint and had almost gone out. The walls were covered with a
gaudy paper and two or three cheap theatrical prints, and that the bare
boards were littered with cigarette butts and spent matches. Facing the
door was a narrow bedstead painted green. On the bed and on the floor
were scattered blood-stained towels, and he saw that the bed-linen and
the pillow where the man was lying were also splattered with blood.

Gardstein was dressed except for his boots and when he saw the
doctor he muttered to himself. He explained that he had been shot,
accidentally, in the back three hours previously by a friend. From his
examination Dr Scanlon concluded that there was evidence of a bullet
lodged in the front of the chest. Later, it was found to be touching
the right ventricle. He suggested that Gardstein should be immediately taken to the London Hospital, but this was flatly rejected by the
dying man. In the circumstances there was little else the doctor could
do except to promise to call back later and to give him some medicine, which Sara could go and collect with him now, to deaden the
pain. He asked what name he should put on the medical certificate and
was told George Gardstein. He then said that his fee was ten shillings.
Gardstein told Sara to look in his pockets. She found a sovereign and
put the change by the bed.

Sara went back with Dr Scanlon to his surgery for the medicine and
then went on to 36 Lindley Street where the men were still hiding.
She told Fritz that Gardstein knew that he was dying and was worried because the papers had not been burnt. Fritz told her to go back
and bring him some clothes, any photographs she could find and his
ship's tickets for Australia. If Gardstein died, she was to pour petrol on

his body and on his bed and burn down the house to destroy all the remaining evidence.

Sara again went back to 59 Grove Street. She gave Gardstein some medicine and nursed him until 7 a.m., when again he told her to leave him as she could do him no good. She went to her lodgings and lay down, still in her clothes, on the bed; she was exhausted by her efforts. After she had rested for a while she went back to the dying man. She offered him some more medicine, but he refused to take it. He again told her to go away as there was nothing more she could do for him.

By this time, Sara was close to breaking-point. Neither she nor Luba knew what to do next. They told Mr Reuben, the grocer in Old Montague Street, who had found them their lodgings, about Gardstein, but Mrs Reuben came to the door and told them to go away as she and her husband did not want to be involved. Sara by now felt that she had to go to the dying Gardstein once more, and this time Luba, who had at last stifled her fear, went with her. It was now 9.15 a.m. Luba, out of habit, knocked on the door, and it was opened by the landlord Max Katz. He was still standing by the open door, fastening his collar, when the two women ran back downstairs with terrified looks on their faces. As they hurried into the street he went upstairs and peered into the front bedroom. Lying on the bed, which was littered with blood-stained sheets and towels, was Gardstein's dead body.

The bedroom at 59 Grove Street where Gardstein died.

Luba was too terrified to go home. She borrowed some clothes from a friend and went to 36 Lindley Street. But Fritz, Joseph and Peter had already gone; only Hoffman was there. She asked the same questions over and over again. Where was Fritz? What had happened? Hoffman would tell her nothing. While they were talking a friend of Peter's, Pavell Molchanoff, who had known him in Marseilles in 1909, came in. Luba at once told him all that she knew and begged him to go to the house and collect the photographs that she had left behind. She was terrified, she said, of being accused of Gardstein's murder. She pleaded with Sara to return with him to the house while she waited for them both in Pavell's lodgings in 36 Havering Street. When she reached them she was not sure which room to go into. She hesitated for a moment and then went into the front room. As she entered the young balalaika-player, Nicholas Tomacoff, got up and shook her hand. The other men there were having an animated conversation and, not wanting to be the only woman present, she went into the back room to wait for Pavell; opening the door she stared with astonishment into the clean-shaven face of Peter the Painter.

Pavell Molchanoff had known that she would find him there but hadn't warned her what to expect. Peter had banged on his door and woken him up at 2 a.m. and asked to be put up for the night as it was too late for him to get into his own lodgings. When Luba told Peter that Gardstein was dead he became very agitated and paced restlessly up and down the room. He ignored her questions and said that he could not tell her anything of what had happened. As she became more frightened she asked if she should leave the country. Peter ignored her question and asked her if she had any money. As she was looking into her purse Pavell came into the room alone. His news was bad. When he and Sara had tried to leave Grove Street the landlord had stopped them and told him that one or other of them must remain behind. Quite what he intended to do they did not know – it is doubtful whether he knew himself – but Sara had had to stay as his hostage.

Peter hurriedly put on his coat and waistcoat and asked how much it would cost to get to Poplar. Pavell gave Luba the half-sovereign, the change from Dr Scanlon's fee, which he had taken from the dead man's bedside table. Peter asked her for some of it to help him get away, and she gave him half a crown. Luba said that she would go to her brother's house and wait until Pavell and Hoffman called later in the day, which they had promised to do. When she reached home she heard her two younger brothers talking excitedly about the Houndsditch murders. Luba felt instinctively that the murders were connected in some way with Gardstein's death.

Meanwhile Sara was waiting beside Gardstein's body for something to happen. Already her delicate mental balance threatened to topple her over into insanity. While she waited she picked up the papers and photographs she found and burnt them in the grate but there were periods of blackness and depression, which gradually grew longer as the morning progressed, when she would sit in front of the small jets of flame and stare blankly into nothingness.

Clearly the landlord had no intention of doing anything except keeping her there and waiting on events; but Dr Scanlon had a clear duty to inform the police. He had been called to attend a dying man suffering with a bullet wound which he knew could not possibly have been self-inflicted, and the circumstances were such that he must have strongly suspected foul play. But there were strong reasons of self-preservation for not going to the police. Most immigrants, particularly those from Russia and the countries under its domination, believed that there was little or no difference between the Tsarist police system, which used murder and torture and systematically carried out pogroms against a suffering population, and the English policeman. Already, by late Saturday morning, there was astonishment among the Russian immigrants that the police had not carried out a pogrom. If Scanlon had told the police what he had seen and this information had got back, he would instantly have been branded as a police informer by every immigrant and his practice shunned, which would have meant financial ruin. He therefore delayed telephoning the local police at Arbour Square, until just before it was time to make his midday visit in case the situation had resolved itself.

This new information was passed on to Detective Inspector Frederick Porter Wensley, nicknamed 'the Weasel' and, by foreigners who could not pronounce the word, 'Vensel', an animal he in no way physically resembled. In fact, his small dark eyes, the long nose, and brushed-back hair and the face sloping downwards from the narrow skull to the broad heavy jaw and jowls made him resemble more accurately a sorrowful elephant, an unfortunate impression which the luxuriant walrus moustache did something to eradicate. He was a Somerset man who had joined the Metropolitan Police in 1887. Part of his probation had been spent in Whitechapel during the Jack the Ripper murders, and two years after he had joined he was transferred to H Division permanently. At first he was resentful of the transfer but gradually he adjusted to Whitechapel and came to enjoy it. His overriding ambition was to become a detective but he was too keen for some of his colleagues, and in spite of his dogged devotion to duty he was held back until the divisional superintendent insisted that he should be taken into the department. Again he was denied promotion, and after four years he asked for an explanation. He was told that promotion would mean his automatic transfer to another division and that he had become too useful to the department. He immediately appealed to the Assistant Commissioner to intervene on his behalf. A special exception was made in his case and, instead of automatic transfer to another division each time he was promoted, he was kept where he was.

Wensley contacted the City Police and he was soon joined by Detective Inspector Thompson. Because of Wensley's own unrivalled knowledge of the East End, it was arranged for him to collaborate in the investigation. The two men hurried to Dr Scanlon's surgery and told the doctor to make his call on Gardstein and then to return to his surgery where they would be waiting for him. In this way he would not be connected with the raid that would inevitably follow. The doctor stressed again – he was most insistent on the point – that nothing should be said or done to indicate to anyone that he had helped them. The detectives agreed; they only asked one thing of him in return: it was vital that he should tell no one, and more particularly the press, of what was happening.

The doctor's visit to 59 Grove Street is unrecorded, but he must have seen the brooding figure of Sara Trassjonsky as well as the stiffening corpse. He got past the landlord and then, ignoring everything that he had been told, he telephoned the Coroner's Officer; it was either the Coroner's Officer or Dr Scanlon himself who then broke the story to the press. When he got back to the surgery he told the astounded policemen what he had done. They were furious and raced with several armed detectives to the house, reaching it only minutes before the reporters.

Mrs Katz – 'a fat old Jewess' was Wensley's unflattering description – opened the door. She could not or would not understand their questions, not even when Wensley cut short her babble and pushed her up the stairs ahead of him, guessing that if there were armed men at the head of the stairs no power on earth would have got her up. (He reckoned that her ample bulk would protect him from any possible bullet, but her weight would have crushed him if she had fallen backwards!)

As the bedroom door swung open, he saw Gardstein lying on the bed with his eyes open, facing them. It was hard to believe that he was dead. He was lying there in a crumpled dark-grey suit and white shirt, with white stripe facings, pulled out at the waistband.

Detective Sergeant Benjamin Leeson, who had joined Wensley, pushed open the door of the back room. Sara Trassjonsky was thrusting more papers into the flames as he reached forward to stop her, his revolver ready, and seized the hunchbacked little woman by the wrist. She was hustled away to City Police headquarters in Old Jewry, off Cheapside, and policemen were stationed outside the house to keep back the reporters who by then were milling about on the pavement. A young man pushed through the small crowd and, ignoring the policeman outside, knocked on the door. When it was opened he asked for Fritz. His name, he told the astonished detectives, was Nicholas Tomacoff.

6

A Face like Adonis

A *Daily Chronicle* reporter who visited the house in Grove Street wrote:

The street door opens into a narrow and ill-lighted passage, in which badly washed and ragged clothing was hanging from bits of string. Towards the end of the passage a sharp turn to the left led me on to a narrow and almost perpendicular staircase, without handrail. Here was more washing suspended from the ceiling. At the top of a staircase was a small landing, and immediately in front was the room in which the assassin died.

The room itself was about ten feet by nine, and about seven feet high. A gaudy paper decorates the walls and two or three cheap theatrical prints are pinned up. A narrow iron bedstead painted green, with a peculiarly shaped head and foot faces the door. On the bedstead was a torn and dirty woollen mattress, a quantity of blood-stained clothing, a blood-stained pillow and several towels also saturated with blood.

Under the window stood a string sewing machine, and a rickety table, covered with a piece of mole cloth, occupied the centre of the room. On it stood a cup and plate, a broken glass, a knife and fork, and a couple of bottles and a medicine bottle. Strangely contrasting with the dirt and squalor, a painted wooden sword lay on the table, and another, to which was attached a belt of silver paper, lay on a broken desk supported on a stool. On the mantelpiece and on a cheap whatnot stood tawdry ornaments. In an open cupboard beside the fireplace were a few more pieces of crockery, a tin or two, and a small piece of bread. A mean and torn blind and a strip of curtain protected the window, and a roll of surgeon's lint lay on the desk. The floor was bare and dirty, and, like the fireplace, littered with burnt matches and cigarette ends – altogether a dismal and wretched place to which the wounded desperado had been carried to die.

On the bedside table was a tweed cap containing a handful of ammunition – six .297/.230 short cartridges for Morris-tube and small rook rifles, six .30 Mauser pistol-cartridges and seventeen 7.9 mm Mauser rifle-cartridges of Austrian 1904 manufacture – which had been gathered together and put there by Sara Trassjonsky as she ransacked the room. In Gardstein's jacket and trouser pockets were thirty 7.65 mm Belgian cartridges of F.N. manufacture and in the dark overcoat, with a bullet hole in the back, which was slipped over the end of the bed, a clip of seven cartridges and seven more loose of the same make. Thrust between the mattress and the palliasse was a loaded Dreyse pistol and two more clips of ammunition.

Two immediate links with the shootings were two upholstered chairs matching four others in 11 Exchange Buildings, and the door key of No. 9 which was found in Gardstein's pocket.

The papers which were found scattered about the room and in Sara's lodgings, which had been taken there by her and Luba during the night, firmly dispelled police doubts that they were dealing with a conventional criminal gang. In Gardstein's pocket book was a member's card, dated 2 July 1910, certifying that the bearer was a member of the Lettish Anarchist Communist Group 'Leesma', as well as detailed instructions for exploding bombs by electricity, exploding quicksilver, stuff for fuses, and the specifications of several guns including their calibre, length and weight. There were also two letters from Zurich, one apparently from his brother complaining that he had worked all summer like a mad dog but that he could not save a farthing and hoping that Gardstein, at least, would have had a full purse. There was one cryptic line, 'Have you written to the finger of God in Libau?' He ended, 'The devil take it, I have spent 15 francs although I have not much money.' The other letter was also from Zurich asking him to send some money to buy an overcoat. Gardstein was also carrying a passport in the name of Schafshi Khan.

The core of Fritz's letters that survived referred to prisoners in the Central Prison, Riga, and were nearly all addressed from the Hard Labour Section. His main correspondent was Charles who, in one letter, complained of the number of 'dogs' (spies) that were already hovering around. One friend is sentenced to two years' imprisonment and another is sent to Siberia. In his longest letter to survive Charles complained of the anguish of seeing their friends suffer and of how helpless he was to help them. Mary (he mentions her Christian name only) was sentenced to ten years' imprisonment less the 3½ months she was awaiting trial. Bail was fixed at 1,000 roubles (£100) but it was impossible to raise such a sum. Now she was in N-4.

All around I see awful things which I cannot tell you. I do not blame our friends as they are doing all that is possible, but things are not getting better.

   The life of the workman is full of pain and suffering, but if the suffering reaches a certain degree one wonders whether it would not be better to follow the example of Rainis [an author of Lettish poems] who says burn at once so that you may not suffer long, but one feels that one cannot do it although it seems very advisable. The outlook is always the same, awful outlook for which we must sacrifice our strength. There is not and cannot be another outlet. Under such circumstances, our better feelings are at war with those who live upon our labour. The weakest part of our organisation is that we cannot do sufficient for our friends who are falling. For instance, such an incident occurred last week. I had to send 10 roubles to Milau Prison for S. Cerman who is to be transferred to another prison. I [also] had to secure the necessary for Krustmadi, and this evening I received news from Libau prison that one of our friends of last summer has been taken there without any money. We ought to help but we have only 33 kopecks and the treasury of the Red X is quite empty. It is terrible because the prisoner may think we will not help him!

A more personal demand was from Fritz's sister Liza, who was two years older. In September she wrote to him from Hamburg advising him against carrying on with a Jewish girl (Luba) as he already had a wife. Between June and September she had been ill in hospital, it was thought with tuberculosis, and the money she had saved from teaching had all been spent, as well as their parents' money, on doctors' bills. She still hoped to join him one day, but on the next instant realised that she never would. Some of the cards and letters the police found were unintelligible without the code. Written on one postcard was 'They who live in Neva Street have received, as you ask me to get the information'; another began with the verse of 'A Dog' (A Spy?), and two more were about an old miller woman who grumbled that she had been forgotten. There were personal cards and letters belonging to Peter the Painter from his girlfriend, Anna Schwarz, living in Kiev – they were mostly love messages. 'The moon is for the night/The Sun is for the day/But your eyes are always for me!' 'This is my picture. I have had two more taken. This is your old wife. If you have no money I will send your money back.' She always referred to herself as 'your black girl'. There were others asking whether he was going to give her up, should she wear her hair long or short, and how did he like her in this Russian costume?

Other letters were from an unknown correspondent in Baku, where there was a Lettish Society of about 200 members. There was correspondence with the Lettish group Zensonis ('Industrious'), Brihwiba and the Black Flag, the largest group in Paris; a statement of accounts from the Executive Committee of the Social Revolutionary Party in Baku with the motto 'In the fight you will get your right'; a collection list for impartial prisoners belonging to no party to make their suffering easier; notices to prisoners in Riga and leaflets against conscription. Running through the whole of the correspondence which survived – and one can safely assume that the furrow was just as deeply ploughed in the correspondence Sara burnt – is a constant plea for money.

Before the body was taken away, or Sara Trassjonsky to the station, Inspector Thompson brought the boy Solomon Abrahams from Exchange Buildings – he was as far as they knew at that time the only witness to the shootings – to the house to make a positive identification. Whether by chance or by design – one suspects the latter – he saw Sara Trassjonsky as she was being taken away and identified her as one of the people he had seen. He said he recognised her because of her hunchback. Gardstein's body was then taken away and, after the post mortem, photographed and placed in a special apparatus for preserving it. A journalist was dining at the London Hospital when a young medical student came in and said excitedly, 'We've got him. There was great competition, and he's as handsome as Adonis – a very beautiful corpse.'

'Great work!' said the host.

By Sunday evening, 18 December, several more pieces had fallen into place. Most important was the willingness of Tomacoff to help the police. Within hours he had given them a complete list and description of the men he had seen the previous afternoon in Fritz's room, together with the names of those he knew. He also knew the address of the locksmith, Osip Federoff, who in an unguarded moment had carelessly given it to him. On the Sunday evening, between seven and eight o'clock, Tomacoff took the police to Federoff's lodgings at 141 Romford Street. He was lying on his bed when Tomacoff knocked on the door of his room and told him to get up as the police were waiting outside. He also took them to 36 Havering Street where Peter Piatkow and Pavell Molachoff, who had accompanied Sara Trassjonsky to Grove Street, had spent the night.

When Luba had left Pavell at Saturday lunchtime and gone to her mother's home, Pavell had promised to call and see her later that day. At 5 p.m. he had arrived with a newspaper containing a description of the woman who was wanted in connection with the murders. Its very vagueness made Luba suspect that it was her, although in fact it was a description of Nina Vassilleva. It was also the first time that she had heard a full account of the murders. She was understandably terrified. She did not dare to tell her mother or her elder brothers of her involvement, and asked Pavell if he could find her a room where she could hide out. Pavell said that he would try but his efforts proved unsuccessful. Luba then asked a girl, Esther Weiner, who was lodging with her mother, if she would go to Sara Trassjonsky's lodgings and pick up some photographs. Esther agreed. Presumably Luba told her something of what had happened, because the girl took her to her sister's house at 41 Great Garden Street while she went alone to Sara's lodgings. On arrival at 10 Settle Street Esther was arrested by the waiting policemen and was not released until late the next morning. She then told Luba's mother of what had happened and Luba's brothers, Jack and Nathan, when they found out, went looking for their sister.

When Esther did not return, Luba left at 11 p.m. and went to a friend in Columbia Road. She begged to be allowed to stay with the friend but was told there wasn't the room. One of the lodgers took her to a house somewhere near Victoria Park Road and she spent the night there. In the morning, about eight, the landlord burst into her room and told her to get out as her description was in the morning papers. Wearily she dragged herself back to Columbia Road which was where her brothers found her. They dragged her away to Leman Street police station. Sergeant Mackenzie was at the desk when they brought her in. 'This is the young woman the police are looking for,' they said fiercely.

'She lived at 59 Grove Street, in the back room first floor, where the dead man was found yesterday, with a man named Fritz.'

The printed description of the woman who was wanted for questioning was 'Age 26 to 30; 5 ft 4 in; slim build, full breasts; complexion medium, face drawn; eyes blue; hair brown; dress, dark blue, three-quarters jacket and skirt, white blouse, large black hat trimmed with silk'. But it was such a vague description that nobody, least of all Isaac and Fanny Gordon, connected it with their own lodger, Nina Vassilleva. As far as they knew she was still living in the country where, after three weeks nursing a sick friend, she had gone to manage a small cigarette-making business for her employer, who was also ill. She had been gone six weeks so far. About 8 p.m., nearly twenty-four hours after the murders, Isaac went into her room to put a penny in the meter as the gas was fading. He realised with a shock that somebody was lying on the bed. In the darkness he could only see the body outline. He was relieved at hearing the familiar tones of Nina Vassilleva, but when he turned up the gas he was appalled by the change in her appearance. Her hair had been dyed a harsh, ugly black and she was clearly showing tremendous signs of strain. He called to his wife, who had gone to the yard to fetch some water, and it was she who gently persuaded Nina to get up.

Nina followed them into the front parlour with ill-concealed reluctance but after only a few minutes' stay went back to her own room. Fanny Gordon tried to question her but Nina only wanted to know what had been happening in London. 'There is no good news in London,' Fanny said, and added almost as an afterthought, 'but there has been a pogrom yesterday and some of the police have been shot and murdered.' Later, when she had gone and her twelve-year-old daughter Polly came into the room to pick up the school books she kept on the dresser, Nina asked her to fetch a newspaper and to read to her what it said about the Houndsditch murders. She sat on the bed and listened intently as the child read every scrap of news about the murders, including the description of the woman wanted for questioning. Afterwards she saw Nina measuring herself to see how tall she was.

Isaac Gordon waited until his wife and daughter had gone to bed and then he went into Nina's room. She was kneeling in front of the grate burning a mass of letters and papers and in a completely hysterical state. He begged her not to burn the papers. 'This is not right of you to burn [them] like this, it is not right.' Hysterically she told him that she was the woman who had been living in Exchange Buildings and that she had heard that the police were going to carry out house-to-house searches; she did not want them to find these papers. Isaac pleaded with her to let him have them for safe keeping. 'You must not burn any papers as I can take them [to a place] where they will be looked after. You can trust me as I have known you for eight months. Your friends come here and I do not talk to anyone,' he wheedled. He went to bed but spent a restless night, as he thought that in such an over-wrought state Nina might kill herself. At 8 a.m. he knocked again on her door and it was only when he knocked for a third time that she let him in. She climbed back into bed and said that she felt ill. 'Don't make life any more miserable,' Isaac implored.

'It would have been better if they had shot me,' Nina answered, 'instead of the man they have shot. He was the best friend I had.'

'You need not go on like that because he is dead and you can't fetch him back,' Isaac told her brutally.

'Without him I might just as well be dead,' she cried. Lifting her head from the pillow she took a brown-paper parcel from underneath it and handed it to Isaac for safe keeping.

For the rest of the day she brooded and in the evening got up to wash her hair with spirit vinegar soda to take out the dye. She was disturbed by a knock on the door. When she opened it John Rosen was standing there. 'Have you brought trouble,' she asked coldly. He gave a slight shrug. 'I don't know.' She did not want to talk but told him that she had left the house when the men went in to commit the robbery. Rosen watched her brush her naturally brown hair which was streaked with large patches of black dye, and then left after ten or fifteen minutes' stilted conversation. He had only been gone ten minutes when there was a second knock on the door and Detective Inspector Wensley walked in.

The instigator of this visit was Isaac Gordon, who had taken the parcel for safe keeping to his son-in-law, who had quickly wheedled the secret out of him. He had then persuaded him to take the parcel to Arbour Square police station and had gone along with him to interpret for him. A cursory examination of the parcel showed that it contained a passport issued to Minna, daughter of Indrik Gristis, a peasant woman resident in Courland, some papers, photographs and several books including *History of the Revolutionary Movement in Russia, On the Revolution and on Revolutionary Government, A Tale about an Unrighteous*

Czar and *The Government: Its Role in History and Positive Science.*
The photographs that it contained were now in Wensley's pocket. He
ignored the dyed hair and kept his questions to a minimum. Nina, it
seemed, did know a little English and could answer him if he spoke
slowly. Her name, she said, was Lena Vasilev. ('I am a Russian, I make
cigarettes.') Wensley asked if she was a member of the Anarchist Club.
She denied this but admitted having gone there on several occasions.

'Do you know that some police officers were shot at Houndsditch
on Friday night?'

'I heard of it.'

'Some of the men who were engaged in the shooting are said to have
been members of the Club. Do you know them?'

'Perhaps I do, perhaps I don't.'

'We are told you have been from home three weeks and you only
came back yesterday?'

'That's a lie. I have always been here.'

'I am also told you have some bullets and cartridges here.' This was a
complete fabrication but Wensley was looking for an opening and she
handed it to him.

'I haven't but you can look, gentlemen, if you like.'

Wensley had no doubt that they had found the woman they wanted.
Among her clothes was a dark-blue jacket and skirt fitting the description, and on the front of her coat were large stains of what appeared
to be blood. Scientifically there was no way of telling whether it was
animal or human. She also fitted the witnesses' descriptions perfectly.
Wensley decided not to arrest her, in the hope that she would lead
them to the rest of the gang. As yet she did not know of Isaac Gordon's
betrayal; she was stunned when Wensley reached into his pocket and
laid in front of her the photographs that she had placed in the brown-
paper parcel. One of them was of Gardstein. As she stared at them
Wensley asked, 'Whose photos are these?' In his pocket was the last
one – the thirteenth – of Nina herself.

'I don't know,' she answered.

She could not understand why he let her go. Next morning she said
she felt ill and asked Isaac Gordon to go to a doctor that she knew; he
was to tell him that Nina was ill and ask him to come at once. She was
about to give him the name when she changed her mind and said
that she would go herself. She confided that she was going to beg the
doctor to give her an alibi and plead with him to say that she had been

sleeping at his place for the past two or three nights. Certainly Nina felt that the risk was justified as the doctor was the same one that she had gone to for help for the dying Gardstein. Since he had not gone to the police as he had threatened, and had said nothing since, there was a slim chance that she could get him to agree to this. Also he was an old acquaintance, which was why she had gone to him for help in the first place. They had met three years before, when Nina was in domestic service in Dalston and used to do cleaning for the doctor's wife. Later, when she was self-employed as a cigarette-maker, she had gone to the doctor for orders, but after the first he had refused to give her any more as her prices were too steep. They had occasionally met since at Russian concerts. Four months before the murders the doctor, Mengle Freedman, had opened a practice at 54 Whitechapel Road, which was where Nina had gone for help and where she now went to see him.

When she appeared at the doctor's door, Nina later told Isaac Gordon, it seemed that he 'would have soon seen the devil as see her.' He told her to clear out and said that he would not do any of her dirty work, which would soon ruin his practice. He was badly frightened by her visit and later, when he was interviewed by the police, he stressed that Nina had not stayed with him at any time, either before or after the murders, and, like Dr Scanlon, he was most anxious that his name should be kept out of the affair.

Nina went back to her lodgings by now equally frightened. She saturated the dark-blue blouse that she had worn on the night of the murders with paraffin and set it alight. She also burned her black hat, but gave the feather trimming to Isaac Gordon, who asked for it, and the lining of her blue skirt, which was also consigned to the flames, to Fanny. She unwisely kept her blood-stained coat. She packed some clothes in a brown-paper parcel and made a present of the rest to Fanny Gordon. She was determined to escape. Next morning she said goodbye and tried to get away to Paris. She did not get very far. The same evening she returned in despair. She was terribly distressed and said that she had been followed everywhere by detectives. 'If I go to Russia I shall be killed and if I stop here I shall be hanged,' she moaned, and added fatalistically, 'What is to be, will be.'

Nor did the police succeed in lulling her suspicions by including the description of the woman they wanted for questioning on the reward posters. Five hundred pounds was offered for the capture of Fritz Svaars and Peter the Painter. The most likely claimant looked like being Nicholas Tomacoff. After bringing Federoff into the net, he was lodged in a hotel and all his expenses paid for the next five weeks as he hunted about for information. Everywhere he went he was accompanied by a policeman. From 24 December to 28 January the police showered him with gifts as the search switched between the West End and the East End. On 23 December the policemen bought him boots, a shirt, a collar and socks (15s 6d); on the 28th underpants, vest, socks and collar (8s 4d); on 2 January a hat and overcoat (14s 9d); on the 5th a new collar (6d); on 12 January more underclothes, handkerchiefs and collars (17s 3d). His five weeks' hotel-expenses cost £7 10s and there were other day-to-day expenses, fares, etc., as well. On 22 December he took them to 48 Turner Street where Fritz's cousin, Jacob Peters, was living. Tomacoff was not employed by the police on a day-to-day basis until the twenty-fourth; possibly he delayed giving them this information to demonstrate his usefulness. Fritz had, in fact, given him Peters' address some time before. The police were waiting in Peters' room when he came in. He was surrounded by armed police and searched. An interpreter, Casimir Pilenas, from the Thames Police Court, was with them as the arrested man apparently did not speak English, and spoke to him in Russian. He told him why he was being arrested. Immediately Peters answered, 'It is nothing to do with me. I can't help what my cousin Fritz has done.' His revolutionary experiences had taught him how to survive. Certainly he had no intention of hanging if he could shift the blame onto someone else.

Among the things the police had found in Grove Street was a small watercolour signed 'Yourka 16/12/10' and a slip of paper 'G. Dubof, 20 Galloway Road, Shepherd's Bush'. The house was watched but the police made no contact until 22 December and then only because their hand was forced. From Tomacoff's description they thought that Yourka was another of Salnish's aliases. The Special Branch knew that he was on intimate terms with a man they knew only as Printer or Compositor, who in reality was Joseph; they knew that this man had worked under another name for a jeweller in Houndsditch. According to their information he had visited the Anarchist Club once or twice but was not known to have expressed any political opinions. They also knew that he was married to, or living with, a woman; but that was all. They did not know her name, which they subsequently found out was Betsy Gershon, or where she lived, which was 100 Sidney Street.

Observation was kept on Dubol's address, but on 20 December there was an apparent leak of information. A journalist, George Mumford, working for the *Evening News*, was told by the news editor to go to the address and see what he could find out about a man called Yourka. As with Nina Vassilleva, the police had issued a description of Yourka and the others to lull suspicion. Mumford explained to the German landlady, Elsa Petter, that the police were offering a £500 reward for a man named Yourka and that she had a lodger of that name. The woman laughed and said that her husband had told her about it. 'He came home and said to my lodger, "Why, Yourka, they want you!" He was nothing like the description, she said, but the journalist could judge for himself as Yourka was at the back of the house painting. She brought him through and as he spoke very little English she interpreted for him. Yourka Dubof apologised for his appearance. He was wearing a brown waistcoat and trousers and was without a collar and tie. The wanted man was described as aged twenty-one, 5 feet 8 inches in height, of pale complexion, with dark-brown hair and heavy moustache – the description, in fact, of Jacob Peters, although because of lack of information this was not realised yet. Dubof in contrast, had a good colour, a small moustache and fair hair which the journalist described as 'brown with a dash of bronze'. He said that he had only come from Switzerland three months before and went to the Petters because his brother had once lived with them. This was true. Dubof had left Perelman's lodging-house in Wellesley Street at about the same time that Nina Vassilleva had quarrelled with Fanny Perelman, which would be about March 1910. He had gone to Switzerland and returned to England about the end of September. He had been living at his present address since then.

The landlady very largely monopolised the conversation. When the journalist asked Yourka if he ever attended meetings of Russians in London, she said that she had made it a condition of his coming to her house that he would not join any Russian or political organisation. Dubof was obviously at a disadvantage in not speaking English, thought the journalist. He seemed to want to give explanations but most of the time he stood with his arms folded, looking at the landlady and then at the reporter as if not knowing what to make of it. However, he assured the journalist, with broken words and gestures that the names of Fritz and Peter the Painter meant nothing to him. His evenings, he said, were spent talking with his landlord. The journalist dictated a short paragraph which was published the same day.

It began 'Yourka – A common name leads to confusion. The tale of a painter. Yourka is Russian for George.'

Next morning the journalist was interviewed by a detective, and the following afternoon Detective Inspector Newell called on Dubof and asked him to make a statement. Halfway through he suggested that they should finish it at City Police headquarters. 'You make mistake. I will go with you,' Dubof said. Dubof quickly admitted that he knew Fritz and Peter and had been at 59 Grove Street on the afternoon of the sixteenth. He knew that Peter was a painter and had gone to him to find work as he had been sacked on the Monday. He had taken a watercolour as a present.

He was the fifth prisoner in custody. Isaac Levy unhesitatingly identified him and Jacob Peters as the men he had seen dragging Gardstein out of Exchange Buildings, and who had threatened him with their pistols.

The hunt was intensified. For several days and nights the detectives had very little sleep. One detective's Christmas dinner was some bread and butter and tea in an alley down Petticoat Lane. Wensley and his men and City detectives combed all the lodging houses in the

The watercolour given by Yourka Dubof to Peter the Painter on the day of the murders.

Whitechapel area, some sleeping 6–700 men nightly. On 23 December detectives followed Nina Vassilleva to St Paul's Cathedral to watch the funeral of the three murdered policemen. She bought a small black-and-silver memorial card, with wood-block portraits of the three men inside, which was later found in her handbag. The streets were choked with spectators. The Cathedral was crowded with people in black and dark blue. The Home Secretary, Winston Churchill, and Mrs Churchill were followed by the Lord Mayor in his state robe of black and gold, preceded by the Black Mourning Sword and accompanied by the Sheriffs and Aldermen in scarlet gowns trimmed with crêpe. As the three coffins were carried into the Cathedral the voices of the choir floated down the long nave. In front of the coffins was carried the great gilt cross; the coffins were placed on catafalques in front of the choir by the opening to the crypt. On each coffin was the dead man's helmet, Bentley's having a hole in the rim where the bullet had crossed his face.

Before the funeral, photographs were taken of the murdered policemen. As was then customary with mortuary photographs the corpses were dressed in their clothes – in this case their uniforms and greatcoats buttoned to the neck – and they were strapped to stretchers and photographed against the wall with their helmets on their heads. They were photographed standing up because the cameras of the day, which were on tripods, could not be deflected downwards. Photographs were also taken of Gardstein. He lay on a mortuary slab but his head was propped up on a block and the eyelids propped open so that a lifelike portrait could be taken for the poster. His identity was still uncertain and it was hoped that somebody would make a positive indentification of him from the poster; it was marked 'Portrait and description of the dead murderer'.

Jacob Kempler, passing by Arbour Square police station a few days later, recognised the dead man from the photograph as his lodger 'P. Morin'. The subsequent discovery of Gardstein's lodgings at 44 Gold Street was widely publicised as 'The Stepney Bomb Factory'. In his room, it was said, were 'materials suitable for the manufacture of bombs, a supply of deadly acids, piles of cartridges sufficient to kill crowds, and a quantity of anarchist literature'.

As the investigations gathered momentum, Tomacoff began to lose some of his usefulness. In the immigrant community he was already being pointed out as the informer helping the police. When the police were finally given the whereabouts of Fritz and Joseph the source was not Tomacoff but someone completely unknown. The informant came to City Police headquarters in the late evening of New Year's Day. It was snowing heavily. Only scribbled notes were kept of the conversation. Fritz Svaars and Joseph, the informant said, were hiding in 100 Sidney Street with a woman lodger, Betsy Gershon.

Who was the informer? The police kept his name secret, but in the pencil notes that survive he referred to his cousin's lodgings in 83 Nelson Street. It might have been possible to trace the name of the tenant from the rate books or electoral rolls, but the former were destroyed in the war and, as the tenant was an immigrant and had not been long resident, he was excluded from the latter. Other trails have proved equally

THE KING'S MESSAGE TO THE WIDOWS.

The King has heard with the greatest concern of the murder of three constables belonging to the City Police, and he requests you to express to their widows and families his sincere sympathy and his assurance that he feels most deeply for them in their sorrow.

His Majesty will be glad also if you would likewise express to the wounded constables his sympathy with them on the severe wounds which they have received in the execution of their duty, and his hope that they will make good progress towards a complete recovery.

The King would wish to be informed of their present condition.

Memorial cards to the three policemen.

fruitless. But we do know from the notes that the informer went to 100 Sidney Street at 2 p.m. the next day to see the two men and incredibly, in the evidence given to an investigating committee some months later, the landlady described not only his visit but the man himself, although she did not know his name. She said she opened the door to a gentleman

who wore a cap and a Chester and boots with leggings on, but he had a little parcel under his arm, it was simply like an umbrella, but it was a long thing, and it was white and covered with American cloth carried under his arm. He wanted to speak to Mrs Gershon who called down, 'Mrs Fleischmann let him up, he is a photographer'; and I let him up, and he might have been there from a quarter past two till about ten minutes to three when he came down...

Sacred to the Memory of
SERGEANT   THOMAS   TUCKER,
AGED 46 YEARS.
SERGEANT   BENTLEY,
AGED 40 YEARS.
P.C.   JOSEPH   CHOATE,
AGED 32 YEARS.
who were murdered in the execution of their duty
on Friday December 16th 1910.
Interred at the City of London Cemetery, Ilford
on Thursday December 22nd 1910.

Almost certainly the informer was the gang's old landlord from Great Garden Street and Wellesley Street, Charles Perelman, who still earned his living as a photograph-enlarger.

His information ran as follows:

> The woman Gershon came to me on Sunday last at six o'clock [and] said the men – Yoska and Fritz [were] hiding in her house, that they went there on Saturday the 17th and enquired for the address of Abraham and Pavell as she said they were friends of Fritz and Yoska and would help them. I told her I did not know the address but I volunteered to assist the two men. I told her this [in] order to find out where the two men were staying, I also told her that a young Russian [Tomacoff?] would call at eight o'clock the same night and would be calling upon me and would know Abraham and Pavell's address and I advised her to call back at that time. She returned as arranged but I was unable to give her the addresses and it was then I told her I would do all that was necessary for the men.
>
> She then said can I speak openly and I took her into another room. When we were alone she then told me that she had Fritz and Yoska in her house since the murders but was afraid they would be discovered and wanted to find another address for them. I told her I would find a room for them and made an appointment at Newark Street to see her the next day at 1.20.
>
> I saw her as arranged and she told me that the best thing for me to do was to go and see the men at 100 Sidney Street.
>
> I went to Sidney Street at 1.45 p.m. and was admitted by a woman [Mrs Fleishmann] living on the ground floor. I went to the front room on the 2nd floor with Gershaw [sic] who was waiting on the stairs, where I saw Fritz and Yoska standing with their hands in [their] overcoat pockets. I told them I would find other rooms if they had money. Fritz said I have £20 and would like me to find a room in Dalston. As I was leaving Fritz asked me to post the letter produced. I asked my cousin to find a room at 83 Nelson Street (back room on 2nd floor). It was arranged for the woman to see me in Russell Street at 8.30 p.m. for the address and she then told me they would not move until five or six the next day. I also said they wanted a fourth digs.
>
> Shortly after 9 a.m. she called in Russell Street and said they would not take the bed but would buy another and said Fritz would leave at nine the next night and Yoska would want a reply from Fritz that he was safe upon which Yoska would go to the same place.

He added that the total number of those involved was fifteen and gave descriptions of two of them: Papko, age 24–25, height 5'9", hair dark, complexion ordinary, broad-shouldered, walks with a stick and puts his feet well to the ground; seen the previous week with the girl in the photograph shown by Superintendent Ottaway (44 Gold Street); and Osovoki (Osovsky), age 18–19, height 5'6" or 7", hair fair, complexion fresh, large eyes, English-looking.

The letter (*see* Appendix), which Perelman handed to the police, was in an envelope marked in Lettish in red ink: 'Please hand it to J. F. Svaars No. 8 Boschu Street, Libau.' This was enclosed in another envelope, also in red ink, but addressed in Russian: 'To Jahn Ludman, No. 64 Pastbischna Street, Libau, Courland.' The letter itself was written in Lettish in black ink. In it Fritz explained how he had been planning to leave for Australia between 7 and 10 January, by which time his wife should have joined him. He had sufficient money for the voyage (£20). He explained how Gardstein had borrowed sixty roubles (£6) from him with the prospect of getting it back with considerable interest. Gardstein was expecting to get a couple of thousand pounds from which he would give Fritz one thousand roubles (£100) at which Fritz was naturally delighted. Instead, the dying Gardstein had been brought to his flat by two acquaintances, and because he wasn't sure that he hadn't been seen Fritz could not risk staying there, for although he was innocent he would be arrested and certainly hanged. He grabbed a weapon and ammunition and went to a friend's place. He narrated the rest of the night's events: how he had ordered the girls to burn the house down to conceal the fact that Gardstein had been shot and to destroy any other evidence. One of the girls had brought away the ship's tickets but nothing else. He said that the police were looking for another 'lad' (Peter Piatkow) who had been living at his place and they were being sought as participants in the shooting of four policemen. He didn't know what had happened to Peter whom he did not mention by name. He too would be arrested and hanged if caught because the guilty ones were not known and 'my landlord said that he didn't know if we had been at home or not'. (Confirmation that Fritz and Joseph were hiding in Grove Street when the others were breaking into Harris's.) His next sentence revealed that Jacob (Peters) had been arrested and, clearly a white lie for family consumption, 'if anyone didn't know he didn't.' The letter ended despairingly, declaring that he had been on the run for two weeks and didn't know how much longer he could hold out. He had already said that if caught he would hang and he would resist and even shoot himself rather than be taken!

> I'm not at all depressed because everyone knows that one has to die at some time and the good a person such as I can bring to humanity is not worth talking about. And to you it's all the same because up to now I haven't been able to help you and in the future, what luck would I have had? So be peaceful. If I'm lucky then I'll still live and I'll share joy and sadness with you, and if not, you also know that at some time that same hour will come to you and you'll be ashes the same as everyone.

He sent kisses to them all.

Perelman's motives for betrayal are obscure. Subsequent events would show that he had helped Smoller to escape on the night of the murders and one can only assume that his motive for betrayal was greed. He was an old man, lazy, selfish, chronically short of cash, dependent on his wife for money and possibly suffering the added humiliation of knowing about her casual affairs with other men to which he could only respond with brutality. If he had ever been a committed revolutionary he probably felt, as many others did at this time, including Lenin, that he would never live to see the revolution itself. His idealism had probably gone. Possibly he did not care for the young men who were so much more dashing than he and so much nearer his wife's age. His callousness and brutality were well known. Once before he had had his foot on his daughter's throat. Now it would be on Fritz's and Joseph's.

The hurriedly jotted-down police notes don't make it clear that the end of it is a partial recapitulation omitting important time breaks.

After Perelman had been to see the two wanted men he must have gone straight to the police who had swiftly responded by sending armed men to Sidney Street. Late on the Monday afternoon two large horse-drawn vehicles had driven into the street and waited for the two men to leave. Perelman arranged a room in Nelson Street and then met Betsy Gershon in Russell Street at 8.30 p.m. and gave her the address. She told him that they would not move until five or six the next day. She must have told him to wait while she went back to Sidney Street and told them what he had arranged. Obviously they didn't like the

Fritz Svaars' last letter from Sidney Street brought out by the informer.

arrangements because she immediately returned and told Perelman that they would not take the room but wanted something else. Fritz would not leave now until nine o'clock the next night and Joseph would want a coded reply from Fritz that he was safe before he left 100 Sidney Street to join him.

7

The Siege of Sidney Street

A bleary-eyed Wensley was still working at Leman Street police station when the telephone rang just before midnight. The voice at the other end of the line was Superintendent Ottaway's and he sounded anxious. 'We don't like the look of things,' he said. 'The informant is not all that can be desired and seems shifty. It will never do to let these people slip through our fingers now – there's no guarantee that they will move tomorrow night. We propose if you agree, to act tonight.'

Wensley agreed. As soon as it was daylight it would be impossible to conceal the light scattering of detectives watching the house and, in such a sensitive area, this information might quickly be passed to the two gunmen. He offered to bring the rest of his detectives but Ottaway thought that by themselves they might not be enough, and proposed bringing a stiffener of uniformed men. As this meant bringing men from another force and from another police district into H Division, Wensley told him to bring his men to Arbour Square police station while he sent Sergeant Leeson with a message to the home of Divisional Superintendent Mulvaney in Commercial Road telling him of what was happening.

Ottaway swung into action and ordered the single men out. Shivering in their blue greatcoats they straggled through the empty streets, with their faces turned away from the bitterly cold wind which by now was gusting sheets of snow and rain. As yet they did not know what had happened, but when they heard that the married men were to be left behind they realised that there was likely to be some shooting and guessed the rest. At Arbour Square police station they stamped their feet and tried to get warm again while in a nearby office the officers held a hurried consultation.

The meeting began at 12.45 a.m. None of the officers, including Wensley, had an intimate knowledge of the locality and it was left to one of Wensley's detectives, Sergeant Girdler, to brief them. Snatching up a piece of paper he began to draw as they leant over his shoulder. Superintendent Mulvaney turned up the gas flares to give him more light. Sergeant Girdler scored the paper with two parallel lines to indicate Sidney Street, which runs between the Mile End Road and Commercial Road. He then blocked off a square on the right side of the road. All the houses in this square faced outwards, and in the centre were the yards. The streets going round the square, starting with Lindley Street in the north, were Richardson Street, Hawkins Street and Sidney Street. The house where the two men were hiding was part of a block of ten four-storey houses built in 1900. Not only were they bigger than the usual grey two-storey houses in the area but they had facings of red brick and were grandiloquently known, after the landlord, as Charley Martin's Mansions. The house they wanted was next but one to the surgery on the corner of Hawkins Street.

The three superintendents and Wensley then discussed ways and means of getting the gunmen out. Even as they made their plans they were uncomfortably aware that there was no guarantee that the murderers had in fact been located, or that they were the right men. John Stark, one of the City Police Superintendents, spoke for them all when he said, 'This whole operation could make us a laughing stock.' As they talked, Superintendent Mulvaney ordered that a hundred of his own men should be mustered in the parade room to match the City's hundred men. They finally agreed to Wensley's suggestion that men should be placed in the houses on either side of the house, in case the gunmen should try to escape by breaking through the adjoining walls, and that it should be covered front and rear from the yards at the back and from the houses opposite. As Sergeant Girdler knew the locality and some of the people who lived there he was sent with twelve detectives, carrying revolvers and truncheons, to Sidney Street to make the preliminary moves.

Sergeant Girdler divided them into parties of four and left two at the corner of Richardson Street and Hawkins Street. The third party went with him to 3 Hawkins Street where he knocked on the window of the ground-floor flat of Mrs Rubenoff. She opened her door and then went straight back to her room without saying a word. Girdler crept

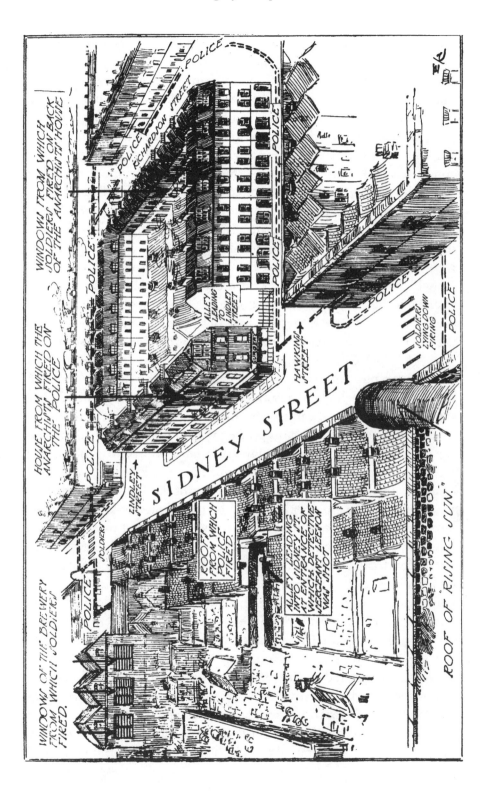

through the passage with the four men and in the back yard directed them to climb over a low wall into the yard of 1 Hawkins Street, which was directly opposite the back of 100 Sidney Street. Having posted them there he returned to the corner of Hawkins Street and knocked on the door of No. 98, which was a doctor's surgery. He posted four more men in the yard, and repeated the same operation again at No. 102 with the last four men. Soon after 2 a.m., the rear of the house was completely sealed off. At the same time the whole block was cordoned off on the perimeter with 200 men to cut off all chance of escape.

In the meantime, Wensley and the City officers had been considering their next move, which was to place armed men in the houses and shuttered shops which were immediately opposite. Some of the City men were armed with Morris-tube rifles, and others with revolvers which were so antiquated that most of them had to be reloaded after each shot. Wensley asked George Weston, one of his sergeants, if there was any chance of getting into the wood yard next to Cohen's the chemist at No. 109 on the other side of the Street. Weston said, 'Yes – I know Cohen well.' He crept across the Street and tapped at the door but got no answer. He then tried the door of the yard but that too was locked. 'Frank,' he whispered, as Sergeant Girdler slipped in beside him, 'can we get this wicket door of the yard open?' Girdler grinned and felt in his pocket; within minutes he had opened the door with a skeleton key. He crept back to his post in Lindley Street as more men moved silently into the yard. From the yard some of the uniformed men broke into the back of the house and woke up the couple who were sleeping in the bedroom overlooking the street. There was a hurried explanation, and as the startled owner and his wife dressed and hurried downstairs they watched with dismay as more policemen trampled into their bedroom and trod snow and water into their fur carpets. The policemen positioned themselves with their rifles behind the lace curtains and partly barricaded the window with the mattress which they yanked off the bed. More armed men were positioned in the shop doorways facing the house and, shortly after 3 a.m., the house was completely surrounded.

Wensley suggested to the officers, 'If I were you, I would get into No. 102 and find out from the occupier the character of the landlord and landlady of No. 100. If they are respectable we shall be doing a good thing if we can quietly get them out.' Detectives were already in the yard of No. 102 but although the landlady, Mrs Bluestein, had co-operated, somewhat unwillingly, with the police so far she bristled at the mention of her next-door neighbour, Mrs Fleishmann, with whom she was on extremely bad terms, and Wensley had great difficulty in finding out what he wanted to know. Eventually he got from her a grudging admission that she was a respectable woman, but when Wensley explained that he proposed waking her up and bringing her into the house Mrs Bluestein, after expressing her disapproval with considerable force, went to bed rather than have to meet her neighbour in her own home. The Fleishmanns, Wensley had already learned, slept in the front room on the ground floor and so, taking with him the Jewish interpreter the City officers had brought with them, he rapped on the window shutters of the house next door. Rebecca Fleishmann half rolled over in bed and listened to the insistent tapping.

'That's the milkman,' she said, nudging her husband. Samuel grunted and snuggled deeper into the feather mattress. 'I won't get up,' he muttered. 'You go as you arrange for the milkman.' Rebecca did not waste any time arguing as their youngest daughter, Leah, was asleep in the same room, and crept over to the window. 'I don't want any milk,' she hissed.

'No, not the milkman,' she heard someone say. The interpreter, Henry Wagner, spoke in Yiddish. 'It is the police.'

Rebecca crept back to her bed and pummeled her husband awake. 'It is not the milkman, it is somebody else,' she said doubtfully. 'Get up.'

Samuel staggered irritably to the window. Like his wife he thought that the time was about 7 a.m. 'We don't want any milk,' he shouted.

'I am not a milkman – I am from the police,' Wagner persisted. Samuel snapped up the blind and stared through the glass. 'I don't believe you,' he said. Wagner held up a truncheon. 'Don't be afraid – come out,' he pleaded with him.

Samuel told his wife to come outside with him. Mrs Fleishmann in particular was disturbed at seeing so many policemen; she was so distressed that in her haste she did not put her stockings on. Wensley asked them how many lodgers there were. She told him that there was an old couple named Clements in the ground floor back room next to her bedroom; in the first-floor front room there was another lodger David Schiemann, his wife and four children. The Fleishmann's twins were in the back room on the first floor. On the second floor the front room was let to Mrs Gershon, and Mr Fleishmann used the back room as a stock room. He also used the large attic as a tailor's shop.

They asked her about Mrs Gershon. Mrs Fleishmann described her as a tall thin woman with glasses. No, she didn't know if there were any strange men with her. Wensley then turned to her husband and told him that he must go and fetch Mrs Gershon down. Samuel Fleishmann was horrified. He was a very nervous man by nature and seeing so many policemen had frightened him still more. 'Not for £1,000,' he said. He explained later, 'I can tell you, if I see so many officers in the night time, nobody would be fool enough to go upstairs.' Wensley tried Mrs Fleishmann again. He had heard that she was a respectable woman and would not tolerate two men living with a woman in her house. He suggested that she went upstairs and saw for herself if this were so. He again met with a stubborn refusal. 'I would not do it for £5,000 nor let my husband do it.' Wensley's manner changed. He began to infer that both of them knew something more sinister and ignored their strenuous denials that they didn't know what he was talking about. Samuel Fleishmann by then was coughing so badly that Wensley suggested, 'Go up and ask Mrs Gershon to come down as your husband has been taken very bad and you want her to help you.' Rebecca said nothing – but went.

The stairs were in darkness, but she had lived in the house for eleven years and could find her way without a light. She knocked on Mrs Gershon's door. There was no light showing under the door so she knocked again. To her chagrin the stock-room door behind her opened and Mrs Gershon came out with bare feet and wearing only a petticoat. For a moment Mrs Fleishmann's outraged sense of propriety got the better of her, but she recovered sufficiently well to explain that her husband was very ill and she needed assistance.

'Give me a little help,' she said.

The two women crept downstairs but as they reached the first-floor landing Mrs Gershon was seized and carried next door. She indignantly denied having anyone in her room until Wensley told her that he was going up there to see for himself. If he was killed, he said, she would be hanged as she knew who the two men were. She then said that there was a cousin of her husband up there and only then reluctantly admitted the presence of a second man. They had called the previous evening, she lied, and refused to go when asked. When she insisted that they leave they had made her take off her skirt and boots so that she could not run away, and had forced her to sleep on an old sofa in the stock room. So the two men were still there. That was all the police

The Tottenham Outrage: the capture of the tram.

Christian Salnish.

The Tottenham Outrage: the bedroom in Oak Cottage where Jacob shot himself.

The Tottenham Outrage: Ching Brook where Hefeld failed to climb the fence and shot himself.

Karl Hoffman, Christian Salnish and 'Bifsteks'.

A contemporary artist's impression of the shootings in Exchange Buildings.

Yourka Dubof: arrest photograph.

Nina Vassilleva: arrest photograph.

Jacob Peters: arrest photograph.

George Gardstein.

Fritz Svaars.

Max Smoller.

Sergeant Tucker.

Police Constable Choate.

'State' funeral of the murdered policemen at St Paul's Cathedral.

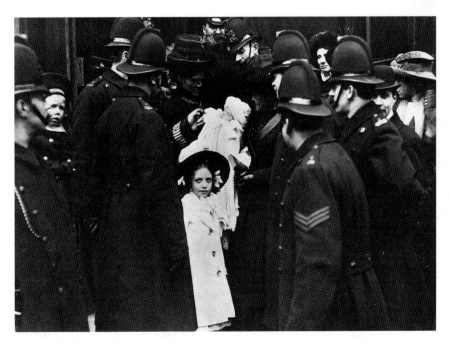

Christening of baby Bentley, son of Sergeant Bentley.

Mortuary photograph of Sergeant Bentley showing the bullet hole in his helmet peak.

Sergeant Bentley.

Exchange Buildings the morning after the murders.

The ringed bullet holes in shop front.

Luba Milstein: arrest
photograph.

George Gardstein: the mortuary
photograph used on the police
notices when trying to identify him.

Sara Trassjonskey:
arrest photograph.

Above Scots Guards and police at Sidney Street.

Left Peter Piatkow (Peter the Painter).

EAST END SIEGE. — *Guards lying prone on ground firing at assassins.*

"The Battle of Stepney": The Anarchists' House on Fire

This page and opposite below The Siege of Sidney Street: a pictorial story published in postcard form.

The EAST END SIEGE,
. The Fort, No. 100 Sidney Street,

EAST END SIEGE. — Police searching the ruins.

East End Siege: searching the ruins.

Sidney Street: the end of the siege.

The kitchen where the body of Fritz Svaars was found.

Winston Churchill at the siege.

John Rosen: arrest photograph. Osip Federoff: arrest photograph. Karl Hoffman: arrest photograph.

Churchill giving evidence at the inquest on Svaars and Joseph.

John Rosen giving evidence
at the magistrates committal
proceedings.

Sara Trassjonsky and Nina
Vassilleva at the magistrates
committal proceedings.

Lenin and Jacob Peters at
Sverdlov's funeral on 16 March
1919.

Clockwise from above
Jacob Peters in Russia in 1917.

Jacob Peters in 1930 about to purge the Red Army of its 'disaffected element'.

Jacob Peters – 'Hero of October'

Karl Hoffman,
Luba Milstein
and daughter
Catherine.

Karl Hoffman and Luba Milstein in old age.

Karl Hoffman and Luba
Milstein with Luba's son
by Fritz Svaars.

Jacob and May Peters with their
daughter May in 1916.

May Peters after her release from a prison
camp in 1956.

needed to know. A coat was flung over Mrs Gershon's shoulders and she was taken away to City Police headquarters.

The police now had a problem. If they went into the house they could not, according to law, open fire until they had been fired on first; this would put them at an impossible disadvantage. In addition, the staircase was narrow (3½ feet wide), with a bend at the top, which would make the operation extremely hazardous. Superintendent Mulvaney later explained:

> The measurements of the passage and staircase will show how futile any attempts to storm or rush the place would have been, with two men … dominating the position from the head of the stairs and where, to an extent, they were well under cover from fire. The passage at one discharge would have been blocked by fallen men; had any even reached the stairs, it could only have been by climbing over the bodies of their comrades, when they would stand little chance of getting further; had they even done this the two desperadoes could retreat up the staircase to the first and second storey, on each of which, what had occurred below would have been repeated.

They decided that it would be best to bring everyone out of the house and then wait for daylight before making their next move. Mrs Fleishmann brought out her children, and then went back again to the first floor, woke Mrs Schiemann and told her to get up quietly. She took the two babies and the Schiemanns' two other children safely downstairs. Old Mr and Mrs Clements on the ground floor were more of a problem. She was quickly persuaded to leave, but her ninety-year-old husband obstinately refused to move out of his bed; to make things more difficult, he was stone deaf. Fleishmann tried to frighten him by saying there were burglars in the house, but the old man only snuggled deeper into his bed of which, said Mrs Fleishmann later, he was very fond. About this time somebody blew a police whistle, and when Fleishmann came to the street door and told the waiting policeman that the old man did not want to come out someone growled, 'Put him in his trousers.' The interpreter went back with him and together they forced the whining old man into his clothes and then struggled out of the house with him on their backs. Nothing was to be gained by gagging him as he was the last to leave. The two inspectors, Wensley and Thompson, propped the street door open and the first-floor lodger, David Schiemann, turned up the gas. The policemen in the house opposite clutched their rifles; they stared intently at the empty hall and lower staircase, and waited. Slowly it began to get light. The policemen cordoning off the block were tired, hungry and very cold. The snow was turning to slush, but the wind had not dropped. At the back of the house, the detectives pulled their caps down further over their eyes and rested their arms on the chest-high walls with their revolvers numbly clutched between their stiff fingers. In Hawkins Street a new baker's shop was opening. Three men and several boys had been hired to hand out 20,000 leaflets, but only three of them had turned up. The leaflets were to publicise a brass band which had been specially hired for the grand opening and, at 7 a.m., policemen and neighbours alike were treated to the band's opening piece from the top floor of the shop. A policeman told them to stop playing but the baker ignored him; the band, in fact, went on tranquilly playing for the next hour.

The streets were still largely deserted, but people were just beginning to hover about, uncertain what they were to see, behind the police cordon. At about 7.30 there was another hurried conference in the wood yard and it was decided to try to attract the two men's attention. Sergeant Weston ran across the road and banged furiously on the still-open door of the house and then ran back. Nothing happened. Then Wensley asked his men to throw some pebbles at the second- floor windows. They spattered against the glass, but still without producing a reaction. Then somebody picked up a brick to throw and, as it was flung at the same window, a pane of glass in the window of the floor below shattered and half a dozen shots sprayed the group of policemen at the entrance to the yard. One bullet passed through somebody's bowler hat. Sergeant Leeson yelled, 'Jack, I am hit', and ran into the yard with Sergeant Weston behind him. Shots were spurting from the stones in the yard as they ran for cover and the gates were slammed shut behind them. Leeson collapsed against the rear of a van as Wensley ripped open his shirt and coat which were soaked with blood. Wensley had little doubt that the Sergeant was dying. Leeson himself thought so too. He is recorded as saying melodramatically, 'Mr Wensley, I am dying. They have shot me through the heart. Goodbye. Give my love to the children. Bury me at Putney.' Wensley pressed his hand. 'We will be with you to the last,' he said. Superintendent Mulvaney ran upstairs to the bedroom where the City men were positioned with their rifles to find out if they had seen the men who had fired the shots or had returned their fire. They had not seen anyone or opened fire as yet, but as he stood talking bullets started ricocheting off the walls and smashing into the glass chandelier. He went downstairs again and sat by Leeson who had been carried into the kitchen.

Someone ran across the street to the corner surgery next to the besieged house and brought back Dr Krestin but Leeson, even though he thought he was dying, waved him away as he doubted his medical qualifications! In the meantime Louis Levy, who kept his coffee stall in the yard and who had been trapped by the shooting, climbed over the roofs to fetch Dr Nelson Johnstone from his surgery in Mile End Road. Dr Johnstone arrived about twenty minutes after the detective had been shot. A bullet whistled by him as he crossed Sidney Street. Once in the yard Levy pointed to an outhouse and told him that he would have to climb over it and the adjoining walls to reach the wounded man. Johnstone handed him one of his bags and together the two men climbed onto the roof with the help of a ladder, crawled along the coping and eventually reached the wood yard. Leeson was lying on a couch in the kitchen. His coat, waistcoat and shirt were open. The bullet wound was level with the left nipple and about two inches in towards the centre of the chest. Johnstone was about to probe the wound when the detective said, 'It is not there, doctor, it has gone out the other side.' Johnstone pulled back Leeson's coat and found another wound about four and a half inches beyond and about three-eighths of an inch below the right nipple. The bullet had apparently struck the rib, passed under the breast bone, glanced along another rib and passed out at the right side. Leeson was spitting blood and in a state of total collapse. 'Someone take this,' he said, remembering the revolver in his right-hand pocket. The doctor took it and gingerly placed it in his hip pocket to give to Wensley. He plugged the wounds and revived the wounded man with a large dose of brandy.

It was obviously vital to get Leeson to hospital. The only way out was over the outhouses at the rear which backed onto Mann & Crossman's brewery. Wensley scrambled over them and came back with a stretcher, which was hauled into the yard. He then got a van in the yard, pushed it up against a dung pit and placed a ladder at a slant from the van to the outhouses, which were about fourteen feet high. Leeson was brought out on the stretcher, lifted from the ground to the van, then dragged across the ladder and onto the roof of the outhouse. Wensley and the others on the roof were hampered by a blinding fall of sleet but had so far been unobserved by the two gunmen although they were now above the level of the gateway. Suddenly a man's helmet appeared; he was mounting a ladder from the brewery side of the wall. Wensley shouted at him to get back, but it was too late. They had been seen. Shots began to smash against the wet and slippery tiles. A bullet grazed Dr Johnstone's forehead; he shouted to Wensley to lie down. Wensley flung himself forward onto the broken tiles and for about ten minutes he and Leeson, who was still lying helpless on the stretcher, were exposed to the constant stream of fire. Eventually Leeson, unwilling to let anyone else expose themselves to the fusillade, rolled off the stretcher and over to the wall and was helped down to the safety of the brewery yard. Wensley now found himself a solitary target on the roof just as the gunmen were getting their range; the bullets were coming unpleasantly close. His only chance of safety was the gutter of the outhouse which was apparently shielded by the ridge of the wall. He lay at full length in an inch or so of sleet and water; he was frozen stiff, and the slightest movement was greeted with a shower of bullets. It never occurred to him, he reflected later, that he could have escaped by loosening the tiles near him and dropping through the roof to the interior of the outhouse. He was trapped there for half an hour. Meanwhile, a rumour that he had been shot was steadily gaining circulation.

The shooting had been going on for about an hour now and it was clear that the gunmen dominated the situation with their superior fire-power. Stark and Mulvaney conferred again and guessed that the two men were using Mauser pistols, which were far superior to the police's Morris-tube rifles. In a lull in the firing which released Wensley, they scrambled over the outhouses into the brewery and tried unsuccessfully to telephone Scotland Yard. They were forced to hurry back to Arbour Square police station. This time they were more successful. Mulvaney spoke to the Assistant Commissioner, Major Wodehouse, and asked for the necessary authority to bring in troops from the Tower of London.

Wodehouse could not give this authority without consulting the Home Office, who passed on his request to the Home Secretary, Winston Churchill. Churchill was in his bath when he was surprised by an urgent knocking at the door. 'There is a message from the Home Office on the telephone. Absolutely immediate.' Dripping wet and shrouded in a towel, he hurried to the telephone and was told of what had happened, and that his authority was requested to send for troops to arrest or kill the two men. He at once authorised the police to use whatever force was necessary and in about twenty minutes was dressed and at the Home Office. There he found that no further information was available other than that the house had been surrounded and that the anarchists were firing in all directions. No one knew how many anarchists there were or what other measures were to be taken. In the circumstances he thought it best, and his advisers concurred, that he should see for himself what was going on. Later on he admitted 'that convictions of duty were supported by a strong sense of curiosity which perhaps it would have been well to keep in check'.

Armed with the Home Secretary's authority, Superintendent Mulvaney hurried to the Tower, stopping only to tell Mrs Leeson that her husband had been wounded but that he was all right, and spoke to the officer commanding the Scots Guards. After telephoning the G.O.C. he was told that he could have the help of a Lieutenant Ross, two non-commissioned officers and seventeen men; they accompanied him back to Sidney Street, arriving there shortly after 10 a.m. The soldiers in their heavy grey coats and their distinctive caps, with the diced cap-bands, halted in Richardson Street. Three of them went with Superintendent Stark to Mann & Crossman's brewery and climbed the high building which was used as a bottling store. The upper part of the building, which was at right angles to Sidney Street and overlooked the wood yard, had three large slatted windows. Through the slats the soldiers could just see the attic and second-floor windows of 100 Sidney Street. Stark pointed out the house to them by indicating a broken chimney pot which was directly in their line of fire. Within minutes they shattered it and had got the range, and were soon firing round after round into the upper windows of the house. This forced the gunmen to move down to the first and ground-floor windows where they were exposed to an equally devastating fire from another party of soldiers who were now occupying the windows formerly manned by the police. Superintendent Mulvaney posted three soldiers at the corner of Oxford Street and Sidney Street, two at the end of Hawkins Street, two at the corner of Lindley Street and three at the Mile End Road end of Sidney

Street. Between eleven and twelve noon some sixty policemen from the surrounding divisions were brought up armed with revolvers, and a gunsmith also arrived with shotguns and ammunition; these were handed out to policemen with military experience.

Since daylight there had been a steady stream of rumours of fighting in the East End, and sightseers had followed the small squads of policemen they saw marching through Whitechapel to Sidney Street. Throughout the morning the cordons had to be strengthened again and again to keep the crowds out of range of the Mausers, which were sighted up to a thousand yards. They watched awe-struck as the soldiers from the brewery tower kept up a sustained fire. The snow turned to a drizzle, and by mid-morning the street was lit up with a watery brightness. Every now and again there would be a puff of smoke and a spit of flame from the house and an answering rattle of shots from the soldiers' Lee Enfields. Some of the policemen had heard a rumour that Leeson was dead and were in a frenzy to rush the house; it was only with the greatest difficulty that they were restrained. One detective was foolhardy enough to run down the street with a rifle and smash the windows on the ground floor; he ran back again to great cheers from the crowd. Similarly a postman insisted on delivering letters to within a few doors of the house, and an old woman close by came to her door at frequent periods throughout the morning and, arms folded, calmly watched the pistol flashes and bullets streaking the red façade.

From the roof of the Rising Sun public house the *Daily Chronicle* reporter had a bird's-eye view.

At both ends of Sidney Street the Scots Guards were in position, taking cover behind the angle of the houses. Around them were groups of policemen in uniform armed with shotguns, and numbers of plain clothes detectives with heavy revolvers. In the shadow of doorways and archways men crouched down with barrels of rifles and pistols pointed towards the house next to the doctor's surgery, with its shattered window-panes and broken brickwork. Looking down into the backyards of the houses opposite Martins-buildings, I could see soldiers and armed policemen moving about, climbing over fences, and getting up tall ladders, so that they could fire between the chimney pots.

On the roof of a great brewery on the same side of the way as the Rising Sun public-house were scores of the work-people, and as far as

the eye could see across the sloping roofs, the chimney-pots and para-
pets, the sky-line was black with heads, while in the streets below, as
far as a quarter of a mile away, there were vast and tumultuous crowds,
kept back by lines of mounted policemen. The voices of those many
thousands came up to me in great murmurous gusts, like the roar of wild
beasts in a jungle. It seemed as if the whole of London had poured into
Whitechapel and Stepney to watch one of the most deadly and thrilling
dramas that has ever happened in the great city within living memory.

But my eyes were now fixed upon one building, and no other impression could find a place in my mind. The anarchists' house had the
horrible fascination of a house of death. Bullets were raining upon it.
As I looked I saw how they spat at the walls, how they ripped splinters
from the door, how they made neat grooves as they burrowed into the
red bricks, or chipped off corners of them. The noise of battle was tremendous and almost continuous. The heavy barking reports of Army
rifles were followed by the sharp and lighter cracks of pistol shots. Some
of the weapons had a shrill singing noise, and others were like children's pop guns. Most terrible and deadly in sound was the rapid fire of
the Scots Guards, shot speeding on shot, as though a Gatling gun were
at work. Then there would come a sudden lull, as though a bugle had
sounded 'Cease fire', followed by a silence, intense and strange, after the
ear-splitting din.

It reopened again when a few moments later there came the spitting
fire of an automatic pistol from the house next to the surgery. From
my vantage point I could see how the assassins changed the position
from which they fired. The idea that only two men were concealed
within that arsenal seemed disproved by the extreme rapidity with
which their shots came from one floor and another. As I watched,
gripped by the horror and drama of it, I saw a sharp stabbing flash
break through the garret window. The man's weapon must have been
over the edge of the window sill. He emptied his magazine, spitting
out the shots at the house opposite, from which picked marksmen of
the Scots Guards replied with instant volleys. A minute later by my
watch shots began to pour through the second floor window, and
before the echo of them had died away there was a fusillade from the
ground floor.

So this amazing duel went on, as a distinct clock chimed the quarters
and half hours. From 11 o'clock until 12.30 there were not scores or

hundreds of shots fired, but thousands. It seemed that the assassins had an almost inexhaustible supply of ammunition.

At about noon the Home Secretary's car was stopped on the fringes of the crowd. The crowd, thought Churchill, as he got out, were not particularly friendly. There were several cries of 'Oo let 'em in?' in allusion to the Liberal Government's refusal to restrict alien immigration. With the help of the police he pushed his way through the cordon to the corner of Hawkins Street and Sidney Street. Almost at once the situation became embarrassing. He had no wish to take personal control but his position of authority inevitably attracted to itself direct responsibility. He saw that he would have done much better to have remained in his office but it was impossible to get into his car and drive away while matters were so uncertain, and – he wrote later – so 'extremely interesting'. Anxious to have a better view of the house he crossed the road and sheltered in the doorway of a warehouse.

'Plans were now made to storm the building from several sides at once,' he later wrote. 'One party, emerging from the next-door house, was to rush the front door and charge up the stairs; another party of police and soldiers would break into the second floor at the back through a window; a third, smashing in the roof, would leap down on the assassins from above.' All of these plans, with the exception of the first, were hopelessly impractical, and on Churchill's suggestion a search was made of the foundries in the neighbourhood for steel plate or shield which would protect them if they rushed the stairs. Such a plan could only have resulted in some loss of life and fortunately was never tried. At about 1 p.m. there was a shout from the crowd followed by a few moments of silence in which not a single shot was fired. From the garret window a thin haze of bluish smoke curled up towards the roof.

'The house is on fire! They will be smoked out like rats or burnt alive!' As the minutes passed the smoke increased in volume. The wind was not strong enough to carry it away and soon the whole roof was shrouded in clouds of grey wispy smoke. Soon there was another shout:

'The second floor is alight! They must surrender or suffocate.'

Gradually the smoke became thicker. Slowly it funnelled through the shattered windows and rolled in billowing clouds out through the front and the back of the house and gathered over the roof like an angry storm-cloud. Presently scraps of torn paper and the ashes of burnt paper floated out and mingled with the smoke. From the roof of the Rising Sun a reporter could see a gas jet burning steadily in the first-floor room and guessed that the men had deliberately set fire to the house before attempting to escape. The most likely route was through the back of the house where earlier the waiting detectives had seen two men come to an upstairs window. One of them was carrying two pistols which he fired simultaneously through the window; minutes later a defective cartridge containing a very small charge of powder jammed in the rifling of one of the Mausers putting it out of action. As the thousands of pieces of black and white paper fluttered like butterflies over the heads of the crowd the soldiers increased their volume of fire. But the men inside were still alive. Once, one of them leaned too far through the window. Instantly he became the target for concentrated fire; it seems likely, from subsequent evidence, that he was killed at that time by a bullet through the brain. At about 1.30 p.m. the first tongues of flame flickered through the attic windows and licked the roof. Lower down there were still the black, heavy billowing clouds of smoke. Suddenly there was a gasp of horror from the watching thousands. It looked as if a smoke-charred figure was climbing through the first-floor window and standing huddled up on the sill outside. Again there was a concentrated burst of firing and then the 'figure' fluttered in the wind, the smoke drifted away and it was seen that it was only a torn and charred curtain. Once more there was the short, sharp flash of shooting from the burning house.

The houses on either side were now evacuated in case they should catch fire, or in case the gunmen should try to escape by breaking through the wall. The Fire Brigade stood by to put out the flames; they had been dissuaded from advancing on the house only on the personal intervention of Churchill himself. His orders were to let the house burn. 'Flames now burst out in a fury,' wrote the *Daily Chronicle* reporter.

> The garret was burning like matchwood. From my position on the Rising Sun I could hear the roar of those fire-demons. In another quarter of an hour they had burned their way through the topmost rafters; with a great uproar they surged skywards and made a fiery crown upon the roof. By this time the first floor also was a seething furnace of flame. The angry tongues were thrust out three yards from the gaping jaws of that awful house.

About a quarter of an hour passed and then the flames broke through the roof and curled about the gables. The crackle and the roar steadily increased and with a great crash the roof fell in, exposing the charred and burning ribs. From the first-floor window great tongues of flame shot out against the bullet-scarred walls. Only on the ground floor could anyone survive; Again there was a tremendous crash as another part of the house collapsed. 'The first floor fell in with a shock of splintered wood and cracking iron, and again a pillar of fire with a whirlwind of dancing sparks rose high into the clear sky, where the winter sun was shining.' Moments before the first floor collapsed a gust of wind lifted the smoke from the ground-floor window and the watchers opposite looked into the blazing inferno that had once been the Fleishmanns' bedroom. They distinctly saw a man lying on the bed with his face buried in a pillow and the flames streaking up the walls and floor about him. This was Joseph. Then the smoke rolled back, obliterating him completely, and the ceiling collapsed.

Blazing timbers were flung into the street, masses of masonry crashed down, fiery splinters, like shooting stars, were hurtled a hundred yards or more. Broken glass fell upon the pavement again and again with a dreadful sound of destruction. And into all this turmoil and fury there poured a terrific artillery of shots. The soldiers were volleying now from every window and every roof on the opposite side of Sidney Street, and their shots had thunderous echoes, for other soldiers and many police were firing into the back of the blazing house from the yard.

Standing behind the Scots Guards, with the tears rolling down his cheeks, was the tiny schoolboy figure of Carlusha Perelman. He was crying because he knew that Fritz and Joseph were inside.

Detectives with their revolvers ready walked slowly towards the house and re-entered the houses on either side to make sure that the men had not broken through the walls. A whistle blew and the firemen walked cautiously down the Street, their helmets gleaming in the dull afternoon light, escorted by soldiers and armed policemen. A detective walked up to the door and, lifting his foot high, kicked it open. As it swung back a great belch of flame roared out but it was clear that nobody could still be alive inside. Within minutes the hoses were pumping out great jets of water into the house and soon there were only great clouds of black smoke left hovering over the charred ruins, the twisted metal and the crumbling walls.

On the way back to the Yard, where poached egg and whisky were waiting, the refrain of an old comic song kept running through one detective's head: 'I say what a day we are having, my boys! I say what a day we are having!'

8

Headless Bodies

Once the front door had been kicked open the firemen soon got into the building. As heavy jets of water were poured into the back of the house, they dragged their hoses into the passage and quickly doused the flames. After half an hour they began to search through the flooded debris, which they threw into the yard. Almost immediately a bulky mass was noticed about three feet from the fireplace. The head was missing and there appeared to be just the stump of the neck and the bone of an arm protruding. As the firemen pulled away more debris they saw that most of the clothes had been burnt off and that the legs had disappeared. The body itself was sitting in a half-upright position which suggested that it had fallen through from one of the upper rooms. A fireman started digging with a spade in the centre of the room and began to work his way towards the window; two feet from the wall he found a skull cap and brains with 'only about an inch of stuff underneath the brain pan'.

As they were working the upper floor and part of the side wall collapsed on top of them. Five firemen were dragged out of the rubble, with bleeding hands and faces, and taken to the London Hospital where one of them later died from his injuries. The search was soon resumed. The charred body was bundled into a coffin, which was tied up with string, and taken to Horseferry Branch Road mortuary.

It was nearly 8 p.m. before the firemen found the second body lying on its left side in the back room. One of them caught hold of an arm, but the hand and wrist were missing and a small piece of skin about six inches long came away in his hand. Carefully he scraped away some of the rubble and uncovered a pistol apparently lying on the man's back about halfway between the neck and the hip. The police surgeon, Charles Grant, caught hold of the charred arms sticking up through the ashes and pulled on the bones; the body rose up to meet him but the head was missing. Most of the body had been destroyed by fire but in places it had been protected by falling debris. A brain pan was handed to him and some pieces of feet and limbs in a towel. This second body was also taken away for post-mortem examination. The firemen later found two wigs belonging to old Mrs Clements, which promptly led to rumours that Fritz and Joseph had tried to escape as women.

Most newspapers correctly assumed that the bodies were those of Fritz Svaars and Joseph, but others were beginning to find the plethora of names confusing. Joseph was wrongly identified with Yoska alias Jacob Fogel or Vogel, and the *Daily Mail* completely baffled its readers by claiming that 'Mouremtzoff alias Gardstein and Levi, the dead assassin of Grove Street and owner of the "arsenal" in Gold Street, Stepney, resembled, by a coincidence, the elusive "Peter the Painter", and like the latter, was known for his skill with the brush.' Several days later, even more confusingly, it claimed there were two Fritz Svaars! In America, Pinkerton's Detective Agency publicly announced that they thought they could identify the Houndsditch murderers with three burglars who had committed a jewel robbery in Boston the previous March and subsequently jumped bail; fortunately for the harassed police this was quickly disproved with photographs.

The identification of both men, in fact, rested almost exclusively on Betsy Gershon's evidence to the Coroner's Inquest on 9 January 1911. She explained that she and her husband had come to England in 1905 but because of poor health he had gone back to Yalta in the Crimea eighteen months previously, where she occasionally sent him money. (Because of his wife's involvement in the 'siege', the Russian police subsequently searched his house and exiled him to another town.) She said that she had met Joseph since her husband left, and that he used to visit her once a week or once a fortnight. When he came on New Year's Day (not the day after the murder which was the real date) the first thing she noticed about him was that he had shaved off his moustache. Fritz was with him, but Joseph referred to him only as 'a pal'. When they came again the next night they refused to leave. They threatened her with their fists and made her take off her skirt and shoes to stop her going downstairs. She took a pillow and went to sleep in the stock room where there was a discarded sofa. About an hour later she heard Mrs Fleishmann knock on her door.

She described Joseph's peculiar limp, and her description of the man who was with him tallied with the official police description of Fritz Svaars. Dr Grant found on examination that body no. 1 had a spine more than an inch longer than that of body no. 2 and in every way was that of a bigger man. His right thigh-bone showed an old fracture well knitted, but which might have caused a limp in consequence of the shortening of the limb. It was safe to assume this was Joseph's body. From the position of the entrance and exit wounds in the head, the hole in the occipital bone behind the ear and the haemorrhage in the brain showing that the victim was alive when the wound was made, there was little doubt that he had been shot and had not committed suicide. From the fact that there was a considerable amount of rubbish under the body and that it had assumed a half-upright position among the accumulated rubbish, it was inferred by both Dr Grant and Station Officer Clark who found it that the body, although lying on the ground-floor back room when found, had fallen into that position from one of the upper rooms.

Body no. 2 was found by the doorway of the same room but without any rubbish under it, which suggested that Fritz had died where he was found lying. The body had been splashed with molten lead but had been protected to some extent by the debris which had fallen on top of it. Some clothing still remained; as far as Grant could judge it was the remains of two shirts (16½ collar) and two blue serge waistcoats. The remains of male genital organs were quite visible but the other organs had been so destroyed by fire as to make any examination of them quite futile. The lower part of the face, including the mouth through which the tongue was protruding, the nose and parts of the orbits were present, and the signs unmistakably pointed to death by suffocation. The Coroner's jury brought in a verdict of justifiable homicide.

The bodies were enclosed in two plain elm coffins, one bearing the name Fritz Svaars and the other Joseph. They were taken to Ilford Cemetery and carried into the church together with several other coffins. When the chaplain was told of their identity he expressed his strong disapproval of their bodies being brought into the church and said that it was an outrage to public decency that they should be buried in the same ground as two of the murdered policemen. The first part of the church service was read over their coffins, but a cemetery official directed that they should not be interred pending a decision of the cemetery authorities. The coffins were carried from the graveside and replaced on the hearse. Later the same day they were buried in unconsecrated ground without a religious service being read over them.

The 'siege' had created a sensation both at home and abroad. Foreign capitals reacted with humour, amazement, contempt and admiration. An American newspaper, wrongly reporting the death of Peter the Painter, said: 'It had been hoped, according to some ironical news papers, that when he was run to earth an opportunity might have been given to the navy to share in the credit of the extermination of the Houndsditch murderers. The suggestion was that a torpedo boat destroyer should be anchored at the nearest point in the Thames and bombard the desperadoes' lair while 5000 policemen marshalled the London populace at a safe distance.'

In France there was nothing but admiration for British methods. There had been no 'hesitation, carping criticisms, vacillation, temporising' as would have happened in their own country. Most French newspapers believed that the two men, by attempting to stab in the back the country that had given them asylum, had swayed moderate opinion against them and perhaps dealt a deadly blow to international anarchism.

In Germany new restrictions were put on immigrants. The *Lokalanzeiger* sneered: 'As for us, a thousand policemen, troops, firemen, and machine-guns, would never be necessary to capture a criminal in Berlin. Our police would also think it their business to take the criminals alive. The action of the London police is comparable to the shooting of sparrows with cannon.'

Both at home and abroad, liberal journals hoped that the right of asylum would not be curtailed, while the anti-Semitic press capitalised on the fact that the percentage of Jews in the revolutionary enterprises was high; it mocked the liberals for having praised the Russian terrorists as martyrs as long as they operated in Russia and condemned them as criminals as soon as they threatened the position of aliens in England. The Jewish newspapers blamed St Petersburg, and the Russians asked for international co-operation to stamp out anarchism.

At home there was heavy criticism of the police, and particularly of Churchill, for their handling of the affair. The police were blamed for not bringing out the men alive and there were dramatic suggestions that they should have climbed onto the roof and hurtled glass bowls of sulphurous acid down the chimney, or bored holes through the walls on both sides, at floor and ceiling level in each room, and fired through these until the men surrendered. An early newsreel of 'Mr Churchill directing the operations' was nightly received with unanimous boos and shouts of 'shoot him' from the gallery.

There was general astonishment at the poor quality of the weapons the police were armed with, and firearms manufacturers were invited by the Home Office to a basement shooting-gallery in Kennington to demonstrate new weapons. The gunsmith Robert Churchill was in charge of the tests. As well as police and Home Office officials, the Home Secretary was present. Before the gunsmith could begin, the Home Secretary, thinking he was the Mr Churchill being asked to start the trials, stepped forward eagerly and picked up a Mauser similar to the one he had carried in the cavalry charge at Omdurman and in the Boer War. A policeman obligingly shone his lamp along the barrel so that he could see the sights.

Neither the Home Office nor the City Corporation would accept any liability for the damage that had been done in Sidney Street. Churchill suggested that claims totalling more than £2,000 should be referred for investigation to a board appointed by himself, consisting of representatives of the Metropolitan and City police and the Metropolitan police district. As far as he was aware there was no legal liability upon the police, or upon any public authority, to pay the claims, but it had always been the practice of the Metropolitan police to pay reasonable compensation, as an act of grace, to innocent bystanders whose property had been destroyed or damaged in efforts to make arrests. He suggested that, in the circumstances, this practice should be followed and any amount awarded paid in equal moiety by the Metropolitan police and the City Corporation. The City agreed on the understanding that they admitted no legal liability, and nominated the former Deputy Chairman of the Police Committee, Alpheus Morton, MP, as their representative. Churchill nominated Sir Henry Dalziel, MP, as the Home Office representative and W. J. Wilby of the Receiver's Office, Scotland Yard, as Secretary and Financial Adviser.

Most of the claims were wildly inflated. Charles Martin, the owner of the house, was bluntly told by the Committee that it had no intention of rebuilding it like Buckingham Palace. Nor would it compensate shopkeepers for lost profits and business, spoiled bread, advertising and brass bands, nor neighbours for miscarriages. Its only concern, it seemed, was for the former tenants who had had everything destroyed. Mrs Schiemann had died three weeks later, apparently from post-natal causes; her husband, left with four motherless children to support, could only find broken cups and plates in the ruins, and was compensated with £65. Old Mr Clements, whom he had carried out, was represented at the hearing by his grandchildren, who unwisely included in his claim nearly £12 for books he did not possess. They copied the titles from a bookseller's catalogue, and stupidly included the catalogue numbers and prices!

The Committee was even more disbelieving with the Fleishmanns' claims. Eyebrows were raised when Samuel Fleishmann honestly, if mistakenly, admitted that he had not paid income tax for the past eleven years. His equally frank admission that nothing had been insured placed the Committee in a quandary; it was not sure whether to let him suffer for his negligence or to compensate him out of pity. As a businessman he was a failure and for some years had obviously been living on capital. Losing his stock and machines had put him out of business. His claim for more than £900 was nearly half the total amount being claimed. Not unnaturally the Committee scrutinised each item in great detail. It was highly sceptical of the silver spoons, and of the beaver coats, diamond rings, gold chain, and the evening dress-suit the landlord claimed he wore. It gave him just over a quarter of what he asked for.

The only tenant the Committee refused to compensate was Mrs Gershon. No charge had been brought against her and she was released, but few people were willing to help her. The Committee was openly hostile and crudely implied that she had been Joseph's mistress or worse.

On 20 January 1911 the City Police Commissioner asked the General Purposes Committee of Aldermen to give him the money to pay the informer who had led them to the wanted men. He was not mentioned by name. If Charles Perelman had expected the full £500, he was disappointed. The full sum was for three people – Fritz Svaars, Peter the Painter and the unnamed woman. Since he had led them only to one of those wanted he was only entitled to a third of the reward. He was paid £166 13*s* 4*d*. In old age Carlusha remembered the unexplained money that his father had suddenly come into.

Joseph was worth nothing.

The Judas Window

Rain gusted across the Guildhall yard as the committal proceedings of the Houndsditch murders began. Gas flares were burning brightly in the eighteenth-century court-house on the left of the yard, even though it was late morning, as the horse-drawn prison van rolled through the line of policemen surrounding the square and the armed policeman, who had been sitting by the driver, climbed stiffly to the ground. Under their water-logged capes every policeman was carrying a revolver.

Sara Trassjonsky was gripped by the arms and hurried into court between a detective and a prison matron. Since her arrest she had broken down completely. The lingering hours of watching Gardstein die, her abandonment by everyone, including Luba, the hours of waiting by the body for the police to come and arrest her, and her present plight, had nudged her over the edge into hopeless insanity. There were occasional patches of lucidity, but these were getting fewer and fewer and would shortly disappear altogether. Since she was thirteen years old her life had been nothing more than 'agony, hunger, cold, misery and illness'. There had hardly been a day when she was free from the pains in her head and crippled back. Her home life had been brutalised by her father's shoutings, and the occasional beating-up of her mother, when the children huddled in a corner of the room, not daring to go out; afterwards her mother, to relieve her own misery, would give them a punch or smack.

In the notes she had scribbled in the police station after her arrest, and which were taken away by the police for possible clues, she had described how Gardstein's body, like Banquo's ghost, had loomed up suddenly before her eyes; how she could hear voices shouting at her that she had killed him; then there was the relief when she thought that she had betrayed everyone and, could run free in the streets because there was nobody left to kill her; and finally, a recurring theme, that it was for her mother's sins that she was suffering.

Her letters, written in moments of lucidity, as well as the other prisoners' letters, were handed to the police for translation in the hope of yielding possible clues. Those in Russian were translated by the Russian Consulate, who were thus in a position to pass to the Tsarist police not only information on the prisoners themselves but also the whereabouts of their friends and families and other possible dissidents. The prisoners' most frequent demands were for books and linen. Jacob Peters asked for books by Gorky and Zola, and Luba Milstein, in the martyr's role she had created for herself, De Profundis.

Jacob Peters, after an initial nervousness, was indifferent, genuinely so, as to what happened to him. His strength was his indifference to death. As the son of a Latvian farm-labourer he had experienced all the burdens of degrading forced labour. His schooling had lasted only a few winters; at the age of eight he was tending cattle, and at fourteen he had become a farm-labourer like his father. In 1904, when he was eighteen, he had left the farm and moved to Riga where he joined the illegal Latvian Social Democrats Labourers Party. During the war with Japan, Peters founded a party cell in the Libau shipbuilding yard and had openly agitated among the sailors of the Baltic Fleet. He led a strike in the shipbuilding yard, but in the terror which swiftly followed the 1905 uprising he was flung into prison on a fake attempted-murder charge. Not realising his importance, or the part he had played in the uprising, his captors had limited his torture to beatings-up and ripping out his fingernails.

Peters was detained for nearly two years. In the autumn of 1907 he and other prisoners went on hunger strike and demanded to be manacled whenever they were taken out of the prison, as batches of prisoners that had formerly gone out had always been shot for allegedly escaping.

He had been released in 1909 and fled to England before the full extent of his complicity in the uprising was known. Peters joined several left-wing groups to improve his 'theoretical and political education', and studied English which he apparently spoke with a Cockney accent acquired in the sweat shop where he worked as a tailor's presser. Unquestionably his share of the expropriation, if it had succeeded, would have gone to Lenin and the Bolsheviks. He had no intention of shouldering responsibility when the police and press were blaming Fritz and Peter the Painter for the murders, and there was a possibility of his wriggling out. His first words when he was arrested had been, 'It is nothing to do with me. I can't help what my cousin Fritz has done.'

He had been contemptuous of his change of politics. A subsequent comment was 'Fritz called himself an anarchist, but he did not know anything about it'. However, the readiness with which he was prepared to blame his cousin for the murders suggests something other than a change in politics as the cause of their quarrel. There was more than a hint of this in his subsequent cross-examination by counsel, who asked him if Fritz was a Socialist. Peters reportedly smiled and answered, 'He would have been a better friend with the Russian gendarmes than with the Socialists.' Clearly he is implying that Fritz had been a police collaborator and this can only refer to the time when Fritz broke down under torture and gave the police a particular piece of information. The fact that he had done it once is what made Fritz so terrified of being captured and tortured again. Had Peters himself been a part of that betrayal? And is that why he was so ready to see Fritz punished?

Now that the two men were dead they, like Gardstein, could become scapegoats for the others. In his more confident moments Peters thought that he might get away with five or six years. Yet even he must have wondered how he was going to shake the evidence of the eyewitnesses who had seen him and Dubof with guns in their hands dragging the dying Gardstein from Exchange Buildings.

His prison correspondence makes it clear that in writing he was trying both to confirm alibis and to give warnings to those on the outside. One letter from Brixton prison dated 27 January 1911 and addressed to Mr Aladin in Chiswick asks him to find out whether he, Peters, was attending evening class on a particular night. The letter continues, 'If I was not there on the night, I was seeing my friend Grishka off at a railway station, but I think Grishka left on 1 December etc.' Grishka was one of Salnish's aliases. If it was Salnish he was referring to this can only mean that he was in London throughout the planning stages of the Houndsditch expropriation, and, if not directly involved, must at least have been aware of what was going on.

Dubof had been arrested on the same day as Peters. By an incredible coincidence he had been recognised in the prison hospital by another prisoner, John Hayes, who was completely unknown to him but who had seen him in Exchange Buildings on the day of the robbery, not once but three times. Hayes had been a policeman for twelve years, before being dismissed and sentenced to a month's hard labour for theft; several minor convictions had followed and he was on release when he saw Dubof. He hadn't been surprised at the close scrutiny Dubof had given him as the years in the force had left their mark and he was used to being mistaken for a detective. When he saw Dubof in the prison hospital he immediately recognised him again and suspected at once that he might be connected with the murders. He slipped him a newspaper with Gardstein's picture on the front page to see how he reacted. Dubof went deadly pale and repeatedly kissed the photograph before folding it up and putting under his pillow.

Hayes immediately told the prison governor and the police of his discovery. His story was checked out and found to be true. In his statement he described a woman who had been standing with Dubof in Exchange Buildings, but he omitted to mention another man who had been standing only a few feet away. On 15/16 February 1911 he saw this man exercising in the prison yard. Hayes only knew him as B 1–26, the prison governor as John Rosen alias 'the Barber'.

Rosen's whereabouts hadn't been known until mid-January. Inspector Wensley had missed him by ten minutes when he visited Nina Vassilleva two days after the murders, and soon after that he had disappeared. Tomacoff knew him only by his nickname. The trail might have ended there except that Rosen became careless and told Rose Campbell, a girl he had been courting for eight months, that he was involved with the group. She in turn confided in her mother, who told her son-in-law Edward Humphreys, who went to the police. Humphreys said that on Christmas Eve Rosen had taken Rose Campbell to a house off the Commercial Road and introduced her to a man he said was Peter the Painter, a friend of his and the man wanted by the police. Rosen had also told her that he was a member of the gang and that if anyone had fallen out on the night of the murders he would have taken his place. He said that he knew about the Tottenham Outrage, although he didn't go into details, and that a reward had been offered by the Russian Government for the arrest of Gardstein for a similar outrage in Russia. Mr Humphreys ended by saying that in October Rosen had taken Rose Campbell to his room where he had assaulted and seduced her. The police had not started proceedings against him as the girl had gone to his room of her own free will. Rose Campbell promptly denied the whole story when she was questioned and, on 31 January 1911, married her alleged seducer. Her mother would only go as far as saying that, as Rosen was a foreigner, she thought that he might be connected with the gang. She identified a photograph of Gardstein as a man she had once seen with her son-in-law. On 2 February Rosen was arrested at the barber's shop where he worked. His first words were, 'I know you have come to arrest me.'

For three days he denied everything. Then, on Sunday morning, 5 February, he called through the Judas window in his cell door and asked Police Constable Woodward, 'What will they do with me, if I know something and don't tell them?' Woodward answered, 'Do you know anything about this affair?' Rosen nodded. 'I could show you where a man and a woman live, or were living who are concerned in it, but I don't know if they have moved since I have been here.' His cell was unlocked and he was taken to the headquarters in Old Jewry to make a statement.

Rosen had arrived in England from Riga in January 1909 and had gone to live in a sailors' lodging-house at No. 1 High Street, Poplar, run by a carpenter called Stroch; according to police information, Stroch was an anarchist and a police spy, allegedly on the run from Russia for murder; he was also supposed to arrange robberies and then inform the police. Rosen not only lived but worked on the premises in a small barber's-shop. After he had been there about three or four months he struck up a casual acquaintance with Bifsteks, who came to live there, and through him he was introduced to the Perelmans and the rest of the group at the lodging-house in Great Garden Street. He admitted going to Grove Street on the day of the murders but said that he had spent the evening with Hoffman at the pictures, and later in his room, before going home. Next day, when he had heard of the murders, he had gone back and asked Hoffman what had happened. Hoffman had told him briefly what he knew, how Fritz, Joseph, Peter and Luba had come to his room and how he wouldn't let them stay. Apart from that he knew nothing. Rosen had visited him twice more. The third time he went to 36 Lindley Street Hoffman had fled.

Nina Vassilleva was already being watched, but the whereabouts of Hoffman's lodgings opened up a completely new line of enquiry. Only Luba Milstein could have given them his address, but since her arrest she had been detained in the prison hospital and would say nothing to the police, possibly on her solicitor's advice. When questioned by the police Hoffman's landlord said that he had ordered him out of the house the day after the 'siege'; the tenant on the next floor had complained that he could not sleep because Hoffman paced about the room and continually opened and shut the windows. He had left the same night at about 10 p.m. but nine or ten days later a woman had brought the landlord a note from Hoffman asking for some clothes he had left behind and for any letters to be forwarded to Mrs Janson, 114 Cannon Street. The woman said that Hoffman was afraid go to out, and that she herself was afraid she would suffer through him.

Mrs Janson's husband, Theodore, had been helping the police as an informer since 23 December at least, which was when he made his first statement, but it was now clear that he was playing a double game. He was twenty-nine years old and had emigrated from Riga with his wife and children in 1905; he earned his living as a bicycle-maker. In his first statement he had given the police a false name, and an accommodation address used by Fritz in Stepney. Subsequently he had related how he had met Hoffman on Christmas Day and asked him if Peters, Dubof and Federoff, who had been arrested, were the men involved. Hoffman had laughed and said, 'No, there were nine men in the plot, none of them are yet arrested. It's a pity the man is dead [Gardstein], he was the ablest of the lot and leader of the gang. He also managed it that some members of the gang didn't know the others.' Janson had said, at the time, that he didn't know Hoffman's address, but this now seemed unlikely. He had also said that he knew Gardstein lived in Stepney and would try to find out his address, but to do that he needed money. Next day, at the same time that Gardstein's landlord recognised the photograph on the reward poster and went to Arbour Square police station, Janson called back and said that Hoffman had sent a message asking him to go to 44 Gold Street to collect from the landlady three leather trunks belonging to Gardstein. He was too late. The Stepney Bomb Factory, as it was called by the newspapers, had already been found.

Now that they knew Janson was playing a double game the police made their preparations accordingly. They raided Janson's house at 2.15 in the morning of 8 February. There were to be no more 'sieges'. Armed police surrounded the house and got the other tenants out, including Janson and his family, without waking the wanted man. Hoffman was still asleep when he was yanked to his feet and half dragged, half carried to the shop next door. He tried to bluff his way out with the help of Janson who said that he wasn't the man referred to in his statement.

His protests were ignored. A jacket which Janson had lent him, and which was in the room where he was sleeping, had in one of the pockets a passport in the name of Trohimtchick, which was the alias Fritz had used at Newcastle Place; but Hoffman denied that the jacket belonged to him. In the other jacket were five letters and the return half of a ticket to Antwerp. From these the police were able to piece together his movements over the past month. Hoffman had gone back to Riga, but on 27 January the Tsarist police had surrounded the house where he was staying and he had only just managed to escape back to England via Antwerp. He had been living since then with the Jansons. Letters for him had been addressed to Mrs Janson and he had identified those which were his by the handwriting. The only one of the group he would admit that he knew was Fritz, and then only by his Christian name; the others were just faces he said that he had seen at clubs and concerts.

A few hours earlier the net had also closed around Nina Vassilleva. She had been watched for nearly eight weeks and followed wherever she went. Ironically, she was arrested while walking through Sidney Street. Incredibly, although she had expected her arrest at any time, the detectives found in her room not only newspaper cuttings on the murders but the blue three quarter-length coat she had been wearing on the night of the murders, and which still had large patches of dried blood on the front. On 14 February she and Rosen were formally charged in front of the magistrates with conspiracy to rob, and next day Hoffman was charged with the same offence.

From the prisoners' point of view the most disastrous day of the magistrates' court hearing so far was Rosen's committal, since the police read out not only his original statement denying everything but his subsequent statements as well betraying Nina Vassilleva and Hoffman. The latter was appalled that he should have said so much. Rosen wanted to explain his motives but although he, Hoffman and Dubof were on the same landing in Brixton Gaol, they had no way of communicating until Rosen struck up a conversation with a prisoner called Arthur Weeks, a farm-labourer awaiting trial for the carnal knowledge of his nine-year-old stepdaughter. He had already served one sentence for killing sheep and had other convictions for drunkenness and poaching.

Either on Friday, 17 or Saturday, 18 February he was working outside cell B 1–23 when Rosen called out, 'What are you in for?'

'Carnal knowledge,' Weeks growled.

Rosen's English was not good enough. 'Don't understand,' he said.

'What are you in for?' Weeks asked.

'Conspiracy,' Rosen said, and pushed his card through the door.

Weeks studied it for a moment. 'You are charged with breaking into somebody's shop.'

Rosen nodded his head. 'How do you think I shall get on? Two witnesses say I was carrying a bag twice.' (He had been identified as carrying a green bag out of Exchange Buildings on two occasions.)

'Did you carry a bag?' Weeks asked.

'Yes.'

'Did they see you?'

'The witnesses say they did.'

'You will get eighteen months.' Weeks sniffed and walked away.

Later the same afternoon he was cleaning cell tins on the landing when Rosen pushed through the grate part of an envelope with a message scrawled on it in a foreign language. 'You, 27,' he said. Weeks took it to Dubof in cell B 1–27. About an hour and a half later he was sorting Bibles and prayer-books when Dubof gave him a message scrawled on lavatory paper to take back.

Weeks was not on the landing again until Monday morning at 7.30 when he gave the prisoners their tea. When he was outside B 1–4 Hoffman pushed three pieces of lavatory paper through the grate and asked him to give them to Dubof. Instead Weeks took them to his cell, but when he discovered that he couldn't read them he folded them up again and passed them to the warder. He did the same thing with a message Dubof threw to him that afternoon to give to Hoffman. Both were translated by the police.

Hoffman thought that the Barber was trying to save his own neck at the expense of the others. His own view was that there was no point in confessing as the police were looking for twenty-eight people – they believed this to be the size of the group – and wouldn't call off the hunt for the others. The Prison Governor questioned him about the note but Hoffman said it was only a friendly message and denied knowing Dubof before his arrest. He persisted in his denial even when the Governor produced Dubof's note suggesting that they should say that they had only known one another since March or April 19th, when Dubof was living at Wellesley Street. From April to September, the note continued, Dubof had been in Switzerland but they had kept in touch and afterwards met intermittently when they were both looking for jobs. They had gone to Grove Street on 16 December to discuss the decorations for the Lettish concert. Dubof was worried because he had told his lawyer that he had gone to Hoffman's lodgings on 18 December, but if possible he didn't want this mentioned although he had been seen there on that occasion by Hoffman's landlord and landlady; if they didn't mention this in their evidence neither would he. Since then, they were to say, they hadn't met. Dubof wasn't sure whether it was wise to make a confession or not; he would ask his lawyer if it meant a lighter sentence. Until then he advised against it. There was no point in making trouble unnecessarily. It was best to wait and see. They must continue to stress that they were just ordinary working men and casual acquaintances.

About the same time, Weeks, having handed their notes to the warder, was in the exercise yard walking along two yards behind Jacob Peters.

'How are you getting on with your affair?' he muttered.

Peters turned his head and looked over his left shoulder. 'I shall get about five or six years,' he said in broken English.

For a man standing in the shadow of the gallows this seemed unduly optimistic.

10

Red Circles in Court

The most telling point in the defendant's favour, although they didn't realise it at the time, was that the arrests were made over a period of nearly two months – from the time of the first hearing on 21 December 1910, when Trassjonsky and Milstein were brought before the Guildhall Court, to 15 February when the last prisoner, Hoffman, was charged.* Evidence was consequently introduced in a piece-meal fashion, and points vital to the prosecution's case were lost in the increasing complexity of evidence.

On 23 January 1911 Mr Bodkin opened the case for the Crown against the five who were then in custody – Peters, Dubof, Federoff, Milstein and Trassjonsky. None of them were supposed to have more than a smattering of English, but it quickly became apparent from their gestures that they were having little difficulty in following the evidence. He began by saying that the three men were implicated in the murder of the three policemen, that the two women were accessories after the fact, and that all five were concerned in the attempted burglary of Harris's shop.

> It was an enterprise which could not be entered upon and carried out in a few hours, required some long time to get into proper working order, and therefore we hear that as early as 21 November there were enquiries for a house in Exchange Buildings.

* The committal proceedings were actually spread over four months. See below, page 171.

He told the court that Joe Levi, who had rented No. 11, had never been traced but later in the hearing the police learned from Luba Milstein that Joe Levi was, beyond question, Max Smoller. The prosecution's two principal witnesses were Isaac Levy and George Richardson, a jeweller's assistant in Houndsditch, who was also friendly with the boy Solomon Abrahams, who on several occasions had pointed out the new tenants of 9 and 11 Exchange Buildings to him when he had seen them in the street. Consequently Richardson had recognised Gardstein at once when the latter had tried to draw him into conversation late one evening and get him to discuss the better kinds of jewellers' shops in Houndsditch, mentioning Harris's by name. On another occasion he had seen Gardstein drinking in the Three Nuns in Aldgate with Federoff, Peters and Dubof. Other prosecution witnesses had come forward with equally damning evidence.

> So that not only at the Jubilee Street Club, but at 59 Grove Street, in the public house, the Three Nuns, and in the neighbourhood of Cutler Street and at this very house No. 11 Exchange Buildings, there will be evidence to these prisoners, Federoff, Peters, and Dubof, being in direct association with Fritz and 'Peter the Painter'.

Mr Bodkin blundered badly from the beginning. His first and greatest mistake was when he deduced that, since Gardstein was the man who opened the door to Bentley, it was Gardstein also who started the shooting.

> Gardstein was the man who came in flinging open that back door and shot Bentley at his right front; there were also other shots from the man on the stairs ... Several shots were fired at Bentley by the man Gardstein from the back, he advanced to the front door of the house, of that there is no doubt, for we have the hand, according to the evidence of Strongman, protruding through the door of No. 11, so as to sweep the place, firing at Woodhams, Bryant and Martin. That man Gardstein advanced further, for you will remember in the evidence of Strongman he said he came out and fired at him and Sergeant Tucker while they were in the roadway of Exchange Buildings.

The later finding of the Dreyse pistol which had fatally wounded the three policemen, with Gardstein's body, apparently confirmed this interpretation as the correct one.

Unfortunately it wasn't. It was a blunder of colossal proportions. Only two alternatives had been open to Gardstein after he partly closed the door on Bentley. Either he could go up the stairs behind him or through the ground-floor room, which didn't have a connecting door with the hall, into the yard. From where he was standing outside, Constable Martin had had a clear view through the partly open street door into the brightly lit room and must have seen Gardstein if he had crossed his line of vision. As he didn't Gardstein must have gone upstairs. He was self-evidently the man standing at the top of the stairs with his face in darkness when Bentley pushed open the door a few seconds later.

The next point to be borne in mind is the survivors' description of the man who, in fact, did come in from the backyard. Only two policemen saw him – Sergeant Bryant, who had been standing in the doorway with Bentley, and Constable Strongman who had dragged the dying Tucker out of the firing line. Bryant told the court that just before the shooting started Bentley had been speaking to the man on the stairs. As Bentley had moved further into the room Bryant had stepped into the passage after him.

> Immediately I saw a man coming from the back door of the room between Bentley and the table. On 6 January I went to the City of London Mortuary and there saw a dead body and I recognised the man. I noticed he had a pistol in his hand, and at once commenced to fire towards Bentley's right shoulder. He was just in the room. The shots were fired very rapidly. I distinctly heard 3 or 4. I at once put up my hands and I felt my left hand fall and I fell out on to the footway. Immediately the man commenced to fire Bentley staggered back against the door post of the opening to the room. The appearance of the pistol struck me as being a long one. I think I should know a similar one again if I saw it. Only one barrel, and it seemed to me to be a black one. I next remember getting up and staggered along by the wall for a few yards until I recovered myself. I was going away from Cutler Street. I must have been dazed as I have a very faint recollection of what happened then.

Bryant's positive identification of Gardstein as Bentley's attacker is certainly open to question. 'Immediately' twice, and 'rapidly', stress the speed at which the shootings began. Bentley is staggering backwards towards Bryant as the bullets tear into his throat and shoulder. At the same time Bryant himself is under fire from the man on the stairs and is stumbling into the street with bullets in his arm and chest. At best, Bryant could only have had a snap impression of what was happening. His positive identification of Gardstein three weeks later is in line with the, by then, official version of the incident.

Still more erroneous is his evidence that the pistol being fired had a long black barrel, suggesting a Mauser, two of which had been found in Sidney Street. If, in fact, the man who came through the door was carrying a Mauser, it couldn't have been his shots which hit Bentley, because the post mortem showed that the only bullets which hit the sergeant and fatally wounded Tucker and Choate had been fired from the same Dreyse, a much smaller pistol. (Choate had also been shot with a Mauser but the shots that killed him had been fired from the Dreyse.) The same Dreyse also killed Sergeant Tucker. Constable Strongman again identified Gardstein as the attacker, although his original statement, which includes a description of the killer, shows that it could not have been him. Worse still, Strongman only identified Gardstein from a photograph and did not even see the body. In his statement Strongman wrote:

> The door was opened by some person whom I did not see. P.S. Bentley appeared to have a conversation with the person, and the door was then partly closed, shortly afterwards P.S. Bentley pushed the door open and entered, about a minute later I heard several shots and saw P.S. Bentley fall from the doorway across the step. Other shots followed in quick succession and a hand holding a revolver, firing rapidly, protruded from the doorway of No. 11 Exchange Buildings and was pointed at P.C. Woodhams who I saw fall forward into the carriageway. That hand was followed by a man age about 30, height 5' 6" or 7", pale thin face, dark curly hair, and dark moustache, dress dark jacket suit, no hat, who pointed the revolver in the direction of P.S. Tucker and myself, firing rapidly. P.S. Tucker and I stepped back a few yards when the P.S. staggered and turned round. I caught him by the right arm, and we walked towards Cutler Street. I looked over my left shoulder and saw the man fire two more shots in our direction, then he turned and went back in the direction of No. 11 Exchange Buildings. The whole of the shooting appeared to be over in ten seconds.

In court he expanded on some details. He was standing with Sergeant Tucker when:

I heard 3 or 4 shots fired, and we made a step towards the door, when I saw a hand holding a pistol protrude from the street doorway of No. 11, firing rapidly, pointing towards P.C. Woodhams, who was opposite No. 11 Exchange Buildings. I saw P.C. Woodhams fall towards the carriageway; this man came out of the doorway still holding the pistol and pointed it towards Sergeant Tucker and myself, firing rapidly all the time. We stepped back, Sergeant Tucker turned round and staggered. Seeing he was wounded I put my arm round his and led him towards Cutler Street. I looked over my left shoulder and saw the man fire two more shots in our direction, and I could also see the flashes coming from the doorway of No. 11. He turned and went back in the direction of No. 11 … I could only see the barrel as he came under the lamp and it looked a long thin one. The shooting only lasted about 10 seconds and may have been less.

Only Strongman was able to describe the killer in detail. The only doubtful evidence in his two statements is that relating to the pistol which he suggests, but does not positively identify, as a 'long thin one'; suggesting again a Mauser. Possibly he did see a Mauser barrel protruding from the doorway because it was from the doorway that he saw Constable Woodhams shot and a Mauser bullet was later extracted from Woodham's leg. However, the man who stepped into the street and, walking towards him and Tucker, shot the sergeant twice – once in the hip and once in the heart – was firing the same Dreyse pistol that had been used moments before to kill Bentley. Ballistics evidence showed it to be the same one. Apart from his curly hair the most important thing Strongman noticed about him was his jacket suit.

At this point in his statement, the shootings were reaching their climax. Bentley and Tucker were dying, Strongman was dragging the latter out of the firing, Martin was hiding, Bryant and Woodhams were wounded and unconscious, one propped up against a house and the other lying in the roadway, and Piper and Smoothey were running from Houndsditch to the cul-de-sac. From this it is reasonable to infer that when the killer of Bentley and Tucker turned, as Strongman said he did, he did so because he had heard or seen Gardstein grappling with Constable Choate.

Choate's wounds included four in the left leg, thigh, calf and foot. One bullet was extracted from the leg and was identified as having been fired from a Mauser or Borchardt auto-pistol of .30 calibre; another

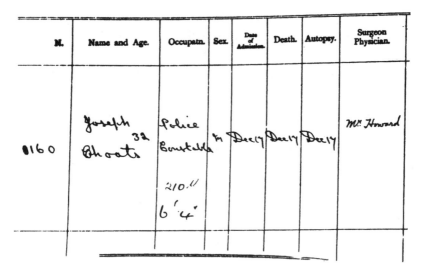

M.	Name and Age.	Occupatn.	Sex.	Date of Admission.	Death.	Autopsy.	Surgeon Physician.
0160	*Joseph Choate* 32	*Police Constable* 210." 6'4"	*m*	*Decr 17*	*Decr 17*	*Decr 17*	*Mr Howard*

Clinical Notes.

Another victim of the shooting affray.

Post-Mortem Findings.

[handwritten post-mortem report, largely illegible]

Post-mortem report on Police Constable Choate.

N.	Name and Age.	Occupatn.	Sex.	Date of Admission.	Death.	Autopsy.	Surgeon Physician.
1159	Charles Tucker 46	Sergeant of Police	M.	Dec 16	Dec 16	Dec 17	B.I.D.
	1844 6'-1"						

Clinical Notes.

Shooting by aliens surprised near
Houndsditch in house next a jeweller's.

Post-Mortem Findings.

Accident. Two revolver wounds. Perforation of heart (1233) lung intestines
Bullet wound in skin over 4th L intercostal space, 1" from sternal margin, track
passing through the sternal _ of the 6th costal cartilage, the pericardium R ventricle,
inner aspect of auricolo ventricular ring + attachment of to antr cusp of the tricuspid
valve, the R auricle, grooving the R side spine of the body of the 7th dorsal vertebra,
passing through the middle lobe of the R lung from L to R, + fracturing the scapula
R rib in the mid-axillary line. Bullet (nickel cased: intact) lodged in substance
of R serratus magnus. Bullet wound in skin by L loin in mid axillary line 2
above the iliac crest. track grooving the lower pole of the L kidney perforating the
_ colon just below splenic flexure passing _ in + out of its anti surface,
jejunum 8" from the duodeno-jejunal junction, perforating the mesentery of the ileum
12" from the caecum, passing through the upper border of the 4th lumbar vertebra upwards
+ to R, through the third lumbar intervertebral disc. Bullet (intact) lodged in the _
of the R psoas. Haemoperitoneum. Haemothorax R. Haemopericardium. Haemorrhage in
_ of L kidney. _ in medulla of L kidney. Slight emphysema of lungs _
of R apex. Calcareous nodule in lower margin of R lower lobe. Slight fatty atheroma of aorta
_ of both epididymes. Sebaceous cyst in fold of R nates. Large muscular man. _ _
_ _ _

fragment in the leg also came from a Mauser. Choate was a big man, 6 feet 4 inches, and Gardstein a mere 5 feet 8 inches. The brief struggle between them was obviously an unequal one except that Gardstein was armed and Choate was not. There were burn marks on Choate's uniform where the pistol had been pressed against the cloth, and it is not too fanciful to suggest that, when Choate ran towards Gardstein and caught him, he gripped him by the wrist which was holding the Mauser. Gardstein, trying to break free, pulled the trigger four times as Choate pushed his hand down and away to deflect the shots. Although the shots missed his vital organs, Choate could not stop them from hitting him in the leg, thigh, calf and foot.

As Choate's leg buckled beneath him, he was shot twice, with two carefully placed shots in the back, from the same Dreyse that had already killed Bentley and Tucker. He fell backwards dragging Gardstein with him, and as they fell Gardstein was accidentally shot in the back by Max Smoller.

Now the importance of Strongman's evidence becomes obvious. Under the street light he had noticed not only the curly hair of the man firing the Dreyse but that he was wearing a jacket suit. It could not have been Gardstein firing the Dreyse because he was wearing an overcoat when he was shot. It was found with the bullet hole in the back, just under the bloodstained left shoulder, and matching the wound in his body. Clearly it was impossible for Gardstein to have been grappling with a man who was not only bigger but nearly a foot taller than himself, to have fired four shots into his leg with a Mauser pistol which the policeman was trying to take away, and in the same instant that he himself was shot in the back to have got behind his opponent who was dragging him to the ground and killed him with a completely different gun!

Who was firing the Dreyse, then? Who was the man who killed Bentley, Tucker and Choate? It could not have been Max because he shot Gardstein with a Browning. Besides, he was clean-shaven, and whoever was firing the Dreyse was similar enough in appearance to Gardstein to be mistaken for him by both Bryant and Strongman – they had described him as 'age about 30, height 5' 6" or 7", pale thin face, dark curly hair and dark moustache…' This only leaves Jacob Peters and Yourka Dubof. Both were of similar height and build to Gardstein – there was only 1½ inches difference between all three – and both had moustaches. But, as can be seen from the photographs taken after their arrest (see plates), only Peters had the dark curly hair and moustache to be mistaken for Gardstein. Dubof's light-coloured moustache barely shows.

Jacob Peters – not Gardstein – was the killer of Bentley, Tucker and Choate. And he was in custody. But the whole of the prosecution's case rested on the mistaken assumption that it was Gardstein who had killed Tucker, Bentley and Choate. Though Mr Bodkin realised that there were doubts about the firearms the police had described, he glossed over their statements. He said that one could well understand that these officers – he thought Bryant was one – were wrong in saying that the man who was firing at Bentley had a 'long thin barrel pistol'. 'I hope I may never have to observe the kind of pistol a person is firing at me.' Any further doubts as to who really did the shooting were stifled completely when he came to describe the finding of Gardstein's body.

> Now Gardstein – under his pillow at 59 Grove Street was found exhibit No. 2, which was a Dreyse pistol. A pistol with a magazine, which on examination had been recently fired. It is difficult to say – for any expert to – when it had been recently fired. It was a pistol rifled in four grooves, and Mr Goodwin, a gentleman who has kindly examined this pistol … has fired some shots from that pistol into sawdust.
>
> The cartridges which can be fired from that pistol are quite common cartridges which are standardised and are used for various automatic pistols, but the peculiarity of this Dreyse pistol is that it has four grooves. It appears that six bullets – two from Tucker's body, two from Bentley's body and two from Choate's body – were fired from the Dreyse pistol as they all have four groove marks upon them…. It is clear that Gardstein was the man who fired, and under his pillow a Dreyse pistol was found, and it seems quite proper to assume that he it was who used the Dreyse pistol. The only one to hit Bentley was Gardstein, and Bentley's bullets were from a Dreyse pistol.

Now even a cursory examination of the basic statements would have shown that the Dreyse was most emphatically not found under the pillow and, by inference, within easy reach of Gardstein's hand to defend himself. The officer who had found the Dreyse when the room was searched was Detective Sergeant Leeson who had subsequently been wounded in the opening shots of the 'Siege'. Because of his lung wound he had been promoted and pensioned off with the higher pension. In his official report he wrote, 'Between the mattress and the palliasse I found one magazine pistol containing seven cartridges, two magazines (one containing seven and one containing six cartridges).' Inspector Thompson, who searched the room with him, confirmed this: 'Between the mattress and the palliasse at the head of the bed was also found a revolver loaded with seven cartridges, also two clips, one containing seven and the other six cartridges.' Ernest Goodwin, the prosecution's ballistics expert, was equally specific. 'The cartridges in the Dreyse pistol No. 7065, found between the mattress and palliasse of the bed on the first floor at Grove Street, E., those in the two clips found in the same place, and in Gardstein's clothing are 7.65 Belgian cartridges of F.N. manufacture.'

Now it has been wrongly assumed from Mr Bodkin's statement that the pistol was under the pillow for Gardstein to defend himself and to resist arrest. In support of this theory it has been alleged that a cap containing a quantity of ammunition was placed by the bed within easy reach of his hand. Certainly there was a cap with ammunition by the bed but none of it could be fired from the Dreyse! According to the ballistics expert the cap held 'six .297/230 short cartridges for Morris tubes and small rook rifles, six .30 Mauser pistol cartridges and seventeen 7.9 mm Mauser rifle cartridges of Hirtenberger [of] 1904 manufacture'. According to Luba Milstein's evidence the cap was not there when Fritz, Joseph, Peter and Max left. Since she didn't put it there and Gardstein couldn't it could only have been put there by Sara Trassjonsky when she was gathering up evidence to destroy. The ammunition was put in the cap for convenience as she bustled about the room and was never meant to be fired; it was meant to be thrown away.

If, in fact, Gardstein had owned the Dreyse, it is reasonable to suppose that some ammunition for this weapon would have been found in his lodgings, which were described as an arsenal as well as a bomb factory. None was found. The only ammunition 'consisted of... 308 .30 Mauser cartridges, some of D.W.M. manufacture, and the other with plain heads; also 26 Hirtenberger 7.9 mm Mauser rifle cartridges'. It is inconceivable, that Gardstein would have over 300 rounds of ammunition for the Mauser that he normally carried, and none for the Dreyse that he was supposed to have used!

All of the evidence suggests that the Mauser pistol which Gardstein was using was handed over to, or taken by, Joseph, and was one of the burnt-out Mausers found in Sidney Street. Goodwin thought that the Browning that was also found there might have fired the bullet into Gardstein's back. Owing to the fire damage he was unable to remove the barrel and could only take a short sulphur-cast of the part of the barrel next to the chamber. The cast showed that the barrel was five-grooved and might also have fired the bullet that was found in No. 2 Exchange Buildings by Miss Parker. Nothing much could be gleaned from the Mausers. The cartridges had exploded from the heat of the fire and the leaden cores had melted and flowed away.

Having handed over his own gun to Joseph, why should Gardstein have a cap filled with ammunition he couldn't use placed by his bed and, when he was powerless to move, have a Dreyse thrust between the mattress and the palliasse where he couldn't possibly reach it, instead of under the pillow if in fact, he had intended to resist arrest?

Inevitably the conclusion is that he didn't know that the Dreyse was there. He thought that by getting rid of his Mauser he had rid himself of at least one major piece of incriminating evidence. His bullet wound he would have to explain away as the result of a shooting accident, as he in fact did to Dr Scanlon. What he didn't realise was that, thrust between the mattress and the palliasse on which he was lying in a state of shock, too ill and too weak to move, was the one piece of evidence that could hang him. If this interpretation is correct, the Dreyse could only have been put there by Peters. But, according to Mr Bodkin, Gardstein had been taken to Grove Street by Fritz Svaars and Peter the Painter, and not by Peters, who was last seen with Dubof and Vassilleva dragging the dying man out of Exchange Buildings.

Again Mr Bodkin didn't try to explain the discrepancy. He described how Isaac Levy had seen Peters and Dubof carrying Gardstein, and how they had threatened him and told him not to follow; how the workmen had seen them in Harrow Alley and Bell Lane:

the same group, doubtless, of four men and the middle man supported by one on either side of him, and there at that point the group is lost sight of but we get from the statements of Luba Milstein and Trassjonsky that at 59 Grove Street several men came in very shortly after midnight, and it was, of course – but it is obvious – that Gardstein was practically carried in. How did they get in? Fritz had a key. It is quite possible, but I do not think it is in evidence, that 'Peter the Painter' had a key. He was familiar with that house for he lived there for some time, and up that staircase, which is of a narrow and most awkward description, the man Gardstein was taken by someone entirely familiar with the ways of that house and staircase. That several persons were there is clear from the statements of Milstein and Trassjonsky, for they said they heard footsteps and the voices of several men.

But how could Mr Bodkin say that Fritz and Peter had carried Gardstein into the house when Luba and Sara had heard only foot steps? This is clear from Luba's final cross-examination:

'To the police when you gave yourself up you said, "I heard the steps of two or three persons, I could not see who they were."'

'Yes.'

'That was not true was it?'

'It was true.'

'"I could not see who they were." Is that true?'

'I did not see them when they came in, I saw them afterwards.'

'You went on to say to the police, "We heard someone go down-stairs, I believe two men, I did not see them."'

'I stated that in my first statement, I stated differently in the second.'

'That was not true to say you did not see them?'

'No.'

'How many men in all did you see?'

'Three.'

'Might there have been others there?'

'I do not know.'

But Luba only changed her evidence because the prosecution was insisting that the men she had seen go out were the same men who had brought the dying Gardstein to the house, although all along she had denied that they were. Besides, Fritz himself, in his last letter, had said quite plainly that two men had brought Gardstein to his rooms where he had been all evening. Not surprisingly, as by this time she had been made a witness for the defence, Luba agreed to this inter-pretation of the facts as it increased the other prisoners' chances of acquittal. It also made her evidence that Fritz had told her he had car-ried Gardstein through the streets like a baby much more believable. The dead man had to become a scapegoat if the others were to escape the gallows.

But rarely in any murder trial could the prosecution have contributed so much to the destruction of its own case.

The committal proceedings were spread over four months, from December to March, and comprised twenty-four separate hearings. Luba Milstein's counsel soon protested against the succession of remands which were made without a case ever being opened against her. He pointed out that she had voluntarily surrendered herself to the police and since she had been in custody they had been unable to show that she was in any way connected with the crime. At the opening of the proceedings of 21 February Mr Bodkin told the court that on the evidence which had so far been given there was insufficient evidence for the prosecution to justify her further detention on the charges of accessory to murder and conspiracy. On the advice of her solicitors she had already made a statement supplemental to the evidence that was already before the court and he asked that she should be discharged. Through the interpreter Luba Milstein was told that she was free to go.

She turned at once – she had been sitting between Trassjonsky and Vassilleva – and without a look at the other prisoners she pushed past Nina and stumbled up the stairs to the back of the court, her dull heavy face lit up by a smile. Her brother took her outside at once, but before she reached the outer doors she broke into a fit of hysterical sobbing. Outside she leaned against the wall of the court and continued sobbing until her brother calmed her down and, when she was more composed, led her away.

The previous week, on 15 February, Karl Hoffman had been brought before the court for the first time charged with conspiracy to break and enter. He was more smartly dressed than any of the other prisoners; over a lounge suit he wore a dark overcoat with a velvet collar. In the dock he engaged in an animated conversation with Dubof and Rosen. Possibly this hurried exchange was to flush out their smuggled prison notes to each other. This sudden intimacy surprised the court when Hoffman's statement, with his corrections, was read out to them. Not only did he deny knowing Rosen and Dubof with whom he was having an animated conversation, but also Gardstein, Joseph, Peter the Painter, Federoff, Peters, Trassjonsky, Smoller and Vassilleva! In custody he had been shown photographs of Gardstein, Rosen, Federoff and Peter Piatkow and had recognised them as men he had seen; he identified Jacob Peters, also from a photograph, as some one he had seen at Lettish concerts. The only people he would admit to knowing were Luba Milstein and Fritz, who, he said, had introduced her as his wife. On 16 December he had gone to bed at midnight and nobody had visited his room. He had heard about the murders the next morning and later heard from a Russian acquaintance that Fritz – he did not know his name was Svaars – was concerned in the murders.

Not unnaturally he was appalled at just how much Rosen had given away and at the extent of his revelations as to what had really happened. He frankly disbelieved him when he said he had done this to help them, and was convinced that the Barber wanted to 'come out with a whole skin' himself. In fact, Rosen's statement did help him and it was because of it that Hoffman was released. Rosen had stated correctly that Hoffman had refused to let Peter, Fritz or Joseph stay with him, though he did not explain his motives, and by itself this would not sustain a conspiracy charge. The only witnesses against Hoffman were the landlady at 35 Newcastle Place and Tomacoff who had seen him, on separate occasions, in Fritz's lodgings; but this proved nothing, as Hoffman did not deny acquaintanceship with Fritz. Obviously there was insufficient evidence against him and on 8 March the magistrates discharged him. The verdict had an exhilarating effect on the other prisoners. Vassilleva, Hoffman and Rosen were all smiles. At the back of the court Rosen's wife could be heard sobbing bitterly.

At the same time the magistrates released Sara Trassjonsky on similar grounds – that there was insufficient evidence against her. All the prisoners except her had been legally represented. She had presented a normal appearance to the court but her mind was continually clouding over. She explained through the interpreter that she wished to challenge some of the evidence, but could not remember what had been said the previous day; she also wanted to make some alterations and some additions to the statement the police had taken from her but had nobody to help her. The strain was too much, and when the charges were dropped and she suddenly found herself free after three months' imprisonment she became completely and hopelessly insane.

On 29 May 1911 the Solicitor for the London County Council wrote to the City Police Commissioner informing him that proceedings had been initiated at the instance of the LCC with a view to deporting Sara Trassjonsky, who was being maintained as a pauper lunatic at Colney Hatch Asylum. She was summoned to appear at Bow Street magistrates' court, on 2 June, as being an alien in receipt of parochial relief and to show cause why an expulsion order should not be made against her under the Aliens Act, 1905. She was too ill to attend, but an order was granted for her deportation. The Clerk to the Asylums Committee told the police that she was insane, of suicidal tendencies and had to be tube fed, and that her condition was of such a nature that she might never recover sufficiently to be deported.

At the next hearing, on 15 March, Federoff's counsel challenged the prosecution's opening statement that the evidence would show that there had been a long-concerted and carefully planned conspiracy, and that each of the prisoners had been playing different but important parts in it. He had been carefully through the depositions and there was nothing to suggest that Federoff had taken part in this conspiracy. The witness, Richardson, alleged that he had seen Federoff on three occasions, firstly walking in Aldgate with Dubof and Peters, secondly standing with Peters at the corner of Aldgate, and thirdly on the morning of 13 December in the Three Nuns hotel. Even if what he said was true, which was denied, this was not proof of conspiracy. 'Conspiracies are not hatched in this manner, walking about the streets.' The other witnesses' evidence was equally doubtful. Bessie Jacobs, the teenaged girl from Exchange Buildings who had said nothing of Martin's cowardice, had picked out Federoff on an identification parade, but when she was asked to identify him in court had picked out Peters instead. She said that when she had picked him out the men had had their hats on; the male prisoners were given their hats and stood up again. She apologised for her mistake and correctly identified Federoff, but her credibility had gone. Her brother Harry, who had held the dying Sergeant Tucker, was also a prosecution witness, but when they left court with their expenses in their hands they saw their father standing on one corner of the Old Bailey and their mother on the other. Bessie was hit by her mother for giving her money to her father, and Harry was hit by his father for giving his money to his mother!

Federoff's counsel did not deny that his client had been at 59 Grove Street on the afternoon of 16 December. He was looking for work. Prosecuting counsel had said that it could be inferred what took place, but he submitted that you could not infer anything of the kind. Certainly Federoff knew Fritz but

> if everybody who knew Fritz is presumed to have been implicated in this burglary, I am afraid his friends would not be safe. Hoffman knew Fritz and was seeing him constantly but this did not prevent you from discharging him. Federoff knew him. The other prisoner, Trassjonsky, has

been discharged. She was acquainted with Fritz, and according to two or three witnesses was seen actually taking down the shutters and doing some work there. The fact that Trassjonsky had been seen in Exchange Buildings did not induce you to send her for trial. The evidence, such as it is, of Federoff having been seen in Exchange Buildings, is not that upon which any jury would convict him.

The magistrate agreed and set him free. Federoff was the fourth prisoner to be discharged.

In a lull in the hearings prominent publicity was given to the christening of Sergeant Bentley's son Robert, named after his father, who had been born a few days after the shootings. The City Corporation made grants of five shillings a week to each of the murdered policemen's children until they were fifteen years of age. 'Baby' Bentley lived only three years and in 1914 was buried with his father. A *Daily Express* fund had raised nearly £2,000 in four days for the policemen's dependents. Mrs Amelia Tucker and Mrs Louise Bentley, the widows of Sergeants Tucker and Bentley, were given pensions of thirty shillings a week so long as they remained widows and of good character. Miss Sylvia Choate, sister of Constable Choate, was given five shillings a week so long as she remained single. Sub-Inspector Bryant and Sergeant Woodhams, who had been promoted, were presented with the Police Medal by the King. Woodhams had to be carried into the King's presence on a stretcher. His shattered leg had left him permanently crippled and Bryant, because of his chest wound, was also an invalid. Like Sergeant Leeson, who had been shot at the beginning of the 'siege', their promotions meant that they could be pensioned off at a higher rate. King's Police Medals were privately presented to the murdered policemen's families by the Lord Mayor.

At the same time as the committal proceedings, some of the witnesses and prisoners were also giving evidence at the Coroner's inquests on the bodies of the three policemen and Gardstein. Because the bodies had been taken to separate hospitals, they came under separate authorities, and the evidence had to be given in two courts – one in the City, which was holding an inquest on Sergeant Bentley, and one in the London Hospital, which was holding inquests on the other two policemen and Gardstein. Mr Bodkin drily remarked to one of the Coroners, 'The law is so strict sir, that I believe if a body is found partly in one district and partly in another the inquest must be held in the district in which the head is.' Mr Bodkin, besides prosecuting at the magistrates' court, represented the Treasury at both inquests.

Inevitably the evidence fell into the same pattern and the wrong conclusions were drawn. Mr Wynne Baxter, the East London Coroner, in summing up, said, 'It had not been proved who actually shot Choate, but probably not Gardstein. With regard to the circumstances attending the death of Gardstein, no doubt the shot that caused his death was fired without any intention of hitting him, but that did not affect the crime. It was not accidental death, it was murder. All three of the persons, therefore, about whose death they were inquiring were murdered.'

But he suggested that only in the case of Sergeant Tucker was there any evidence as to the personality of the murderer, and the jury brought in a verdict of wilful murder against Gardstein. They found that Constable Choate and Gardstein had been wilfully murdered by some person or persons unknown. Subsequently the Coroner's jury at the City Court gave their verdict that Sergeant Bentley had been killed by Gardstein.

After these verdicts, the prosecution had to decide on the final charges against the four prisoners still in custody. Mr Bodkin asked that Peters and Dubof should be charged with murder. The principle was laid down in the Sissinghouse case

that where persons go out for an unlawful purpose in combination and if in the course of that combination it is determined to offer violent resistance to any who may hinder them in effecting that purpose and in the course of offering such resistance murder is committed by one of the combination, it is murder in all: and as to the two men, Peters and Dubof, there is evidence before you that within a few moments of this crime being committed they were there, found armed with similar weapons to those with which the murders were committed and in direct connection with one of the assailants, Gardstein.

They were charged as follows (first indictment): Dubof and Peters were charged with the wilful murder of Charles Tucker; (second count) Dubof, Peters and Vassilleva with feloniously harbouring a felon guilty of murder. Second indictment: Dubof, Peters, Rosen and Vassilleva were accused of conspiring and agreeing together and with others unknown to break and enter the shop of Henry Samuel Harris with intent to steal his goods; (second count) conspiring and agreeing together with the same other persons feloniously to steal the goods of Henry Samuel Harris.

The trial of the Houndsditch Murderers opened at the Old Bailey on 1 May 1911 before Mr Justice Grantham. Sir William Grantham was seventy-five years old and had already expressed his feelings, as reported in the *Daily Telegraph* on 6 January, that 'the men who died in Sidney Street were Socialists of the very worst type, men who did not acknowledge God or anything; he hoped the siege would be a warning to people not to disregard religion.' He was subsequently described by Henry Cecil as 'a really bad judge whose decisions were constantly reversed by the Court of Appeal'. This was not a particularly good omen for the prosecution. The judge had also nearly lost his seat because of political bias in a Yarmouth election case. Nina Vassilleva looked pale as she stepped into the dock and moments later broke down and sobbed bitterly. Her tight-fitting black dress was shabby and a slouch hat of green tweed, with a feather, only emphasised her shabby appearance. Peters had let his hair grow long and it was brushed back over his head. They watched with interest as the jurors were sworn in and stared curiously at the sheriffs in their red gowns on the bench.

The court reporters could not remember a case in which there were so many exhibits. Sacks of exhibits, including the oxygen cylinder which had been bought for cutting the safe, were hauled into court by constables and detectives. On the solicitor's table was a perfectly scaled wood-model of Exchange Buildings and Harris's shop. On the plans the bullet holes and scars had been ringed in red.

Mr Bodkin's opening speech lasted two and a quarter hours. In a masterpiece of compression he went through the evidence, which the judge informed the court made 655 pages, and which had been collated and read – twice. After Max Weil and Constable Piper had given evidence he stopped Mr Bodkin from calling further witnesses and told him, to save time, that on the evidence this was not a case in which he could recommend the jury to find a verdict of guilty of murder. There was no evidence that either Peters or Dubof shot at the policemen, though it was assumed that they were there and it was possible that they did. 'You are within the law strictly, but we don't amplify charges of constructive murder in these days if we can help it.' In his view, it would be wiser to drop the charge of murder and go on with the charge of being accessory before the fact.

Mr Bodkin acceded to his suggestion and the judge directed the jury to say that the two men, against whom there was no evidence of shooting, were not guilty of murder. Peters and Dubof nodded their heads as this was translated to them, but otherwise received the news with indifference.

The prosecution's chief witness was Isaac Levy. On 23 December he had picked Dubof and Peters, on an identification parade, out of a row of between fifteen and twenty others as the men who had been carrying Gardstein and had threatened him. He had afterwards picked out Vassilleva as the woman following them. Although, as the judge said, they could not reproduce a December night in May, two jurors went to Exchange Buildings, shortly before midnight the next day, to try a practical test. They wanted to see with certainty if a person could be identified as far as possible in the same conditions of light. In order that the experiment should be as faithful as possible the police took the precaution of seeing that all the lights in the narrow street were the same as on 16 December.

Two chance passers-by were stopped by the police and asked to walk past the two jurors who were stationed at the entrance to Exchange Buildings. Subsequently the two men were taken to Bishopsgate Police Station and put in a line-up to see if the jurors could pick them out. One juryman readily identified both men while the other identified one. One of the men who was wearing spectacles when he was seen by the jurors in Exchange Buildings, removed them before he was put in the line-up with the other men.

Levy came under a fierce attack from defence council. Mr Bodkin later complained of the venom and hostility he had been subjected to. But before this happened the judge intervened once more in an even more startling fashion. Mr Justice Grantham, on taking his seat, at the opening of the second day's hearing, said that since there was no other evidence of identification he could not allow any jury to find a verdict of guilty on Levy's uncorroborated statement! Therefore there was not sufficient evidence to justify the Crown pressing the case. Yet he thought that there was other evidence to confirm Levy's statement that Vassilleva was the woman following Gardstein!

It is quite clear that she was a great friend of Gardstein. In those circumstances there may well have been reason why she was following him. But yet she may have had no part in the shooting. Consequently, I think it would not be wise to press for a conviction against her as being an accessory after the fact of murder.

It does seem to me that assuming these were three people coming away from the scene, you are not in a position to say that they knew murder had been committed. The law is clear. You must show that an accessory after the fact knew that murder had been committed. Wounding is not murder. It may be a technical point; still it is a point to be taken into consideration. It is doubtful whether you could show that at that time they knew they were escaping from justice. It would not be safe, I think, for the Crown to press the case.

Mr Bodkin rose to his feet as another part of the Crown's case collapsed and said wearily,

While there was the evidence of the doctors that Sergeant Tucker must have died a minute or two after having been wounded, it was just possible that those who were there and saw Tucker might not have known that he was dead. There was another indictment preferred against the prisoners of being accessory after the fact of shooting Sergeant Bentley, but as the evidence of Levy would be the main point, his lordship's evidence as to that evidence would have an equal bearing on that charge.

He then withdrew the charge of being accessory after the fact; when this was translated to the prisoners and they were told that they had been found not guilty on that count too, the girl looked at the men and the men looked at her in some bewilderment. The only charge left against all four was conspiracy to break and enter.

Before the trial continued the judge dropped one more bombshell. He said he was strongly of the opinion, and he might be wrong, that three men, who were the chief murderers, had met their doom. Gardstein was clearly one of them. In his view the other two men were burnt in Sidney Street. 'There were three men firing shots and I think they are dead.' The prosecution had to swallow this, but when the defence counsel for Federoff and Peters stood up and said that it was only fair to the prisoners to say that they had given the police all the assistance and all the information in their power and that they had told the police everything they were able to tell, Mr Bodkin said grimly, 'My friend had better not say that. It may provoke an observation on my part.'

Out of the thirty or forty witnesses to be called, Isaac Levy's evidence was the most damaging to the defence. The stout, middle-aged man, firmly believing that his life was in jeopardy by giving evidence, was subjected to a withering and sometimes humiliating cross-examination, which left him reeling. He was easily upset; his replies became more heated as counsel's cross-examination steadily became more taunting and jeering; more than once he had to be urged to be calm.

'This is the first time you have looked down the barrels of two pistols, conceivably loaded,' counsel asked. 'Were you as composed then as you are now?' he asked. He turned as the judge, intervening said: 'Are you asking which is the worse – having to face cross-examination or looking down the barrel of the pistols?'

There was some laughter. Levy agreed that the experience was 'a little out of the ordinary'.

'A little out of the ordinary! Did you run off like a hare?'

'I did not.'

'Did you say at the Guildhall that you ran away?'

'I was asked if I ran, and there was laughter among the audience in court, and I said yes.'

'If people laugh you are willing to assent to a proposition?'

'I cannot pull a counsel up, and the question was not pushed further or I should have explained that I was running towards Exchange Buildings.'

In spite of the jeering cross-examination the defence could not shake his evidence. Fortunately they did not have to now that the judge had ruled that as it was uncorroborated evidence, it was an insufficient basis for a verdict of guilty. The defence was further strengthened by a Crown witness, Constable Martin, 'who stumbled and fell, and had such a miraculous escape'; he was asked by a juror if he had seen Levy near the scene of the occurrence. He answered quite truthfully he had not – though it was not for the reasons the juror supposed, as Martin had actually been hiding.

The defence submitted that there were only four conspirators, possibly five, involved and they were Gardstein, Fritz, Joseph, Max and possibly Peter the Painter. Further corroboration that this was so had been given in the magistrates' court by Luba Milstein and Karl Hoffman who, after their release, were called as witnesses for the defence. Luba swore that Fritz, Joseph and Max had brought Gardstein into the house, in spite of her earlier statement in which she said that she did not see the men come upstairs, and that two men left without her seeing them; she had made it, she said, because she did not want to give them away and was herself afraid of being charged. Hoffman's statement was even more astonishing. After his earlier statement denying that he knew most of the group or that anyone had come to his rooms after the murders, he completely reversed his evidence and said that Max had killed Gardstein, who was carried by Fritz and Max to Grove Street. Cross-examination was deferred, fortunately for him. He was not called any more, but if he had been he might have faced a criminal charge for such a blatant piece of perjury. He was fortunate, too, that his smuggled prison-notes to Dubof were not introduced into the evidence.

Dubof went into the witness box for nearly four hours. His real name, he explained was Yourka Laiwin, but he had assumed the name of Dubof because he was a political refugee. He was twenty-four years old and the son of a small farmer. He had worked on the farm until he was eighteen and then went to Riga to learn painting. He returned to the farm in the autumn of 1905, when the revolt collapsed, but because he was an agitator he had to leave. He had been arrested and flogged with Cossacks' whips.

He explained that he had only gone to Grove Street on the afternoon of the 16th to see Peter the Painter about painting some decorations for the Lettish concert they were arranging. He had left at 4 p.m. and denied ever having been to Exchange Buildings. Tomacoff unwillingly confirmed that while he was there Dubof and Rosen were not conspiring to break into a jeweller's shop. Dubof's principal witnesses were his German landlady, the domineering Elsa Petter, who referred to her lodger as 'my youngest baby', and twenty-six-year-old Hans Bekov who worked, lived and slept with him and boasted that since September there had only been two nights when they had not slept together. In spite of this intimacy between all three, neither Bekov nor Mrs Petter had any idea of the existence of the group or who Dubof's friends were. In fact, Mrs Petter, as she told the *Evening News* reporter before Dubof's arrest, had made it a condition of his stay that he did not join any anarchist clubs or belong to any political organisations. Dubof, they said, had been home all evening and had gone to bed with Bekov at 11.30 p.m. at the time of the murders, and was still in bed when Bekov had got up at 6.45 the next morning. They churned out dates, times and minutiae with such mechanical efficiency, some of it going back four months – which by itself suggests that they had been rehearsed – that they were impregnable to cross-examination.

Rosen's defence was that he had paid friendly visits to Fritz, glad to meet a fellow countryman and for the opportunity to talk in his native tongue. He denied the construction that was put on his visits. It was only two days after his wedding that he was arrested and foolishly made the mistake of denying that he knew Fritz. But two days later he repaired the damage by telling all he knew. Similarly he denied ever being in Exchange Buildings. It was a clear case of mistaken identity. His resemblance to Fritz was uncanny, particularly in profile, Hoffman said. Fortunately for the defence this could be corroborated by Tomacoff and Smolensky, Fritz's landlord in Newcastle Place, who both thought that Fritz and Rosen were brothers.

Jacob Peters, giving evidence in his own defence, said that he had been a grocer's assistant, a dock labourer and an employee in a butter (oil) factory in Libau. For some years he was a member of the Lettish Social Democratic Party and carried out propaganda work among the Army and the working classes.

'As a paid worker?' the judge asked.

'No, voluntarily. Only principal agitators get paid.'

He was arrested in Riga and held for eighteen months before being freed. Subsequently he went to Germany, intending to go to America, but he had insufficient money and found work in Germany. He next went to Denmark, but could not get work and finally arrived in London in October 1909. He stayed with his cousin Fritz in Great Garden Street but eventually left him. He had expected him to be the same man (politically) as he was in Russia, but he had changed completely. Fritz professed to be an anarchist but knew nothing of anarchism. He had worked as a tailor's presser in Spitalfields from July 1910 until his arrest, but some of his alleged employers could never be found! Yet his defence counsel had handed the police a list, which he had from Peters himself of the places where he was supposed to have worked.

In November 1910 Peters had joined an LCC evening class for English but left it because most of the pupils were Jews, and he had learnt more Yiddish than English. There was laughter in court when the judge commented, 'I hope the London County Council will be aware of this. We can hardly call on the ratepayers to teach people Yiddish', which provoked another outburst of laughter. On 16 December he was at work all day and did not finish until after 8 p.m. He arrived at his lodgings about 9 p.m., and spent the rest of the evening repairing a mousetrap and reading. His landlord had last seen him a few minutes after 10 p.m., when he watched him set the mousetrap with a piece of cheese. Peters' room was on the ground floor facing the street – with two shutters, which were never bolted, over the window. As the landlord went out he saw the chinks of light at the top and bottom but when he returned at 11.30 p.m. the room was in darkness and he assumed that Peters was in bed. This was the weak point in Peters' evidence. It was easy enough to infer that he had had ample time in which to get to Exchange Buildings, well before the murders, and later that night climb back into his room through the street window and the unbolted shutters.

But this damning suggestion was counter-balanced by the evidence that he rarely visited Grove Street and was not there on the afternoon of the 16th.

Nina's counsel faced a more formidable array of evidence. One witness after another told how she had dyed her hair, burned papers or tried to conceal them; of her distress at Gardstein's death, her blood stained clothing, her attempts to get away to Paris. Richardson described seeing her in a miniature Merry Widow hat; the judge asked what he meant and he indicated the style of hat by holding his hands out two feet from his head. In the magistrates' court she had aggressively challenged the evidence, particularly Levy's 'lies'. She was quieter now and frequently sobbed. Her counsel implied that she was a Jewish refugee from Russia where her father was a chef in the palace at St Petersburg. Since arriving in England four years before, when she was nineteen, she had earned a respectable living as a cigarette-maker. In his final summing-up, he said that the poor woman was in love with Gardstein, and she was under his influence, but that there was nothing to prove that she knew anything of the conspiracy.

On the eleventh and final day, Mr Bodkin spoke up vigorously for the Crown's two principal witnesses, Levy and Richardson. The former had given his evidence in spite of the threats he feared on his life if he did so. As for Richardson, defence counsel had suggested that he was a dishonest employee because he had been sacked from his job; in fact, he had been sacked because of the time he had spent in court giving evidence. They had been singled out for 'venomous attack and hostile criticism'. How was crime to be repressed, Mr Bodkin asked, if witnesses who came forward were insulted.

In his summing-up which lasted an hour and a half, Mr Justice Grantham observed that if Constable Martin

> had shown greater courage and a greater sense of duty on the occasion of the dreadful occurrences of 16 December he might have acted in a way that would have assisted the aims of justice. It was true that he was in great danger. The wounded man Gardstein must have been carried over the spot where Martin lay, and had Martin not been afraid to raise his head he must have seen who the persons were who were carrying Gardstein and been able to identify them without difficulty.

The police refused to believe that he was a coward or a liar. That he had never been there doesn't seem to have occurred to anyone.

One piece of evidence could not be explained away. In a cupboard, under the stairs, in 11 Exchange Buildings, the police had found two bottles with impressions from the right finger and thumb, including the scar on the forefinger, of Nina Vassilleva.

The jury consequently found her guilty of conspiracy to break and enter but recommended that she should not be deported. The men were found not guilty and released.

Nina was sentenced to two years' imprisonment, but five weeks later the Court of Appeal quashed her conviction on the ground of misdirection of the jury by Mr Justice Grantham! The Lord Chief Justice criticised the summing up, objecting to statements which amounted to misdirection. Beyond her presence at 11 Exchange Buildings there was no direct evidence to show that she was a conspirator. A great deal had been said about her dyeing her hair and lying, but this could have been due to fear of the possible consequences of what had occurred. Under these circumstances these were points that the jury might like to have considered. The Court of Criminal Appeal was not there to express any opinion as to whether she was guilty or not; they had only to decide whether the trial had been a satisfactory one with regard to the summing up. That Nina was Gardstein's mistress was not proof of her guilt. Under the circumstances the conviction had to be quashed.

This decision meant that of the five men and three women brought to trial none had been convicted. Two of the women and two of the men had been discharged at the magistrates' court. Two of the indictments had broken down at the trial, and on the third indictment, three of the men had been acquitted but Vassilleva found guilty; and now her conviction was quashed.

The *Daily Mail* commented:

> Thus five months have passed since 16 December, when three constables of the City Police were murdered by a gang of armed alien burglars and two more policemen were seriously wounded. Not a single one of their assassins has been punished by the law. Gardstein, one of the murderers, was mortally wounded by a chance shot from one of his confederates. Two more of the gang perished in the Sidney Street 'battle' of January. But it is certain that the persons implicated were numerous. It is no pleasant or satisfactory reflection that several of the principals in the crime and many of their associates have escaped and are still at large.
>
> The police can hardly be congratulated upon their success in dealing with this formidable conspiracy; but, in excuse, it must be remembered that in the vast alien population of East London it is a matter of peculiar difficulty to obtain evidence or run down the offender.

11

Hero of October

The trial was still going on when Max Smoller's wife and children slipped out of the country. She must have guessed that she was under some sort of police surveillance because she used a false name to buy tickets. Since the shootings she had moved from 1 Wellesley Street to a new address in Brick Lane. On 25 April 1911 she left it for the last time together with her two daughters, five-year-old Rachel, who had curly ginger hair down to her shoulders, and three-year-old Cecilia (Cissie). All were conspicuously dressed. Both girls were wearing bright red cloaks with hoods, and Mrs Smoller wore a long cream three-quarter- length coat. Possibly this was to make observation easier – not for the police, who were in deep cover and noting everything down, but for the two men, friends or family, who were watching her and the children from forty yards back. One of them the police knew and the other they described as being middle-aged and about fifty-five. A third man, a young man of twenty-seven, was pushing the family luggage, which was a bundle wrapped in sacking, on a coster's barrow. The two men left her at the corner of Leman Street, shook hands and said goodbye. The young man said goodbye at the dockyard gates. Mrs Smoller and the two girls boarded ship in St Katharine's dock and sailed the same night for Bremen. She told the Chief Officer that her husband had been living in America for the past twelve months and that she herself was going to Russia. The ship sailed at 10 p.m. and with it the last possibility of tracing Max Smoller.

The secret was that he had escaped from the country on the same night as the murders and well before the police investigation could gather any momentum. By the time they started looking for him he was safely abroad. The man who made it possible was the Sidney Street informer Charles Perelman which further indicates that he must have known what was happening and been deeply involved. His son said, in 1977, that his father had in fact been the leader of the group. Possibly his betrayal of Fritz and Joseph was a form of insurance against the police looking too closely into his own background. Young Charles Perelman (Carlusha) remembered the knockings on the door and the comings and goings that night as Smoller made his escape. It was essential that he should have some sort of cover story and this was provided by ten-year-old Annette (Nettie) who was taken out of bed and went with Smoller, posing as his daughter. They headed for Paris, catching a boat the same night. They got through customs by Smoller saying that Nettie was unwell and had diphtheria; once through they were left alone in their cabin. In Paris, Smoller took the little girl to her aunt Hannah Mandelbaum, a Rumanian Jew, who had a flower shop in the Lido. After that he disappeared completely.

During the period between the murders and the siege the subject was never mentioned in the Perelman household. Carlusha's remark in old age that he had cried because he knew that Fritz and Joseph were in the burning house suggests that at some point he must have overheard something. Possibly he had been eavesdropping on his father, as he used to do on the group, and that is how he knew that it was them.

He was at his father's bedside three years later when the old man lay dying of stomach cancer in the German hospital in Dalston.

'Forgive me,' his father said and wept for ten minutes.

Nina Vassilleva felt very bitter towards Max. In two wildly contradicting statements she alleged that Gardstein's death hadn't been an accident. She said that he had been deliberately murdered by Max, who had organised the robbery for that very purpose! This could be dismissed as merely the outburst of a hysterical woman, but perhaps she was remembering Gardstein's exploits in Warsaw, how they had embarrassed the revolutionary movement, and of the attempt by two Social Democrats to murder him which ended in him killing them. Had the Houndsditch robbery been part of an elaborate trap to snare and murder Gardstein without embarrassing the revolutionaries abroad? Was this what she was thinking? If so, her bitterness was understandable.

Apart from Gardstein, the only other person Nina seemed to care about was Sara Trassjonsky who was hopelessly insane and, according to the asylum authorities, had suicidal tendencies. Just two years after the murders a small brown paper parcel was sent anonymously to the police. It was from Nina. Inside was a small perfumed sachet and to it was pinned a small envelope on the front of which was written 'Xmas 1912. To the nurse who so kindly tended Carl Garstin (alias Gardstein) during his last hours.' This was forwarded to the asylum with a request to hand it to Sara if she was well enough to receive it. Apart from an official acknowledgement nothing more was heard. Sara died insane.

Nina carried on working for Abdullah's, making cigarettes. Once she was spotted in a tobacconist's shop window hand-rolling them. Later she worked for the Soviet Trade Delegation at 49 Moorgate in the City. Over half the staff of four hundred were Russians, nearly all of them employed by Arcos – the All Russian Co-operative Society Ltd – and all engaged in espionage and subversive activities in Britain. In May 1928 this led to a spectacular raid by City of London Police and Special Branch in search of evidence. The raid lasted three days and resulted in a diplomatic breach with the Russians when the evidence was made public.

Vassilleva continued to live her solitary life of exile in the East End. She ended her days in a small flat in Brick Lane, not far from the scene of the police murders, and died in St Bartholomew's hospital in 1963.

Of all those involved, Peter the Painter is the most firmly linked in the public's mind with the murders. Unquestionably he got his nickname from the fact that at times he earned his living as a painter and decorator. Unlike Yourka Dubof he did not have any artistic pretensions. A contemporary newspaper said, with what degree of truth we don't know, that 'Peter the Painter was colloquial Russian for "Bill Bailey" or "Will-o'-the-wisp", or any other name which indicates a disposition to disappear and reappear with tantalising frequency.' Certainly he lived up to his reputation and sightings were reported in America, Russia and Australia. But it would have been a pointless exercise to have followed up these leads, even if they had proved genuine, to have extradited him and brought him to trial. On the evidence the police had, he would never have been convicted. Mr Justice Grantham had made this quite plain at the trial when he stated that there was no evidence that Peter the Painter was one of the murderers.

From several sources it has been possible to flush out his elusive identity. The primary sources are two letters from the Sûreté in Marseilles and Paris, and some pencilled notes from an informant which further suggest that the Sidney Street informant was Charles Perelman.

On 23 May 1908 the Marseilles police raided No. 19 rue Chevalier Roze where there were a number of suspected refugees, among them Peter Piatkow, born at Pskow (Russia) on 20 June 1883 of Ivan and Marie Antonow. He described himself as a bachelor and a painter. On arriving in Marseilles he had gone to live at No. 11 rue d'Aubagne on 16 April 1908. At that time this house was reputed to be frequented by anarchists. From 7 June to 6 July 1908 he lived in No. 37 rue des Dominicaines (old No. 27). He then lived at No. 11 rue Ste Claire, and finally went to live in furnished rooms at No. 8 rue Chevalier Roze, the street where he had been arrested, from 4 October 1909 to 13 January 1910, at which time he left, saying he was going to Paris. Part of the time he worked as a painter at the rate of five francs a day.

According to the concierge of No. 37 rue des Dominicaines, Piatkow was a very violent character and often disappeared with his Russian friends, and finished by breaking with them. From a friend the police learned that he had abandoned his studies to work as a painter; that he had worked at the docks and at the Exhibition of Electricity, and had left at the end of 1909 for Evians-les-Bains. Somehow this friend was tricked into giving them other information: that Peter had been imprisoned for acts committed in the revolution of 1905 but had escaped and hidden in his birthplace with some friends, where he earned a living painting street doors, numbers, etc. His father had died in 1908 but his mother and sisters still lived at their farm somewhere near Talsen in Courland. He had travelled widely in Europe and said that he knew most of the countries.

He had studied chemistry in Switzerland but had to leave for an unexplained reason. While living in Marseilles, after his father's death, an uncle, who was an army colonel, told him that if he would go to Paris and study – not politics – he would send him money each month. He had come to Marseilles from Oran, shortly after the King of Portugal was assassinated, although there is no evidence that the two events were linked. He had arrived with a little Polish man, and lodged with him for a while, but the Pole was so lazy that they split up.

Somehow the Sûreté managed further to trick his friend into letting them borrow two photographs of Peter long enough for them to be copied, which the friend would certainly not have agreed to. They forwarded three copies of each pose to the City Police who, within two or three days of receiving them, issued a new 'wanted' poster reproducing both.

The Sûreté confirmed Peter's arrival in Paris from Marseilles, and added that he had lodged from 10 December 1909 to October 1910 at 4 rue Danville. From there he had gone to London.

Less than a week before they were given this news the City Police had been given another extraordinary piece of information. A Russian refugee called at the detective office and said that he believed that Peter the Painter was an anarchist, Peter Pilenas, who came from the same town as himself. He had come to England about four years previously and had first earned a living as a cap-maker and then by selling books on anarchism. He was then living in the neighbourhood of Commercial Street. This was about four years ago. Just after the murders, he had gone to live at a house in Bethnal Green but had stayed only a week, saying that he was going to live in Brooklyn, New York. His bombshell was that Peter Pilenas, whom he believed to be Peter the Painter, was the brother of Casimir Pilenas, who was the interpreter at the Thames Police Court, and whom the City Police had been using as an interpreter to interrogate and take statements from the Houndsditch murderers!

The official reaction is not known. Any damage Pilenas could have done would have been done already, if the story was true. Similarly we don't know if he made any official explanation confirming or denying the relationship, or whether the police simply ignored the information as too incredible to be believed. The first public hint of this story and its genuineness came in 1934 with the publication of Sergeant Leeson's memoirs and was finally confirmed in 1967 by Nina Vassilleva's firm of solicitors.

Leeson's source was a letter from Casimir Pilenas written to him some years after the 'siege', certainly after 1916. Unfortunately he does not explain why it should have been written to him. He merely quotes three brief extracts, and the rest of the letter is built into his story. Casimir Pilenas is not identified by name, but Leeson says that 'this man', though brother to the 'Painter', actually worked for the forces of law and order against Peter and his gang. Casimir Pilenas denied that his brother had been involved in the murders and Leeson further quotes: 'My brother Peter, whose name appeared in some of the documents of the Houndsditch murder case, was here already. So I joined him. He did not live very long; he died in the summer of 1914 [sic]* in Philadelphia...'

In the late thirties Sir William Crocker – his father had represented Sara Trassjonksy and Nina Vassilleva – was on business in New York, where he again met Casimir Pilenas. Casimir told him the 'truth' about Peter the Painter, who he said was his brother, Peter Pilenas; In his memoirs Sir William published a photograph of Peter Pilenas taken between 1911 and 1916 when he died in Philadelphia; the date of his death is given as 17 August, although the body was too badly decomposed to determine how and when he died. The photograph is marked 'Peter the Painter'.

According to Sir William Crocker the Houndsditch murderers tried to blame the innocent Peter the Painter for the murders by putting the dying Gardstein in his room instead of in Fritz's to draw the suspicion away from the real killers. This doesn't make sense as both rooms were rented and lived in by Fritz – Peter was only staying with him. In fact, Peter Pilenas had already left for America and was at sea on the day of the murders.

Was his story genuine? Was Peter the Painter in fact Peter Pilenas? If not, why should Casimir Pilenas say he was?

The evidence is firmly against them being the same man. Peter Pilenas was making caps and selling anarchist literature in England when Peter Piatkow was in prison after the 1905 revolution and in hiding at Pskow in Russia; besides, Pilenas was seven years older than Piatkow, and their photographs show that they were not the same man. Certainly there is a strong likeness between them; but then there was also a likeness between Fritz Svaars and John Rosen.

To begin with, the hairline is different. Pilenas has more hair, though this could be explained by a wig. What cannot be concealed is the nose and ears. Even allowing for the slightly different pose, it is clear that Peter Piatkow has a much thicker bridge to his nose and that the ears are a different shape.

---

* It was in fact 1916; see below

But why should Casimir Pilenas say that his brother was Peter the Painter? When the police were told of his relationship with Peter Pilenas, he must have been questioned closely and have been able to satisfy them that his brother was not the Painter. It is inconceivable that he would have been allowed to continue as one of the interpreters if he had not been able to do so, and it is equally inconceivable that the police ignored the information. Yet after his brother's death, and when he himself had immigrated to America, he wrote to the credulous Sergeant Leeson, whom he knew from their East End days, claiming that his brother and Peter Piatkow were the same man. He volunteered this information not only to Leeson but to Sir William Crocker as well, neither of whom had previously suspected the relationship, and both published it in good faith, Leeson (at Pilenas' request) without giving his source. If Pilenas was anxious for the story to be believed, why did not he publish it himself? The answer must be that he daren't because it was not true. The police would immediately have denied it; one can just hear the jeers if they hadn't: while they were hunting Peter the Painter his brother was interpreting for them and helping the killers to go free. No, Peter Pilenas was not Peter Piatkow, but Casimir Pilenas would have liked people to believe the legend that he was.

He also made another claim which, at first, sounds far more incredible. Leeson quotes it in his memoirs: '…but the crime itself was organised by Stalin, now head of the Soviet Government.'

As usual Leeson gets it wrong, but the reason for his assertion was that Jacob Peters, who should have been hanged for the murder of three City of London policemen, was now one of the most powerful men in Stalinist Russia and a former Deputy Chairman of the terrible Cheka – the All Russian Extraordinary Commission for Combating Counter-Revolution and Sabotage. A Soviet biography[*] explained: 'Yakov Peters. That name aroused fear and hatred in foes of the Revolution, in spies and saboteurs. They said of him: he is Dzerzhinsky's right hand.'

In exile, from 1909 to 1917, Peters had been an active member of the Latvian Social Democratic Party London group. He opposed the Menshevik Central Committee, and in the summer of 1912 succeeded in establishing an LSD Bolshevik Foreign Bureau in London.

---

[*] *Geroi Oktiabria* (Heroes of October) (Leningrad, 1967) vol. 2, pp. 234–5.

The revolution of February 1917 opened up the road to Russia for Peters, and the Foreign Bureau sent him back as its representative. In Petrograd he was made a member of the Bolshevik Military Organisation and was sent to Latvia to agitate and propagandise among the Lettish battalions, as he had done in 1905. He seized every opportunity to spread propaganda among the soldiers, and spoke at meetings, conferences, demonstrations and funerals. He became one of the editors of a Bolshevik Latvian newspaper and, so the official sources say, did not hesitate to unmask, ridicule and morally destroy his enemies.

When support for the Bolsheviks waned and Lenin went into hiding Peters continued to agitate for Bolshevik support. On 23 September 1917 he opened and presented the main report to the 14th Conference of the Latvian Territory Social Democratic Party held in Valka. He spoke of the coming revolution and of the inevitable victory of the working class. He urged that only convinced Bolsheviks should be sent to the Second All Russian Congress of Soviets. He urged, 'The situation is grave and time is ripe. We must take power in our hands, save Russia and call the peoples to fight a revolutionary battle all over Europe.' The Latvian delegates responded by sending him as their delegate to the congress where he was elected a member of the All Russian Central Executive Committee.

He became part of the Military Revolutionary Committee of the Petrograd Soviet, which masterminded the October coup d'etat and Bolshevik seizure of power. His loyalty and ruthlessness brought its reward. Two months after the October revolution the Cheka was formed to combat counter-revolution; Peters was appointed Deputy Chairman to the fanatical Dzerzhinsky.

In March 1918, the Cheka was moved to Moscow following the transfer there of the Soviet Government from Petrograd. The Muscovites were lukewarm in their support of the Bolsheviks; the Mensheviks, anarchists and other political groups were openly agitating against Bolshevik authority and steadily gathering support from the tens of thousands of soldiers arriving from the front. Since the Bolsheviks were unable to feed them they started to loot. The main opposition to the Bolsheviks came from the anarchist Black Guard who, Peters recalled, 'issued orders as if they were in authority, rounded people up on the streets, took away weapons and valuables, and handed out the bourgeois rags right and left to the people'. On one occasion the Black Guard seized a large quantity of opium, sold it and used the money to publish the anarchist newspaper *Chernoye Znamya* ('Black Banner'). Later, the Bolsheviks discovered that the Black Guard were also being issued with rifles, bombs and machine-guns from the Moscow Military Commissariat. Within a month, the Cheka was ready to liquidate it.

On 13 April, at 3 a.m., simultaneous attacks were made on the Black Guard headquarters and twenty-five other centres, and their influence was totally destroyed. More than 100 people were killed, and 500 arrested. Later in the day, Peters escorted the British diplomat Robert Bruce Lockhart through the fighting areas. In house after house they entered, the filth was indescribable. Formerly these houses had belonged to wealthy people, but now broken bottles littered the Aubusson carpets; paintings had been slashed, priceless heirlooms and ornaments lay smashed on the ground. Ceilings were punctured with bullet holes and the bodies were still lying where they had fallen.

In the luxurious drawing-room of the House Gracheva the Anarchists had been surprised in the middle of an orgy. The long table which had supported the feast had been overturned, and broken plates, glasses, champagne bottles, made unsavoury islands in a pool of blood and spilt wine. On the floor lay a young woman, face downwards. Peters turned her over. Her hair was dishevelled. She had been shot through the neck, and blood had congealed in a sinister purple clump. She could not have been more than twenty. Peters shrugged his shoulders. 'Prostitutka,' he said. 'Perhaps it is for the best'.★

Although it had no justification in law, this action further confirmed the Cheka's right to carry out summary executions. In February 1918 it announced that it saw 'no other way to combat counter-revolutionaries, spies, speculators, burglars, hooligans, saboteurs and other parasites than their merciless annihilation at the scene of the crime'. Later in the year it unleashed 'mass red terror'. The following year Peters was reported as signing death warrants continuously, and he earned the sobriquet 'Executioner' because of the number it was said he carried out with his own hands.

When, in July and August 1918, the Left Socialist Revolutionaries revolted, assassinating the German Ambassador and seizing Dzerzhinsky

★ Bruce Lockhart, *Memoirs of a British Agent*

and Latsis, Peters played a major part in putting them down and restoring Bolshevik control. For a short time he replaced Dzerzhinsky as head of the Cheka. Numerous executions followed the Bolshevik recapture of towns and cities momentarily seized in the July rebellion. As the civil war heightened so the terror increased. The Tsar and his family were murdered at Ekaterinburg. The next month it was the turn of the Bolshevik leaders. On the morning of 30 August, the head of the Petrograd Cheka was murdered, and the same evening a young woman tried to assassinate Lenin as he left a Moscow factory and wounded him with two bullets. Arrests began in Petrograd on a massive scale. Robert Bruce Lockhart, who had been shown by Peters the anarchist headquarters on the day the Black Guard was liquidated, was among those arrested. He had been approached by Cheka agents provocateurs with offers to bribe the Lettish regiments to turn against the Bolsheviks. Bruce Lockhart had put them in touch with the British Secret Service and was now heavily implicated in the plot. He was bundled out of bed and taken to Lubianka No. 11, which was the headquarters of the Moscow Cheka. After a long wait he was taken along a dark corridor and shown into a long dark room lit only by a hand-lamp on the writing-table.

> At the table, with a revolver lying beside the writing-pad, was a man, dressed in black trousers and a white Russian shirt. His black hair, long and waving as a poet's, was brushed back over a high forehead. There was a large wrist-watch on his left hand. In the dim light his features looked more sallow than ever. His lips were tightly compressed, and, as I entered the room, his eyes fixed me with a steely stare. He looked grim and formidable. It was Peters.

Lockhart was released almost immediately, but a few days later was rearrested and imprisoned for exactly one month in the Lubianka where he had frequent conversations with Peters. Peters apologised for the food – soup, tea and potatoes – but it was the same as that supplied to himself.

> When he had a free moment, he liked discussing England, the war, capitalism and revolution. He told me strange tales of his experiences as a revolutionary. He had been in prison in Riga in Tsarist days. He showed me his nails as a proof of the torture which he had undergone. There was

nothing in his character to indicate the inhuman monster he is commonly supposed to be. He told me that he suffered physical pain every time he signed a death sentence. I believe it was true. There was a strong streak of sentimentality in his nature, but he was a fanatic as far as the clash between Bolshevism and Capitalism was concerned, and he pursued his Bolshevik aims with a sense of duty which was relentless.

As we were talking, a motor van – a kind of 'Black Maria' – pulled up in the court-yard below, and a squad of men, armed with rifles and bandolièrs, got out and took up their places in the yard. Presently a door opened just below us, and three men with bowed heads walked slowly forward to the van. I recognised them instantly. They were Sheglovitoff, Khvostoff, and Bieletsky, three ex-Ministers of the Tsarist régime, who had been in prison since the revolution. There was a pause followed by a scream. Then through the door the fat figure of a priest was half-pushed, half-carried to the 'Black Maria'. His terror was pitiful. Tears rolled down his face. His knees rocked, and he fell like a great ball of fat on the ground. I felt sick and turned away. 'Where are they going?' I asked. 'They are going to another world,' said Peters drily. 'And that man', he said pointing to the priest, 'richly deserves it.' It was the notorious Bishop Vostorgoff. The ex Ministers formed the first batch of the several hundred victims of the Terror who were shot at that time as reprisal for the attempted assassination of Lenin.★

Peters later wrote that about 600 people were shot by the Moscow Cheka alone.

In less than one year the Cheka, not exceeding 500 men, had crushed two large plots and the uprising of the Left Social Revolutionaries. By the autumn of 1918 public attention had turned to the mounting attacks of the White Guard on the different fronts, and there was a relative calm internally. Opponents of the Cheka tried to prove it was no longer necessary and pressed for its replacement by courts. The Cheka had to withstand many such attacks in the Press, and also at party meetings and conferences. But it survived and Peters later wrote that it became 'necessary to mete out justice at a much more ferocious rate than in 1918'. Earlier he implied that they did not shoot enough people in the first year because they were too inexperienced.

★ R. H. Bruce Lockhart, *op. cit.*

The official figure, which is thought to be an underestimate, for the first year's work is 6,300.

Lenin thought Peters a 'brilliant and very dependable man'. To the foreign correspondents who saw him in the early days of the revolution he was a frightening figure. According to J. W. T. Mason of the *Daily Express*, writing in September 1918, 'The most awful figure of the Russian Red Terror, the man with the most murder in his soul, is the present Extraordinary Commissioner against Counter-Revolution and Sabotage, a dapper little blond Lett named Peters, who lived in England so long that he speaks Russian with an English accent.' The report went on to say that he was known and liked best by the American correspondents because he seemed more culti-vated than the rest. This apparent sophistication could be deceptive: Peters had no compunction about shooting anyone denounced as a counter-revolutionary. The correspondent found him kindly and considerate until he asked for help to get a passport for a Russian girl who wanted to visit her parents in England. Peters was sympa-thetic until he learned that her father was a Tsarist officer and then he refused. She belonged to a class that had to be destroyed. No matter that she was a girl and working for her living. She and her family were enemies of the working class. The look on his face told the correspondent that it was useless to argue any further. A few minutes after this refusal Peters turned to a young American correspondent who was present and said, 'Come, dine with me tonight. I feel I need a little Western civilisation. I want to talk about books and art. I am sick of the sight of these untidy revolutionary men.' Peters now had absolute power of life and death over anybody in Russia. According to Mason, when a neutral visited Peters to plead for some lives he had become 'a mere furious little animal, signing death warrants all day, often not looking to see what he was signing. During one visit the neutral noticed he signed an order to shoot seventy-two officers without even glancing down at the paper.'

Peters' importance increased when the civil war broke out and the very existence of the Bolshevik revolution became threatened by the White Russian and invading allied armies. On 8 May 1919 he was made commander of the internal defence of Petrograd and ruthlessly set about crushing pro-White sympathisers. Eight hundred officers were reportedly massacred in one day and three thousand hos-tages deported to Moscow. The wives and grown-up children of all officers defecting to the anti-Bolsheviks were arrested. Wine, spirits, any money above £500 and jewels were confiscated. Nobody could walk the streets without a pass. Wherever there was any evidence that firearms were concealed in a flat the whole family was shot, as were some wives of escaping officers. The newspapers reported that the Bolsheviks were prepared to blowup large parts of the city if they were forced to abandon it, in line with Trotsky's promise: 'When we leave we shall so bang the door behind us that all the world will remember us.' On 23 August Peters was made commander of the Kiev fortified area, assisted by Voroshilov and Latsis who were members of the council. He hadn't been there very long before he was recalled to Petrograd. On 19 October Zinoviev and Trotsky sent a telegram from Petrograd to Lenin in Moscow requesting Peters' immediate return, as the threat from the White Russian army was increasing. Subsequently he returned to Kiev and became a member of the Military Soviet of the Tula fortified area. From 1920 he was a member of the OGPU (Unified State Political Administration) Collegium or inner cabinet. The OGPU replaced the Cheka and its successor the GPU. From 1920 he was a member of the Turkestan Central Committee Politburo and, judging from an article he wrote, seems to have been engaged in weeding out undesirables in a purge lasting eight months from May 1934.

In 1930 the Soviet press reported that Peters had been given the authority to summon two batteries of artillery to Moscow to 'cleanse the Red Army of its disaffected element'. Clearly this was to be the beginnings of another purge. This was confirmed by his appointment to preside over a tribunal of three to whom special powers had been given. By then he was an important member of the Central Control Committee of the Soviet Communist Party. From this appointment it seems reasonably certain that he still had links with the State security forces which were his power base, but possibly these had been severed by 1935 when there were ominous reports that he was out of favour with Stalin.

Before Bruce Lockhart returned from Russia in October 1918, Peters asked him if he would give a letter and photographs to the English woman he had married in London on 9 September 1916 before returning to Russia. Her name was May Freeman and they had met some years before when Peters was working in a tailor's shop in the

Holloway Road. In October 1918, when Peters' notoriety as the Robespierre of the Russian revolution was at its height, she was interviewed by a *Daily Express* reporter at the house in Islington where she had lived since Peters had left for Russia seventeen months before. She was described as a good-looking young woman who refused to believe what was being said about Peters whom she described as a kind husband and father. They had lived together for several years before marrying, and a daughter, also called May, had been born on 3 December 1913. To stop any confusion she was always referred to as Little May. The letters Mrs Peters showed to the reporter were full of domestic details except for the occasional references to the 'hard work' on which her husband was engaged. There were supposed to have been other letters but Mrs Peters believed that these had been stopped by the censor. She explained that she had not joined her husband in Russia because of the uncertainty of conditions there, although she had recently been asked by Maxim Litvinoff to join him and his party who were returning. Contrary to the press reports, however, Peters did not want his wife to join him and did everything possible to prevent her coming at all. When she and Little May did finally arrive in 1921 it was to learn that he had divorced her and married a Russian wife. Although he didn't want them there, neither did he want them to leave and they were installed in a house next door but one of his own and his Russian wife's.

Wife number two had a son, Igor, by Peters and, although Peters wanted nothing to do with Little May and her mother, the two wives and children got on very well together. Because of the harsh conditions and shortages during the civil war, Mrs Peters was forced to sell the contents of the eleven trunks that she had brought from England with her in order to survive. One day she stormed out of the house as Peters pulled up outside in his big American car, complete with bodyguards, and created an angry scene in the street, telling him in no uncertain terms that he'd got to do something to help. He issued them both with Cheka ration books, but when the first ration of meat arrived it turned out to be nothing more than a bone. Mrs Peters was furious and threw the bone out of the window just as Peters' car drew up outside. The bone hit the car and Peters stormed into his house. Little May, trotting along to the house a few minutes later, found Peters raging to his Russian wife that somebody had just tried to kill him!

Once Little May's mother nearly succeeded in getting her out of the country. She had her adopted by Isadora Duncan who was leaving the country for a tour of America but Peters found out at the last moment and stopped May from going. In December 1937 English newspapers reported that Peters had been arrested in the latest round of the Stalin purges, together with Valery Meshlauk, head of the State Planning Commission, his brother Ivan Meshlauk, General Commissioner of the Soviet Pavilion at the Paris Exhibition, and General Alksnsis, chief of Soviet Aviation. Peters' Russian wife panicked and tried to distance herself from him by changing her name and moving away. She told Little May to do the same but although May had nothing to thank her father for, she refused to do so. In the long term this was to stand her in good stead. The Russian wife was arrested in 1938 and it was to be nearly eighteen years before May saw her again. At the same time Stalin eliminated another ghost from the past. In 1913 Christian Salnish emigrated to America. From 1916 to 1917 he was Secretary of the Latvian American Social Democratic Worker's Association in Boston. In 1917 he returned to Russia and rose to the rank of Brigade Commissar (Brigadier-General) on the Red Army General Staff. He seems to have had a flair for intelligence work, and during the Spanish Civil War he became Soviet military adviser to the Spanish communists from 1937–38. His decorations included the Order of Lenin and the Order of the Red Banner, but these didn't save him. On his return from Spain, on 8 May 1939, the former organiser of the Tottenham Outrage was shot by order of Stalin. The Russian euphemism for this action is 'Subjected to illegal suppression'. Like Peters he has been posthumously rehabilitated.

Soviet accounts tended to differ regarding the date of Peters' death which was variously given as 1938 and 1942. The latter used to be given to suggest that he hadn't died as a result of one of Stalin's purges but at the hands of the Germans when they invaded Russia. The official Soviet sources now agree on 1938. According to Solzhenitsyn, Peters was shot. His daughter, May, however, believed that he was alive very much later than that. She heard from one of the old Bolsheviks who escaped the Terror (his name was Podvoisky) that her father was alive in 1944. Her stepmother heard the same thing from another unrelated source. Subsequent events would seem to confirm this, although the reasons for his survival remain obscure.

After his parents' arrest, Igor went to live with Little May and her mother before getting married in 1940. May's mother died in 1942. Little May, now 29, still retained her British citizenship and for some years worked at the British Embassy in Moscow – first in the Embassy dacha as a companion to the children of one of the staff, and then in the Embassy itself as a telephonist. On 6 November 1948 Igor was arrested. The date itself is significant. When Peters had been arrested and tried – the charge is believed to have been treason, i.e. plotting against Stalin – he was sentenced to ten years' imprisonment. According to May her father, if he was not already dead, was due to be released on 28 November, three weeks after Igor's arrest. If Peters was actually alive were the authorities playing some sort of cat and mouse game to keep father and son apart? May now feared for her own safety. She knew that she was being watched and on 11 January 1949 the police called on her and ordered her to leave her job at the Embassy. This she refused to do. She hoped for a room at the Embassy where she would be safe, and was promised one, but before the promise could be fulfilled the police pounced.

On the evening of 17 January, six days after the first warning, she was arrested and thrown into the Lubianka where she was held for most of 1949.

Were the arrests made because Peters was still alive and this was one way of bringing pressure to bear on him for some obscure reason? Why else should Igor have been tortured, as he was, in precisely the same way as his father had been tortured by the Ochrana in 1905? Peters had been friends with Jacob Sverdlov, one of the key figures of the revolution, and had been with Lenin at his funeral. Both men's sons were named Igor and had been close friends. Now, after Igor Peters' arrest, it was this same friend, Igor Sverdlov, who was his inquisitor and had him tortured by pulling out his fingernails. Other than a wanton act of sadism this is only explicable if Peters was still alive and presumably still of some use to the State. One Western source which suggests that this might have been the case was a book about Eddie Pleasants entitled *I Killed to Live*. Before the war Pleasants had been a professional strongman. He would lie on the floor, with a piano on his chest, two girls dancing on top and a third one playing it. When the Channel Islands were invaded he was captured by the Nazis and taken to Germany where, after being interned and miraculously surviving the battle for Berlin, he was taken prisoner by the Russians and sentenced to twenty-five years' imprisonment in a labour camp. It was while he was serving this sentence that he met another prisoner, Pavlov Dudkin, who claimed to be Peter the Painter. What is significant is that Dudkin apparently spoke English with a slight cockney accent. This couldn't actually have been true of Peter the Painter, who was never in England long enough, but it was true of Peters, and other people had noted the same characteristic.

However, the story Dudkin told of the Houndsditch murders had some peculiar twists in it. His opening remarks were more or less appropriate for a former Chekist leader like Peters. He said, 'Your English police are efficient and persistent, but you have curious laws in your country which forbid arrest unless there is sufficient evidence of guilt and even then a man is still considered innocent unless proved guilty; more astounding still, a criminal is given every opportunity to defend himself. If my accomplices had tried to operate in Moscow as we did in London, we would most certainly have been arrested, and jailed for life, purely on suspicion.' He claimed that Lenin had been one of their leaders. They had had their headquarters in Paris and a network of sympathisers throughout Europe. They had been called anarchists, but the only one who would have claimed that title was Gardstein 'who was courageous to the point of fanaticism'. As they were short of funds and needed to raise money for the party, Gardstein had formed a gang of political fanatics and criminals in London. 'The reason why we were friendly with these crooks was that our Party had decided that it was a loyal principle to rob the capitalist classes, providing, of course, that the money went to the Party.' Dudkin said that he had kept watch with Sara Trassjonsky outside in the street and hadn't seen the shootings. So far the story is credible but now it goes all wrong. Dudkin continued that he had gone to Levi's house and then escaped the same night by boat to the Hook of Holland. Levi had made the arrangements for the loot to be smuggled abroad. Where the story strays is that Joseph and Straus (Svaars), according to Dudkin, had gone to Sidney Street because Joseph had planned to meet Luba Milstein (already in custody) with whom he was in love, and suggest that they should escape together to Australia. However, Luba was a loyal party member and told Straus of the proposed treachery. Straus followed Joseph to Sidney Street and, when the police arrived, trapping them both, shot Joseph. Then, to avoid capture and prevent certain compromising documents falling into police hands, he set fire to the house and himself died in the inferno.

In telling his story, Dudkin at times had lapsed into Russian and sought Pleasants' help with words he had long forgotten. 'There was a faraway look in his eyes – the look of a man that had lived and fought for ideals which had crashed around him.'

Philip Ruff puts the probable date of this incident to about 1953 which would have made Peters (if it was him) about 67 years old. By then he would have been in prison about fifteen years.

In 1953 May and Igor were still prisoners, May having been charged with spying. Her friendship with a member of the British Military Mission to Russia was well known to her inquisitors, and they wanted to know what she had told him. She never ever said anything afterwards (about physical torture) but she was certainly knocked about whenever she answered back. On one occasion when a question had been put to her about her British friend she rudely retorted that there was no need for her to tell him anything; he spoke better Russian than she did – 'and better than you do for that matter!' But by the end of almost a year in the Lubianka she couldn't remember whether she had confessed to spying or not.

The British Ambassador's efforts to get news of her met with rebuffs and nothing more was heard of her for seven and a half years until 1956, when her uncle, George Freeman, who lived in London and with whom she used to correspond, received a card from her. It was a 'camp' card, perforated down the middle, one half for the reply, which bore a Moscow Poste Restante address. More cards came from the camp and then she was given a ticket to Moscow. Officially she didn't exist for the next two years. She was spotted wandering the streets by a friend who took her in, and with the connivance of the caretaker of the flats where she lived, looked after her.

Because of her British nationality, efforts were made to get her an exit visa. But the Russians declared, so long as she looked on herself as a British subject she could not expect to be 'rehabilitated', which was the necessary first step. Finally, she gave in and was given a Grade II pension in 1959. Igor was released about the same time as May in 1955. He'd had a reputation as a drunkard before his arrest and within a short time after his release he was almost certainly alcoholic. When May was given her pension it coincided with Peters' rehabilitation and the two events are obviously linked. One reason why May was given the pension was because she had refused to disown her father when he had been arrested in 1938. Now that he was being rehabilitated this loyalty stood her in good stead, and her pension card was marked that she was the daughter of an Old Bolshevik, one of those who made the revolution. Igor was not so lucky. In 1938 his mother had tried to conceal her relationship to Peters by changing her name and Igor had possibly attempted the same deception. This counted against them both and neither was now rehabilitated. Understandably Igor became a very embittered man.

By 1960 May had a room of her own and Peters' rehabilitation was complete. She was asked to contribute to an official book but refused to do so, feeling that there was nothing she could say in his favour, as he had treated her and her mother very badly. She suggested to the author that he ask her step-mother instead, but this wasn't acceptable and the book went ahead without them.

In February 1965 one of May's English friends, Menna Wilders, received a letter saying that May had died of heart disease on the first of that month. May had been cremated and Menna was asked to find out from May's English relatives what they wanted done with the ashes. Naturally they wanted them to be sent to London and Menna was told that this could be arranged through the Russian Embassy. However, when she went there she was told that this was a matter for the Consulate. There they told her it could only be arranged from the Moscow end. Eventually Menna was told that the ashes had been lost in the post!

Today, Peter's place in the pantheon of Bolshevik heroes is more secure. The man who should have been hanged in 1911 for the murder of three City of London policemen is now officially remembered as a Hero of October. According to the official hagiography, 'His educators were the Party and revolution, and he served them loyally and was a model soldier for the socialist homeland.' In the city of Riga, in his home state of Latvia, is the Communards Park and running around the edge is the Avenue of Heroes. There are statues of such heroes. One of them was of Jacob Peters. It was erected in 1960 after his rehabilitation. The inscription read, 'Jekabs Peters (1886–1938) an outstanding Soviet Party and State worker who took an active part in the 1905–1907 revolution and the Great October Social Revolution, and sat on the Central Committee of the Communist Party of Latvia and the All-Russian Central Executive Committee.'

In 1992 it was demolished when Latvia regained independence and destroyed such reminders of the Russian occupation.

Luba Milstein was more fortunate. Some months after the Siege she gave birth to Svaars' son but named him Alfred, not after his father, but after Alfred Dzircol which was the real name of 'Karl Hoffman'. The latter had secretly loved her all along and promised Fritz that he would look after her if anything happened to him. (Alfred and Luba's children were later told 'a rather romantic story of a wonderful martyred friend who intrusted his beloved Luba to Alfred should any thing happen to him'.) When the baby was about six months old in January 1912, Luba sailed for America, followed a year later by Hoffman who entered the country illegally. They lived together in various places in and around New York City. They never married as they didn't feel the need for any governmental approval (especially that of 'imperialistic' governments) for any personal commitment they chose to make. This was difficult to explain when they got older and came to collect their social security. Initially they used the surname of Weinstein. This may have been a derivation of Milstein imposed by Ellis Island officials but the more probable explanation is that it was used to placate Luba's family, with whom she stayed in touch, by suggesting that Alfred was Jewish when in fact he was a Latvian gentile. Eventually they reverted to his real name of Dzircol which was anglicised to Driscoll.

Hoffman worked as a painter, Luba as a seamstress and in the early days they had lots of friends coming and going who shared with them what they had, but at some point they broke with them. They had turned to Marxism as a scientific theory for making a better world and this perhaps had alienated them from their former companions. They rejected terrorism as counter-productive and dangerous to innocent people, suspecting that some people were using it as a cloak for robbery.

At one point Hoffman and Luba returned to Europe to straighten out a particular problem, but it was not a successful trip. Someone left a package in their care and Hoffman's animal instinct for survival made him open the package to see what it contained. Inside was gunpowder. It must have been a very large package as he and Luba spent the whole night flushing it bit by bit down the toilet. By morning they both had raging headaches.

Hoffman, according to his daughter, was never anything but a self-sacrificing and loving father. Both he and Luba frequently did without themselves, but the children didn't remember the family being poor. There was always delicious food, periodicals, library books, a victrola, and records. They had a daughter, Catherine (Kitty), and she remembers the family as being very close to each other but isolated from almost everyone else. Their political opinions, lack of religious affiliation and strange ways made them seem different. As an example of the latter, as a child Catherine wore boys' shoes. Luba had rightly surmised that the girls' shoes of the time were neither healthy nor sturdy, but Catherine did look odd. Education and health, however, and not appearances, came first. Hoffman was not a good provider of money (he was not aggressive and could not express himself well in English) and every penny had to be worried over a hundred times. Luba could love devotedly and possessively. She was tireless in the children's care, worried, nagging, obsessed and frequently angry and depressed at how life had turned out. And yet, Catherine recalled, 'There was always the feeling of being cherished, laughter over cups of tea in the kitchen before bedtime, reading in bed, my parents' voices murmuring in their room for hours as they went over the events of the day, plans for the next. Our poorest apartment was always snug, freshly painted, bugless, and everything worked. Pop saw to that.' But the main gift that the children got from their parents was 'a strong ethical structure that amounted to a religion based on their being such political folk'. (Luba spoke, not very well, at Street corners during the depression) 'We were expected to die, literally, for a principle, to fight for what was right, to practise self-denial and discipline rather than be corrupted by watering down our beliefs. We were to be empathetic to the suffering of others and always loyal to the "toiling masses".' When the children had grown up they bought a tumbledown house in the country, which Hoffman did up, and which had a marvellous garden where tea was served under the trees. The only unhappiness was Luba's growing over-sensitivity and frequent outbursts aimed at anyone she thought was slighting her.

Hoffman was seventy-three years old when he died in 1961. Luba was wild with rage and grief but gradually she calmed down. She settled in a beach area, renewed friendships with a number of old acquaintances from the early days and even fell in love again at the age of seventy-nine. When her demons were not raging she had charm, wit and intelligence. She died in 1973 when she was eighty-one. Her last two guests at the convalescent home were two admiring males.

One of Catherine's most touching recollections concerns her father, whom she remembers as one of nature's gentlemen. She was frequently ill as a child but whenever there was the hint of warm weather he would bring her a sprig of hedge-flower 'broken off God knows where, on a city street, on the way home from work, as a sign that good times were coming, that every spring was new.'

12

Notes for the Curious

Apart from the mystery of Peter the Painter, there are two stories which are consistently linked with the murders and the Siege. They are the murder of Leon Beron, a case which is normally referred to as the 'Clapham Common murder', and (less serious) a story that it was Stalin who masterminded the Houndsditch murders.

Briefly, Leon Beron's body was found on Clapham Common on New Year's Day, 1911, less than forty-eight hours before the beginning of the Siege. The head had been terribly battered about and on each side of the nose were two cuts, each two inches in length and symmetrical in shape like the S-shaped holes on either side of a violin. This form of mutilation, using the letter 'S', was generally taken to indicate that the victim had been either a police informer or spy. Alternatively it could have been a 'J' standing for 'Jew', which was how the 'S' was interpreted in the smuggled prison notes that were passed between Hoffman and Dubof. Inevitably, when the Siege began, the two events were linked by the press and continued to be reported side by side. It was argued that Beron had been killed and mutilated for betraying Svaars and Joseph. Stinie Morrison, who was tried and convicted for the murder, protested his innocence to the end. He was never hanged but died in prison some years afterwards. Many believed then, and still do, that his trial was a gross miscarriage of justice. His counsel argued that the two cases were linked and there is some evidence that they might have been.

Among the Houndsditch papers there is a report to the Deputy Medical Officer at Brixton Prison which was written on 28 January 1911 by Warder T. Russel: 'As Prisoner S. Morrison was leaving the

Hospital for discharge this morning, Prisoner Y. Dubof came towards him and remarked, "Wish you success".' As both men were awaiting trial and obviously anxious about the outcome this can hardly be considered as sufficient evidence that they knew each other and were implicated in each other's crimes.

One of the factors linking the two crimes, however, is locality. At the beginning of December Morrison moved to 5 Grove Street; Svaars was living at 59. The Warsaw restaurant in Osborn Street was where Beron would sit all day from lunchtime to midnight conducting his business, which included fencing stolen goods and backing profitable sounding burglaries. According to Harding, the Warsaw was also Gardstein's headquarters. This immediately raises several questions. Was Beron a backer of the Houndsditch burglary? Was Beron Gardstein's fence? Was it in fact through Beron that Gardstein fenced the watches that Svaars gave him to raise extra cash?

More evidence that the two crimes were linked has been put forward by Frank Clarke in his book *Will-O'-the-Wisp*. According to Clarke, Beron's murder was a pre-emptive operation, not a retaliatory one. He argues that he was killed by unknown members of the group because it was thought by some that he was going to betray them – not that he had already done so. The source for this information was a Lett named August Maren (also known as Peter Jansen, 'Yahnit', meaning 'little John', Peter Johnson and John Johnson). Certainly he was involved with the group as he appears in one of the group photographs seized from Sara Trassjonsky in the police raid on Grove Street and which she was trying to burn. Maren had been a schoolteacher and was presumably caught up in the 1905 revolution. Certainly his known anti-Tsarist views led to him being accused by one of the Baltic counts of being an anarchist and he was consequently imprisoned in Riga from 1906 to 1908. Eventually he was released, as the principal witnesses kept disappearing, making it impossible for the prosecution to prove the charges against him. Maren was almost certainly a Social Democrat; he addressed a meeting of the Social Democrats in London and was an acquaintance of the socialist Hjalmer Branting, who assisted anti-Tsarist refugees in Sweden and was himself an adviser to Lenin in the years of exile.

The extent of Maren's involvement is not clear, but he lived in the same lodgings as Karl Hoffman and when the police came to arrest the latter the landlord, Theodore Janson, told them that the man they should have arrested had already fled. Janson, as his statements make clear, was willing to play the informer in exchange for money. Maren had sailed for Australia three days before, but it was clear before he left that he was a badly shaken man and he told his friends that he was wanted by the police. However, the further the ship sailed the more his confidence was renewed, and he began to boast that he was a member of an association that had planned to rob a gold magazine in London to finance and support their friends in Russia. Four or five of their best men had been chosen to commit the robbery but one of them had been injured when the police had disturbed them and had died in a friend's house. Two others had gone to a house where the group stored its fighting and burglary instruments, until a fight with the soldiers had broken out. Clarke makes the point that if Betsy Gershon had been storing ammunition at Sidney Street, as Maren's statement suggests this would explain the two men's seemingly inexhaustible supplies during the Siege. Maren's statement also confirms Perelman's information that the two men had been staying with Gershon since 17 December and not from 2 January as the official version suggests. Her involvement was much deeper than was publicly admitted which was presumably why she was refused compensation and so harshly treated by the Claims Committee.

Maren claimed that Beron's murder had been carried out as a result of deliberate policy, not because Beron was the informer, but because he was a potential one, while the killing itself would be a warning to others of the kind of reprisals that could be expected if they passed on information about the Lettish revolutionaries to the police. He said, 'A Jew wanted to tell the police about the anarchists' movements and we found out what he was going to do. We got him one day in a paddock and we killed him. We cut his ears and nose and put Freemasons' traitor marks on his face and then cut his throat. We did this to frighten the other Jews so they would be afraid to tell where the anarchists, who were wanted, were hiding.'

Maren was subsequently arrested in Australia in August 1911. The police then cabled to London for information and investigated claims that Maren might be Peter the Painter himself. The City of London police subsequently confirmed that he was a known associate of Peter the Painter, but the failure of the trial had simply underlined the fact that they didn't have enough evidence on which to extradite either Maren or Piatkow if he could be traced. Maren was released in

October 1911. Five years later he enlisted in the Australian army and served in the Middle East and on the Western Front. After 1917 he disappears from the story.

If Maren had been part of the group then how big had it been? Who else was involved? Janson who, besides being an informer, had come from Riga together with his wife, Lonny, and infant son in 1905? If not involved with the group he was certainly a fellow Lett and of the same age and background as the others. Possibly this is why they trusted him. On 26 December 1910 he told the police of a conversation that he had had with Karl Hoffman. Janson said to him, 'Three of the men are arrested, are they the men?' Hoffman laughed and replied, 'No, there were nine men in the plot, none of them are yet arrested. It's a pity the man is dead [Gardstein], he was the ablest of the lot and the leader of the gang. He so managed it that some members of the gang did not know the others.' He also said that he thought that one of the murderers had left the country.

Clearly the last reference is to Smoller, who had got away the same night. Knowing Hoffman's highly developed instinct for survival it is not clear how much credence can be given to his statement. My own feeling is that it was a blind, chiefly because of that reference to 'one of the murderers'. The one word 'murderers' immediately puts Hoffman at arm's length from the rest of the group and places him on the side of law and order. Not only would this give him some respectability but, if his statement is accepted, it exonerates the three already in custody and shifts the blame on to others whose names died with Gardstein. Was Salnish one of them?

If this hypothesis is right (that Beron's murder was a warning) then clearly it failed because it was too late. Apart from Perelman and Janson, who kept their activities secret, there was Nicholas Tomacoff, whose betrayals seem to have quickly become public knowledge. If anyone should have been killed, rightly or wrongly, for betraying Svaars and Joseph, it was him. Not only had he gone voluntarily to the police but the information he had given to them had led to two arrests. Several days before the Beron murder he was being pointed out as a police informer. A salesman warned the police that this was happening on 28 December. What is equally clear from the salesman's statement is that Tomacoff was continuing to play in concerts and clubs where he did not have police protection. Possibly, as has been argued, by then he had passed on all his knowledge to the police, and there was therefore little point in risking a heavier and more protracted police investigation by killing him.

The most recent source for the theory that Stalin organised the Houndsditch expropriation is Richard Deacon's *A History of the Russian Secret Service*. The theory loses instant credibility by the opening account of the Siege:

> This incident, which resulted in a five-hour rifle battle between anarchists and Scots Guards, provided an excellent example of Russian counter-espionage techniques as used abroad. A police sergeant, investigating a report of 'strange noises' coming from a house in Sidney Street, Houndsditch, called there and was shot dead. When other police surrounded the house and demanded that the occupants surrender they were met by a barrage of fire from automatic pistols. Two more police were shot dead and Winston Churchill, then Home Secretary, ordered out the Scots Guards to assist the police. One thousand police, assisted by Guards, kept up a fire on the house, which was eventually burnt down.

He goes on to quote a Mr James Burley who claimed that he regularly went to the Continental Cafe, in Little Newport Street, Soho, which Stalin also frequently used in 1910: 'Jozef Georgi, he called himself. He was a bombastic little man, not very big.' Mr Burley claimed that Stalin knew all about the events leading up to the Siege, that he was looked up to as one of the leaders, that he had a hand in planning the burglary and that he kept a watch on Peter the Painter.

In fact, the earliest that anyone could have started planning the robbery was in May 1910 when the shop was first opened. Stalin's movements can be traced during this period and have been confirmed by both Soviet and western sources. He was arrested on 23 March 1910 and transferred to a prison in Baku some three days later. He was held there for six months before being transferred, under escort, on 23 September to Solvychegodsk in northern Russia, which was later one of Stalin's central NKVD concentration camps. He was still there in July 1911. Nor is it likely that he would or could have masterminded the expropriation from this distance or that he would have hesitated to betray the anarchist involvement to the Ochrana, when he was already betraying the Bolsheviks with whom he was linked politically and trying to gain favour. The theory that he was involved in the Siege is just not credible. Clearly the genesis for Burley's nonsense is the Pilenas letter, quoted by Leeson, which was written when Stalin was dictator of the Soviet State and Peters one of its most powerful men. The story has been given credence because of Stalin's presence at the London Congress in 1907 and his involvement in the Tiflis expropriation which followed shortly afterwards.

There is a related theory that the Houndsditch expropriation was masterminded by a Tsarist agent provocateur, the intention being to incite the exiles into further expropriations leading to their expulsion by the host country. Peter the Painter was widely believed to be an agent provocateur by the East End's Russian community. Laurence Irving, Henry Irving's son, was a popular figure within this community and was told that they believed that Piatkow was acting under instructions from the Russian government to create incidents such as this in the hope that Britain would thereafter deny asylum to the Russian revolutionaries. At the same time public sympathy would be aroused for the Russian government and the steps it had taken to deal with similar outrages. Piatkow was believed to have been allowed to escape because of this secret understanding with the police and the intelligence services. If this had been the intention then it was singularly unsuccessful. Political exiles continued to be given asylum even when, like Nina Vassilleva, they had been given a criminal conviction by the host country and were wanted on a capital charge in their own.

In 2008, Tower Hamlets Community Housing named two houses Peter House and Painter House with plaques which read 'This block was built in 2006 by Tower Hamlets Community Housing and named after Peter Piaktow, who was known as Peter the Painter, the anti-hero of the nearby Sidney Street Siege in 1911'. Understandably there were protests by the Metropolitan Police Federation and the family of Sergeant Bentley at this glorification of a murderer. Tower Hamlets Community Housing denied it was glorifying the police killers. 'There is no evidence that Peter the Painter killed the three policemen, so we knew we were not naming the block after a murderer. there is some doubt as to whether he existed, but he is the name that East Enders associate with the siege and Sidney Street.

Appendix

Translation of Fritz Svaars' letter

outer envelope: To Mr Janis Ludmans
64, Pastbishchna Street
Libau
Courland

inner envelope: Please pass on to
J. F. Svaars
8, Bosh Street
Liepaja★

Greetings dear ones!

I think it's worth telling you now about London, the search for me and still others.

I only want to tell you how it came about, how they're looking for us everywhere and who's been arrested. We are completely innocent and were in no way connected with the attempted robbery for which we are now being hunted. This is the story. Not long ago I wrote to you that I would soon be travelling to that longed for country – Australia.

★ Liepaja is the original name for this major Latvian port. Libau is the Germanicized form used then by the Baltic barons and Russians alike. This name was also used during the German occupation in the Second World War. The inner envelope is obviously addressed to his father as the letter's contents reveal.

That would have happened between the 7th–10th January, 1911. Also, by that time, my wife should have been here and then both of us with three other men would have left England. I had enough money for the journey as I got 300 roubles from Russia. I sent 100 to my wife and I kept 200. Three weeks ago Puika (you remember him – the shoe-maker's son – who had just come from Paris, came to see me and asked me to lend him 100 roubles for a short time, just for two weeks because it was terribly necessary and that there was a brilliant chance of becoming rich after two weeks at the longest. He showed me a telegram showing that his folks had sent out another 300 roubles. I of course didn't have 300 roubles because I'd already bought two ship's tickets for 160 roubles. So I lent him £6 [60 roubles] which left me with £2 in my pocket. A week went by and Puika came to my flat on Saturday evening and said that after 3-4 days I would get my money back with considerable interest. There was the prospect of a couple of thousand pounds in which case he would give me some £100 (1,000 roubles). Of course I was delighted. That same Saturday, about 12 at night, two acquaintances came to my flat bringing Puika who'd been shot and could no longer walk. I could no longer stay in my flat for another minute because I wasn't sure that their bringing in the wounded man hadn't been seen and I, who was clean, would be arrested for nothing and certainly hanged. Those who brought in the wounded man themselves fled immediately and I grabbed the most necessary things, a weapon and ammunition and also went to some known members, from there I sent two girls to go and bandage Puika, to get hold of a doctor, clean out the flat, burn the letters and other papers. Three hours later the girls announced that Puika was terribly wounded and would probably die. The doctor had been and said to go to hospital which Puika wasn't prepared to do. All the papers had been burned except for the books. I told them to try and bring out my new clothes, photographs and the ship's tickets; if Puika should die, to pour paraffin over him and the bed and start a fire so that he is burnt together with the flat, then the police wouldn't even know that he'd been wounded and also all the things would get burnt. That would hide everything from the police. Puika had died and straightaway the police arrived. And so there was no fire. One of the girls had been spotted by the police but had slipped away by the back and brought the ship's tickets but nothing else. I went straightaway and said to keep the tickets safe. After I'd gone the police immediately surrounded the house and arrested the girl. I don't know anything about the tickets or anything else. Another lad was living at my place who also went. The landlord had described us both very well arid they are looking for us both as participants in the shooting of four policemen. The whole of London is buried in police. I don't know anything about the other member except that he has still not been arrested. He like me, if arrested, will without doubt be hung because the guilty ones are unknown and my landlord said that he didn't know if we'd been at home or not. I know that if they get hold of me they'll hang me anyway and for that reason I am going to resist and will even shoot myself. Jekabs has been arrested – if anyone didn't know, he didn't – and another two were arrested because they'd come to my flat and were my friends. I don't under stand how my name has come out, no photograph has appeared as yet and I don't think one will.

Two weeks I've been on the run, how much longer I can manage, I don't know. To leave soon doesn't bear thinking about because they're guarding all the roads intensely. I'm not at all depressed because every-one knows that one has to die at some time and the good a person such as I can bring to humanity is not worth talking about. And to you it's all the same because up to now I haven't been able to help you and in the future, what luck would I have had? So be peaceful. If I'm lucky then I'll still live and I'll share joy and sadness with you, and if not, you also know that at some time that same hour will come to you and you'll be ashes the same as everyone.

Don't say anything to the shoe-maker – she'll find out herself soon enough.

I kiss all of you and my dear friends. Send a kiss to Liza also because I'm not allowed to write. Tell no-one, absolutely no-one where I am, don't write before I write to you through Lud.

[your Fricis]

Select Bibliography

Bermant, Chairn, *London's East End: Point of Arrival* (Macmillan Publishing Co., Inc., 1975).

Chapman, Eddie, *I Killed to Live: the Story of Eric Pleasants* (Cassell & Co. Ltd., 1957).

Churchill, Randolph S., Winston S. Churchill, vol. 2, *Young Statesman 1901–1914* (Heinemann, 1967.)

Churchill, Winston S., *Thoughts and Adventures* (Odhams Press, 1932).

Clarke, F. G. *Will-O'-the-Wisp: Peter the Painter and the anti-Tsarist terrorists in Britain and Australia* (Oxford University Press, 1983).

Crocker, William Charles, *Far from Humdrum* (Hutchinson, 1967).

Deacon, Richard, *A History of the Russian Secret Service* (Frederick Muller, 1972).

Eddy, J. P., *The Mystery of 'Peter the Painter'* (Stevens, 1946).

Fishman, William J., *East End Jewish Radicals 1875–1914* (Gerald Duckworth & Co. Ltd., 1975).

Harcave, Sidney, *First Blood* (Macmillan, 1964).

Hassall, Christopher, *Edward Marsh* (Longmans, 1959).

Hastings, Macdonald, *The Other Mr Churchill* (Harrap, 1963).

Hearst, Patricia Campbell, *Every Secret Thing* (Methuen London Ltd., 1982)

Hingley, Ronald, *The Russian Secret Police* (Hutchinson, 1970).

Hoiroyd, James Edward, *The Gaslight Murders* (Allen & Unwin, 1960).

Leeson, Benjamin, *Lost London* (Stanley Paul, 1934).

Leggett, George, *The Cheka: Lenin's Political Police* (Oxford University Press, 1981).

Linklater, Eric, *The Corpse on Clapham Common* (Macmillan, 1971).

Lockhart, R. H. Bruce, *Memoirs of a British Agent* (Putnam, 1932).

–, *My Europe* (Putnam, 1952).

London, Jack, *The People of the Abyss* (Nelson, 1903)

Macnaghten, Sir Melville, *Days of My Years* (Edward Arnold, 1915).

Moorehead, Alan, *The Russian Revolution* (Collins/Hamish Hamilton, 1958).

Nicholls, Ernest, *Crime within the Square Mile* (John Long, 1935).

Nott–Bower, Sir William, *Fifty Two Years a Policeman* (Edward Arnold, 1926).

Pope, A. U., *Maxim Litvinoff* (Secker & Warburg, 1943).

Rogers, Colin, *The Battle of Stepney: the Sidney Street Siege – Its Causes and Consequences* (Robert Hale Ltd., 1981).

Rose, Andrew, *Stinie: Murder on the Common* (Bodley Head, 1985).

Rose, Millicent, *The East End of London* (Cresset Press, 1951).

Samuel, Raphael, *East End Underworld: Chapters in the Life of Arthur Harding* (Routledge & Kegan Paul Ltd., 1981).

Serge, Victor, *Memoirs of a Revolutionary 1901 1941* (Oxford University Press, 1963)

Seth, Ronald, *The Russian Terrorists* (Barrie & Rockliff, 1966).

–, *The Executioners* (Cassell, 1967)

Shub, David, *Lenin* (Pelican, 1966).

Sims, George R., *Living London* (Cassell & Co. Ltd., 1901).

Sinclair, Robert, *East London* (Robert Hale, 1950).

Smith, Edward Ellis, *The Young Stalin* (Cassell, 1931).

Ulam, Adam B., *Lenin and the Bolsheviks* (Secker & Warburg, 1966).

Wensley, F. P., *Detective Days* (Cassell, 1931).

Wolin, Simon, and Slusser, Robert M., *The Soviet Secret Police* (Praeger, 1957).

Wood, Walter, *Survivors' Tales of Famous Crimes* (Cassell, 1916).

Woodcock, George, *Anarchism* (Pelican, 1963).

INDEX